JUSTICE IN A GLOBALIZED WORLD

Justice in a Globalized World

A Normative Framework

LAURA VALENTINI
University College London

Great Clarendon Street, Oxford, OX2 6DP,
United Kingdom

Oxford University Press is a department of the University of Oxford.
It furthers the University's objective of excellence in research, scholarship,
and education by publishing worldwide. Oxford is a registered trade mark of
Oxford University Press in the UK and in certain other countries

© Laura Valentini 2011

The moral rights of the author have been asserted

First Edition published in 2011

All rights reserved. No part of this publication may be reproduced, stored in
a retrieval system, or transmitted, in any form or by any means, without the
prior permission in writing of Oxford University Press, or as expressly permitted
by law, by licence or under terms agreed with the appropriate reprographics
rights organization. Enquiries concerning reproduction outside the scope of the
above should be sent to the Rights Department, Oxford University Press, at the
address above

You must not circulate this work in any other form
and you must impose this same condition on any acquirer

Published in the United States of America by Oxford University Press
198 Madison Avenue, New York, NY 10016, United States of America

British Library Cataloguing in Publication Data
Data available

Library of Congress Cataloging in Publication Data
Data available

ISBN 978–0–19–959385–9

For mamma, papà, and Christian

Acknowledgements

I began to work on this manuscript in the autumn of 2005, when I was a first-year PhD student. Since then, I have accumulated a giant debt of gratitude towards my mentors, colleagues, family, friends, favourite coffee shops, and chocolatiers. The list of those who have supported me is very long, and the space in which to thank them is very small. What follows only begins to convey how grateful I am to all of them.

I first started to think about global justice as an undergraduate student at the University of Pavia, where I was taught by Ian Carter. Ian was a most attentive supervisor back in Pavia, and is now a much-cherished friend and continued source of intellectual inspiration. I would be glad if my work were half as rigorous as his! I then moved to UCL, where I spent four enjoyable and fruitful years as a graduate student. I am indebted to many of my fellow PhD students, for their friendly support and engagement with my work, and to my supervisor, Cécile Laborde, from whom I have learnt a tremendous amount. She has always managed to strike the right balance between criticism (of outstanding quality) and support, and I would feel very proud of myself if one day I became as good a mentor as she was for me. I also want to express my sincere gratitude towards Bob Goodin, who invited me to spend a few months at the Australian National University (ANU) in 2007 and 2009. I have benefited immeasurably from the time spent at the ANU, with its unique combination of rigorous philosophy and friendly socializing, and from Bob's generous advice and unfailing support over the years. While in Australia, I had the opportunity to collaborate with Christian Barry, who was a great co-author, and with whom I have had many helpful discussions on international ethics. I am grateful to my PhD examiners, David Miller and Jonathan Wolff, for their feedback and encouragement, to three anonymous readers for Oxford University Press, who have provided detailed and thoughtful reports on the book's penultimate draft, and to Dominic Byatt for overseeing the editorial process. The book reproduces portions of already published work of mine, and I am grateful to the publishers for permission.

Chapters 2 and 4 partly draw on L. Valentini, 'On the Apparent Paradox of Ideal Theory', *Journal of Political Philosophy*, 17 (3) (2009), by permission of Wiley-Blackwell, and much of Chapter 6 draws on L. Valentini, 'Coercion and (Global) Justice', *American Political Science Review*, 105 (1) (2011), by permission of Cambridge University Press.

Since 2008, I have been a Junior Research Fellow at The Queen's College, Oxford University, and between 2009 and 2010, a postdoc at the Center for Human Values, Princeton University. The intellectual life at both institutions was strikingly rich, and I feel privileged to have had the opportunity to take part in it. For many instructive and enjoyable conversations on themes related to this book's topic, I am especially grateful to Charles Beitz, Brookes Brown, Simon Caney, Ryan Davis, Kyla Ebels-Duggan, Robert Jubb, Joseph Mazor, David Miller, Nicholas Southwood, Annie Stilz, John Tasioulas, Patrick Tomlin, and Lea Ypi. Philip Pettit in particular has been helpful and encouraging well beyond the call of duty, engaging with my work and providing much-needed intellectual and emotional support while I was on the infamous job market.

Other friends and colleagues who have been helpful along the way include Sara Amighetti, Peter Balint, Richard Bellamy, Enrico Biale (who read the full final draft of the manuscript), Clara Brandi, Geoff Brennan, Alex Brown, Emanuela Ceva, Chiara Cordelli, Pablo Gilabert, Tamara Jugov, David Karp, Eszter Kollár, Steve Macedo, Pietro Maffettone, Larry May, Saladin Meckled-Garcia, Julio Montero, Valeria Ottonelli, David Owen, Christian Schemmel, Henry Shue, Kai Spiekermann, Zofia Stemplowska, Federico Zuolo, and Jennifer Welsh. In addition, I have benefited from presenting work related to this book in departmental seminars at the ANU, Birmingham, Essex, Genoa, Manchester, Oxford, Princeton, Roehampton, Rutgers, and UCL. For questions and comments, I am also grateful to the participants at several graduate conferences (Warwick, Manchester, Harvard, and Pavia) and professional conferences including the Canadian Political Science Association Annual Conference, the International Studies Association Annual Convention, the Association for Legal and Social Philosophy Annual Conference, the European Consortium for Political Research Joint Sessions of Workshops, and the conference on Global Justice: Theory Practice Rhetoric at the University of New South Wales. The latter conference also marked the launch of an initiative, called *The Global Justice Network*, involving myself and some of my closest friends and colleagues. Two of them in particular deserve special mention: Tiziana Torresi and Miriam Ronzoni.

I met both of them when I was an undergraduate visiting student at Oxford University, in 2003–2004, and since then they have been among the most loyal friends and impressive colleagues one could hope to have. With Miriam I have collaborated on a number of projects, from which I have learnt a lot, and which have benefited this book in more ways than I can explain. Both Miriam and Tiziana have consistently been sources of inspiration and encouragement, ready to support me when I needed support, to engage with my work when I needed feedback, and to tell me off when I needed to stop working. I owe them a very big 'Thank you!' for all of this.

Finally, I cannot even begin to express my gratitude towards the people to whom this book is dedicated: my parents, Annamaria and Alfredo Valentini, and my partner, Christian List. My parents' unbounded love and generosity is something I will forever be grateful for: they have always been there for me, sometime at the cost of not being there for themselves. Christian has been an unfailing support, both intellectually and emotionally. He has read two full drafts of the manuscript, engaged with many of its arguments, and instilled confidence in me when I was losing it. Without him, my life would not be the same and neither would be my work.

To all the people I have mentioned (and to those I might have forgotten): *Grazie mille!*

February 2011

Contents

1. Introduction: The Problem of Global Justice ... 1

PART I: COSMOPOLITANISM

2. Assessing the Cosmopolitan Ideal ... 23
3. Justifying Cosmopolitanism: A Methodological Critique ... 44

PART II: STATISM

4. Assessing the Statist Ideal ... 71
5. Justifying Statism: A Methodological Critique ... 92

PART III: A NORMATIVE FRAMEWORK

6. The Function of Justice: Assessing Coercion ... 121
7. The Content of Justice: Freedom and Equality ... 155
8. The Scope of Justice: Global ... 179
9. Conclusion ... 205

Bibliography ... 213
Index ... 223

1

Introduction: The Problem of Global Justice

1.1 INTRODUCTION

Kant famously said, '[t]he peoples of the earth have thus entered in varying degrees into a universal community, and it has developed to the point where a violation of rights in one part of the world is felt everywhere'.[1] This much-cited line from *Perpetual Peace* is now truer than ever before. We live in an age of globalization. The goods that we buy, the news that moves us, the trends we follow, and the people we encounter come from all over the world. Nowadays, if we want to get a sense of what is, or might be, happening at home, we also need to take a look at what is, or might be, happening abroad. Over the past fifty years or so, phenomena such as human-rights violations, poverty, civil wars, genocides, and epidemics have acquired an unprecedented global dimension.

Globalization opens up new possibilities and generates new challenges. As many have noted, whether it is a blessing or a curse very much depends on how it is managed, or on how *we*, humankind as a whole, respond to it. In turn, our responses to globalization may be evaluated from a plurality of different perspectives: one of them is that of morality.

We pass moral judgements on how states, corporations, NGOs, international institutions, and other global actors participate in, and react to, globalization on a daily basis. We judge the rules governing financial and trade liberalization, the particular development policies undertaken by industrialized nations, we blame our countries and ourselves (at least those who live in the wealthy Western world) for failing to assist the poor and destitute, we agonize over whether wars fought in the name of human rights and democracy are morally defensible, and so forth. These are just a few examples of the moral challenges we are confronted with by virtue of living in an evermore globalized world.

One of the difficulties in approaching what might be referred to as the morality of globalization is the lack of a well-developed moral 'toolkit' with

---

[1] Immanuel Kant, 'Perpetual Peace: A Philosophical Sketch' (1795), in Hans Reiss (ed.), *Kant's Political Writings* (Cambridge: Cambridge University Press, 1970), 93–130, pp. 107–8.

which to do so. Most of our political–moral vocabulary has been designed to answer questions arising within self-contained political communities. Now that the context and effects of our actions extend well beyond domestic borders, more versatile moral tools are needed. The process of constructing such tools involves asking whether principles and concepts that are familiar in the domestic arena can be extended to the international one, or at least modified so as to fit it.

Central to domestic *political morality* is the notion of *justice*. We routinely assess political institutions from the standpoint of justice and injustice, for instance, when we complain that the tax burdens imposed by the government are unjust, or that a small subset of the citizenry unjustly enjoys far better opportunities than the rest, or when we approvingly observe that a new pension scheme or labour law is more just than what we previously had; the list could continue almost indefinitely. As increasing international integration is, arguably, turning what used to be a world of separate states into a global society, political theorists have started to wonder whether the notion of justice they appeal to in the domestic context could also be invoked at the international, some would say global, level.

This question also constitutes the focus of the present book. I concentrate on contemporary liberal political theory, whose ideals are most eloquently articulated in the works of John Rawls and reflect much of the political sensitivity of the Western world, and ask whether it is capable of offering a plausible answer to *the question of extension*: 'Can principles of justice be meaningfully extended from the domestic context to the world at large?' As liberal principles of domestic justice are rather demanding – requiring equal civil and political liberties, equality of opportunity, and placing strict limits on permissible economic inequalities – our answer to this question has potentially far-reaching implications.[2] Should these egalitarian principles extend beyond the domestic arena and apply on a global scale?

Liberal theorists are famously divided on this question. Some, who have become known as cosmopolitans, answer it in the affirmative; others, so-called statists (or nationalists, or social liberals), answer it in the negative.[3] The former conceive of global justice as domestic justice writ large. For them, the egalitarian principles of justice that liberals defend at the domestic level should also apply globally. The latter, by contrast, deny that egalitarian justice has

---

[2] These are the kinds of requirements advanced by the most prominent contemporary liberal theories of justice. See e.g. John Rawls, *A Theory of Justice* (Oxford: Oxford University Press, 1999 rev. ed.); and Ronald Dworkin, *Sovereign Virtue: The Theory and Practice of Equality* (Cambridge, MA: Harvard University Press, 2000).

[3] I here understand statism broadly, as indicating those views that place emphasis on individual political communities, be they characterized as nations, peoples, or states. (The otherwise important differences between these notions are of little relevance for present purposes.)

a place beyond the domestic arena, and opt for an account of international morality consisting of principles of mutual assistance and respect between internally well-ordered political communities.

While cosmopolitanism and statism are still popular in the global justice literature, some scholars have recently suggested that genuine progress in this area can only be made by transcending the dichotomy between them. For these scholars, the dilemma between globalizing domestic principles of justice, on the one hand, and denying that justice has any role to play outside state borders, on the other, is a false one. Much more plausible, they argue, is the view that different principles of justice apply to different domains of human action. This allows one to claim that principles of justice should govern global or near-global social practices, without thereby also implying that domestic egalitarian justice should extend to the world at large.[4]

Albeit very promising, this third 'wave' of the debate on global justice is still in its infancy, and most of its representatives have focused on the question of what justice requires in relation to specific global practices, such as trade or health care distribution. That is, so far no comprehensive treatment of the difficulties with cosmopolitanism and statism, and systematic account of how to overcome them, has been offered.[5]

Firmly situated in this 'third' wave of the debate on global justice, the present book aims to fill this lacuna, by providing a sustained critical discussion of cosmopolitanism and statism, and a fresh perspective helping us to steer a middle course between them. The book consists of three parts. Parts I and II look at cosmopolitanism and statism in detail, and trace the difficulties with their substantive moral demands to more fundamental *methodological* shortcomings. Part III puts forward a methodologically sound normative

---

[4] See e.g. Joshua Cohen and Charles Sabel, 'Extra Rempublicam Nulla Justitia?', *Philosophy and Public Affairs*, 34 (2) (2006), 147–75; A. J. Julius, 'Nagel's Atlas', *Philosophy and Public Affairs*, 34 (2) (2006), 176–92; Aaron James, 'Distributive Justice without Sovereign Rule: The Case of Trade', *Social Theory and Practice*, 31 (4) (2005), 533–59; Miriam Ronzoni, 'The Global Order: A Case of Background Injustice? A Practice-dependent Account', *Philosophy and Public Affairs*, 37 (3) (2009), 229–56; Andrea Sangiovanni, 'Justice and the Priority of Politics to Morality', *Journal of Political Philosophy*, 16 (2) (2008), 137–64; Norman Daniels, *Just Health: Meeting Health Needs Fairly* (New York and Cambridge: Cambridge University Press, 2008), ch. 13; Lea L. Ypi, 'Statist Cosmopolitanism', *Journal of Political Philosophy*, 16 (1) (2008), 48–71, and 'Justice and Morality beyond Naïve Cosmopolitanism', *Ethics & Global Politics*, 3 (3) (2010), 171–92; Rainer Forst, 'Towards a Critical Theory of International Justice', *Metaphilosophy*, 32 (1/2) (2001), 160–79; Richard W. Miller, *Globalizing Justice: The Ethics of Poverty and Power* (Oxford: Oxford University Press, 2010); and Anna Stilz, *Liberal Loyalty: Freedom, Obligation, and the State* (Princeton, NJ: Princeton University Press, 2009), esp. pp. 101–9.

[5] Two recent *comprehensive* contributions to the literature on global justice have started to move towards a middle ground between cosmopolitanism and statism: Gillian Brock's *Global Justice: A Cosmopolitan Account* (Oxford: Oxford University Press, 2009); and David Miller's *National Responsibility and Global Justice* (Oxford: Oxford University Press, 2007). Notice, however, that Brock and Miller still explicitly place themselves in the cosmopolitan and statist (social liberal/nationalist) camps, respectively.

framework for thinking about justice, understood as an eminently political virtue, both domestically and internationally.⁶ In a nutshell, on the view I defend, the role of principles of justice is to evaluate the moral justifiability of coercion. Because of their freedom-restricting nature, coercive acts and relations stand in need of special justification. The principles that establish the conditions under which coercion is justified are what I call principles of justice.

I argue that, since coercion exists domestically as well as internationally, principles of justice should apply to both realms. However, since the forms of coercion characterizing these two realms differ, the principles of justice governing them need not have the same *content*. More specifically, I conclude that global justice requires more than statist assistance, yet less than cosmopolitan global equality.

In this introductory chapter, I offer an overview of the theoretical landscape in which the book is situated, describe its structure, and anticipate its central claims in greater detail. In Section 1.2, I set out the fundamental commitments of contemporary liberalism. In Section 1.3, I consider the two dominant liberal approaches to global justice: cosmopolitanism and statism. In Section 1.4, I argue that both approaches encounter significant difficulties from a theoretical as well as a practical point of view. This suggests that the debate between these two outlooks has reached an impasse. In Sections 1.5 and 1.6, I lay out the structure and contents of the book, thereby illustrating my proposed way out of the impasse.

1.2 CONTEMPORARY LIBERALISM: A BRIEF OVERVIEW

It is now widely acknowledged that contemporary liberal theorists share a fundamental commitment to the principle of *equal respect for persons qua autonomous, self-directing, agents*. From a liberal perspective, human beings are the ultimate sources of moral concern. Although every individual has a special responsibility for her/his own life and well-being, from an impartial perspective, each has equal value and a right to form and pursue her/his own conception of the good.⁷ This is why, for liberals, the moral quality of actions

---

⁶ The notion of justice is also used outside the political context. For instance, a child may plausibly complain that it is *unjust* that his brother receives more Christmas presents than him. Even if the child's claim is perfectly intelligible, his use of 'justice' is not one I am concerned with here. Throughout this book, I will understand justice as a political concept, applying in the first instance to political practices and institutions.

⁷ See e.g. Will Kymlicka, *Contemporary Political Philosophy: An Introduction* (Oxford: Oxford University Press, 2002, 2nd ed.), p. 4; Dworkin, *Sovereign Virtue*; and Thomas Nagel, *Equality and Partiality* (Oxford: Oxford University Press, 1991).

and institutions is to be judged on the basis of how they affect each person's life prospects.

Contemporary liberal theorists differ with respect to how they interpret the requirements following from this fundamental commitment. However, most of them share the view that, at the very least, equal respect demands *intersubjective justifiability*. As Jeremy Waldron puts it, 'liberalism rests on a certain view about the justification of social arrangements', that is

> liberals are committed to a conception of freedom and of respect for the capacities and the agency of individual men and women, and... these commitments generate a requirement that all aspects of the social should either be made acceptable or be capable of being made acceptable to every last individual.[8]

Just to mention one prominent example, the justificatory approach Waldron describes is central to John Rawls's outlook on justice. This appears clear in Rawls's derivation of the principles of justice from the so-called original position: a hypothetical choice situation where suitably idealized representatives of citizens are asked to agree on what principles should regulate the distribution of social goods within their polity.[9] This focus on unanimous agreement reflects the idea that such principles should be justifiable to *all* those whose lives they govern. To be just (morally legitimate), a social order must be *in principle* capable of attracting the consent of those who are, in some way or other, subject to it, independently of their actual consent. In Waldron's words '[w]hen we move from asking what people actually accept to asking what they *would* accept in certain conditions, we shift our emphasis away from will and focus on the *reasons* people might have for exercising their will in one way rather than another'.[10]

In short, in this book I shall understand liberalism to require that the ways in which we affect each other's lives – most importantly through participating in social arrangements – be justifiable to common human reason, no matter what one's specific outlook on life, or conception of the good, is. The idea of equal respect for persons interpreted in terms of intersubjective justifiability is what I take to be the hallmark of contemporary liberalism. When liberals approach issues of international morality, they do so from within this particular justificatory standpoint. But how do they answer the *question of extension*, namely the question of whether principles of domestic justice should extend to the world at large?

---

[8] Jeremy Waldron, 'Theoretical Foundations of Liberalism', *The Philosophical Quarterly*, 37 (147) (1987), 127–50, p. 128.
[9] Rawls, *A Theory of Justice*, ch. 3.
[10] Waldron, 'Theoretical Foundations of Liberalism', p. 144, emphases original.

1.3 LIBERALISM AND GLOBAL JUSTICE: THE DEBATE

As anticipated, within liberal quarters, there are two opposite stances on this question: cosmopolitanism and statism. The former answers the question in the affirmative, the latter in the negative.[11]

Cosmopolitans share the conviction that, given the fundamental moral equality of persons, the *egalitarian* principles liberals adopt to assess domestic distributions of liberties, opportunities, and economic goods should apply to the world at large. Specifically, for most contemporary liberals, societies are just so long as they grant their citizens equal civil and political rights, as well as equal opportunities, and place strict constraints on permissible economic inequalities. Only then could social arrangements be justified in the eyes of all.

In light of this, cosmopolitans say, it would be irrational for people to want to live in a world where their fate is in large part determined by morally arbitrary factors, over which they have no control, such as their countries of birth. If the domestic social order needs to be justified in the eyes of all, so does the global one, and it is unclear why common human reason would deliver different answers in these two cases. That is, it is unclear why egalitarian justice should apply domestically, but not globally.

Although different cosmopolitan theorists justify this claim in different ways, they all believe that equal respect for persons requires egalitarian justice both at home and abroad. Some theorists, such as Simon Caney, Kok-Chor Tan, and Charles Beitz (in his more recent work), believe that equality follows directly from the principle of equal respect for persons, and thus automatically extends to the world at large.[12] Others, such as Thomas Pogge, Charles Beitz (in his earlier work), and Darrel Moellendorf, hold that equal respect for persons requires substantive equality only between people who stand in particular kinds of relations *vis-à-vis* one another – for example between citizens sharing a common set of legal, political, and economic institutions, what Rawls calls a 'basic structure of society'.[13] For these 'relational cosmopolitans', such relevant relations can now be said to exist worldwide.[14]

---

[11] This definition is offered in Charles R. Beitz, 'Social and Cosmopolitan Liberalism', *International Affairs*, 75 (3) (1999), 515–29.

[12] Charles R. Beitz, 'Cosmopolitan Ideals and National Sentiment', *The Journal of Philosophy*, 80 (10) (1983), 591–600; Simon Caney, *Justice beyond Borders: A Global Political Theory* (Oxford: Oxford University Press, 2005); and Kok-Chor Tan, *Justice without Borders: Cosmopolitanism, Nationalism and Patriotism* (Cambridge: Cambridge University Press, 2004).

[13] Thomas W. Pogge, *Realizing Rawls* (Ithaca, NY: Cornell University Press, 1989); Charles R. Beitz, *Political Theory and International Relations* with a new afterword (Princeton, NJ: Princeton University Press, 1999); and Darrel Moellendorf, *Cosmopolitan Justice* (Boulder, CO: Westview Press, 2002).

[14] I borrow the distinction between relational and non-relational cosmopolitanism from Andrea Sangiovanni, 'Global Justice, Reciprocity, and the State', *Philosophy and Public Affairs*, 35 (1) (2007), 3–39, pp. 5–8.

Contrary to cosmopolitans, statists hold that a correct interpretation of equal respect grounds duties of egalitarian justice domestically but only more modest duties of assistance and just interstate conduct internationally. On this view – which corresponds to Rawls's own and has been partly defended by scholars such as David Miller, David Reidy, Thomas Nagel, Michael Blake, and Andrea Sangiovanni[15] – what reason demands varies across different contexts. Different practices produce different goods and express different values: while domestic justice assesses the quality of the relations between free and equal citizens, international justice concerns the relations between free and equal political communities. Consequently, statists consider equal civil and political rights and egalitarian socio-economic policies unsuitable for the international arena. At the international level, respect for equal civil and political rights is often replaced with a thinner criterion: respect for basic human rights; and egalitarian socio-economic policies, aimed at achieving equality of opportunity and wealth between individuals, are replaced by duties of assistance aimed at addressing absolute (as opposed to relative) deprivation between peoples. So long as peoples respect one another's right to self-determination, honour basic human rights, and assist one another in difficult circumstances, the demands of international morality are entirely fulfilled.

Even though statists may be regarded as defending an account of international 'justice' based on principles of respect for the sovereignty of minimally just states and mutual assistance between them, the notion of justice they employ at the global level significantly differs from the one they champion domestically. This is why I claim that they answer the question of extension in the negative. No matter how they call their principles of international morality, at least *prima facie*, these seem far from being an extension of principles of domestic justice.

The differences between cosmopolitans' and statists' outlooks on global justice have significant theoretical and practical implications, especially when it comes to how we conceptualize the demandingness and stringency of our duties towards the global poor. From the viewpoint of demandingness, there is a clear difference between promoting cosmopolitan global socio-economic

---

[15] John Rawls, *The Law of Peoples* (Cambridge, MA: Harvard University Press, 1999); David Miller, *On Nationality* (Oxford: Clarendon Press, 1995); Thomas Nagel, 'The Problem of Global Justice', *Philosophy and Public Affairs*, 33 (2) (2005), 113–47; Michael Blake, 'Distributive Justice, State Coercion, and Autonomy', *Philosophy and Public Affairs*, 30 (3) (2001), 257–96; David A. Reidy, 'Rawls on International Justice: A Defense', *Political Theory*, 32 (3) (2004), 291–319; and Andrea Sangiovanni, 'Global Justice, Reciprocity, and the State', *Philosophy and Public Affairs*, 35 (1) (2007), 3–39. As suggested in footnote 5, David Miller's *National Responsibility and Global Justice* does not fall quite as neatly within the statist camp as I describe it. See Laura Valentini, 'Cosmopolitan or Social Liberal? Review of David Miller's *National Responsibility and Global Justice*', *Global Justice: Theory Practice Rhetoric*, 2 (2009), 50–3, for further discussion.

equality, and ensuring that every political community has sufficient resources to sustain itself. Needless to say, attaining the former goal requires much greater sacrifices on the part of wealthy nations than attaining the latter. From the viewpoint of stringency, while cosmopolitans explicitly regard our duties towards distant others as weighty duties of justice, statists are somewhat ambiguous in this respect. In particular, the way they characterize such duties suggests that they are instead weaker – though still obligatory – demands of humanitarian assistance.[16]

The distinction between justice and humanity is a familiar one in our moral vocabulary, and is central to much of the debate on global justice.[17] While principles of justice establish persons' entitlements, principles of humanity ground duties to help those in need with resources that are rightfully one's own.[18] Unlike humanity, justice creates a

> system of rights (and consequently of duties and obligations)... and 'rights' are protected fields for activity within which individuals or groups may pursue their interests.[19]

Infringing a duty of justice thus means violating someone's rights, by failing to respect her/his entitlements. This is why duties of justice are seen as particularly weighty. If you have a duty to help others in need, *a fortiori*, you have a duty not to deprive them of, or prevent them from accessing, resources that are justly theirs.[20]

To see this, consider the following two scenarios. Suppose John finds himself in need after recklessly gambling away all of his money. Moved by John's predicament, Greg decides to help him by offering to pay his rent. In so doing, Greg acts out of a duty of humanity: he generously

---

[16] I say 'suggests' because there are reasonable disagreements on this point. Thomas Nagel explicitly refers to humanitarian duties, but John Rawls is less clear in this respect. For example, some contend that his duties of assistance are, in fact, stringent and relatively demanding duties of justice [see e.g. David Reidy, 'A Just Global Economy: In Defense of Rawls', *Journal of Ethics*, 11 (2) (2007), 193–236; and Rex Martin, 'Rawls on International Distributive Economic Justice: Taking a Closer Look', in Rex Martin and David Reidy (eds.), *Rawls's Law of Peoples: A Realistic Utopia?* (Oxford: Blackwell, 2006), 226–42], while others argue that they are weaker duties of humanity [see e.g. Tan, *Justice without Borders*, pp. 66ff.; and Thomas W. Pogge, '"Assisting" the Global Poor', in Deen K. Chatterjee (ed.), *The Ethics of Assistance: Morality and the Distant Needy* (Cambridge: Cambridge University Press, 2004), 260–88]. I find the latter interpretation more in line with the substance of Rawls's duty. See also footnote 9, ch. 4.

[17] Other terms used to indicate duties of humanity are 'beneficence' and 'charity'.

[18] Brian Barry, 'Humanity and Justice in Global Perspective', in Brian Barry, *Liberty and Justice: Essays in Political Theory 2* (Oxford: Clarendon Press, 1991), 182–210, p. 209. See also Tan, *Justice without Borders*, pp. 66ff., and Sylvie Loriaux, 'Beneficence and Distributive Justice in a Globalising World', *Global Society*, 20 (3) (2006), 251–65.

[19] W. D. Lamont, 'Justice: Distributive and Corrective', *Philosophy*, 16 (61) (1941), 3–18, p. 3.

[20] Barry, 'Humanity and Justice', pp. 204–10.

Introduction: The Problem of Global Justice

supports John, 'he does him good', because John is in extremely difficult circumstances.[21]

Now suppose Greg ends up being destitute because John refuses to return the money Greg had previously lent him. When John eventually pays the money back, under threat of a lawsuit, he certainly cannot take credit for generously helping Greg. It is not that Greg has found himself in trouble and John has big-heartedly rescued him: John has put Greg into trouble in the first place. In such a scenario, John's duty towards Greg is certainly more stringent than in the former case. In other words, it is a duty of justice, not one of humanity.

With this broad characterization of the distinction between justice and humanity in hand, we are now better equipped fully to appreciate the difference between cosmopolitanism and statism.[22] Cosmopolitans, who believe that liberal-egalitarian *justice* should apply to the global arena, hold that the *de facto* system of entitlements defining people's respective 'fields for activity' across the world is unjust. For it to be just, it should conform with liberal principles of domestic justice, granting all human beings equal civil and political rights, and placing strict limits on permissible global socio-economic inequalities. This implies that at least part (if not all) of what liberal citizens, and their governments, ought to do in order to improve the situation of the world's least advantaged is in principle *owed* to them.

For statists, on the other hand, liberal citizens, and their governments, have a duty to *help* the poor meet their basic needs and develop viable social institutions. These international distributive obligations appear to be more akin to duties of humanity than to duties of justice, thereby suggesting that, whatever resources the global privileged *ought to invest* to help the world's poor should be seen as rightfully theirs and not as *belonging* to the world's less fortunate nations in the first place.

In short, the duties advocated by cosmopolitans seem to be both more stringent and more demanding than those advocated by statists. These different moral stances have different implications for action. While by focusing on the global system of entitlements, cosmopolitans implicitly direct our attention towards radical institutional reform at the international level, statists'

---

[21] This is a simplified scenario. Of course, if John and Greg lived in the real world, one would have to wonder whether the best way for Greg to discharge his duties of humanity would be to help reckless John, or to support charities and NGOs helping the distant needy.

[22] In particular, some ways of drawing the distinction, especially those resting on the difference between negative and positive, perfect and imperfect, duties have been challenged in the literature. See e.g. Henry Shue, 'Mediating Duties', *Ethics*, 98 (4) (1988), 687–704. For this reason, at this introductory stage, I have kept my account of the distinction as general and as uncontroversial as possible. I shall offer a fuller characterization of this distinction later on in the book. For a critique of the distinction, see Allen Buchanan, 'Justice and Charity', *Ethics*, 97 (3) (1987), 558–75.

duties of assistance or mutual aid seem to be more aptly discharged through measures other than global institutional change – such as development aid – or, at any rate, through relatively modest institutional change.[23] In light of these differences, which side of the debate offers the more plausible answer to the problem of global justice?

1.4 LIBERALISM AND GLOBAL JUSTICE: THE IMPASSE

The contemporary liberal debate on global justice has reached an impasse. Although both cosmopolitanism and statism appeal to powerful intuitions, the principles they eventually defend do not provide fully satisfactory interpretations of the international requirements of a liberal political morality from both a theoretical and a practical viewpoint. In what follows, I offer a broad outline of their perceived theoretical and practical deficiencies (leaving a more detailed treatment of them to subsequent chapters).

1.4.1 Theoretical Difficulties

From a theoretical viewpoint, taking peoples, rather than individual human beings, as first objects of moral concern, Rawlsian statists are often accused of failing to be true to the liberal commitment to the fundamental equality of persons. If domestic institutions are to be evaluated on the basis of how they affect persons' interests, why should international institutions be assessed in relation to different moral standards? As a result of this shift in perspective, so the critique goes, statists defend implausibly permissive standards of international toleration, welcoming non-liberal societies as members in good standing of a just international order. Within such societies, citizens are not treated with equal respect: for instance, women might be underprivileged; and members of religious or ethnic minorities might be legally forbidden from running for public offices. Statists' criteria of toleration thus seem inconsistent with the fundamental commitments of any plausible liberal outlook on justice.

Moreover, statists are accused of failing to appreciate the deep structural nature of global politics, or at any rate to downplay its normative significance. This appears most clearly in their insistence that liberal peoples owe the world's poor a duty of aid or assistance. On the statist picture Rawls proposes, for example, global poverty is not produced (or partly produced) by international injustice, but rather it results from misfortune or lack of appropriate

---

[23] See Beitz, *Political Theory and International Relations*, pp. 127ff.; and Tan, *Justice without Borders*, pp. 66–74.

social institutions in the countries affected by it. The causes of poverty in developing countries are almost exclusively endogenous, so that all liberal societies have to do is *helping* these 'burdened' nations become 'well ordered'.[24]

Rawls's picture of the relations between states, the critics contend, severely downplays the extent of global interdependence, and consequently misconstrues the nature of liberal societies' responsibilities towards developing countries. Nowadays, what happens in one part of the world is at least partly determined by decisions made elsewhere. Just to mention one example, in May 2008, *Newsweek* reported about the alarming increase in food prices worldwide and the related intensification of food riots across the globe. Interviewed by the magazine, Michael Pollan, a professor of journalism at UC Berkeley and an expert in food politics, suggested that

> The worldwide crisis over food prices is the direct result of the decision, made by the Bush administration in 2006, to begin feeding large quantities of American corn to American automobiles, in the form of ethanol. This fateful decision led to a run-up in corn prices, which in turn led farmers to plant more corn and less soy and wheat – leading to the surge in the price of all grains. But make no mistake: we've created a situation where American SUVs are competing with African eaters for grains. We can see who is winning.[25]

Critics of statism complain that its theoretical framework is either unable to capture these systemic phenomena, or assigns insufficient moral significance to them. Indeed, the fact that statists' descriptive account of world politics is, arguably, incomplete does not suffice to show that their conclusions are morally inadequate. For instance, there may be reasonable disagreement about whether, by turning corn into ethanol, the United States have in any way committed an injustice against the world's poor. Causal responsibility need not translate into moral responsibility.

Critics of statism, however, do contend that many decisions taken by liberal societies both contribute to world poverty and are in fact unjust because of their foreseeability and avoidability. By way of example, they typically point to the unfairness of international financial and trade regulations. Thanks to their greater bargaining power, wealthy liberal states are able to secure for themselves unfairly profitable terms of agreement, to the detriment of less powerful nations. There must be something unjust, the critics complain, in developing countries being forced to open their markets (when only protectionist measures would allow their infant industry to compete on the global plane), while

---

[24] This critique has been forcefully advanced by Thomas W. Pogge in 'Critical Study: Rawls on International Justice', *The Philosophical Quarterly*, 51 (203) (2001), 246–53.

[25] *Newsweek*, 'How to feed the world' (19 May 2008), available online at http://www.newsweek.com/id/136360/page/8 (last accessed 11 July 2008).

the United States and Europe get away with subsidizing their already prosperous textile and agricultural sectors.[26]

In sum, critics of statism complain that, in circumstances of high global interdependence, liberal societies' duties towards the world's poor cannot be regarded as a mere matter of assistance. Before helping the world's poor, so the critics contend, we, privileged inhabitants of wealthy countries, should also make sure not to harm them. Statist assistance alone is thus morally inadequate as a response to world poverty.[27]

If too much toleration and blindness to systemic unfairness undermine statism, moral intransigence and blindness to special relationships threaten the plausibility of cosmopolitanism. First, by championing the application of liberal-egalitarian principles of justice to the world at large, cosmopolitans are routinely accused of failing to appreciate the moral significance of communal ties, of giving up crucial liberal values such as self-determination and national autonomy, and of surreptitiously promoting Western imperialism. In short, on the critics' view, cosmopolitans' globalization of domestic principles of justice is self-defeating: it undermines the values such principles are meant to protect.[28]

These general criticisms take different forms, depending on the particular type of cosmopolitanism at which they are directed. For instance, non-relational cosmopolitans are thought to subscribe to too unsophisticated a methodology, incorrectly thinking that the moral equality of persons always translates into substantive civil, political, and socio-economic equality. Non-relational cosmopolitans, so critics argue, mistakenly believe that the principle of equal respect *per se* tells us what we owe to each other, while a plausible account of our respective entitlements can only be constructed in relation to particular social contexts. Otherwise, we would have to be committed to the implausible view that our duties towards our families and friends are the same as our duties towards our fellow citizens, in fact the same as our duties towards all other human beings.[29]

Relational cosmopolitans, on the other hand, acknowledge the context-dependent nature of moral duties. On their views, equal respect for persons grounds liberal-egalitarian justice only in virtue of the existence of particular kinds of relations between individuals, such as those between fellow citizens. Relational cosmopolitans' mistake, so the critics contend, lies in their

---

[26] See e.g. Pogge, '"Assisting" the Global Poor'; and Darrel Moellendorf, 'The World Trade Organization and Egalitarian Justice', *Metaphilosophy*, 36 (1/2) (2005), 145–62.

[27] See Thomas W. Pogge, *World Poverty and Human Rights: Cosmopolitan Responsibilities and Reforms* (Cambridge: Polity Press, 2002).

[28] See e.g. Timothy Brennan, 'Cosmopolitanism and Internationalism', *New Left Review*, 7 (2001), 75–84.

[29] See e.g. David Miller, 'Against Global Egalitarianism', *The Journal of Ethics*, 9 (1/2) (2005), 55–79, pp. 66–7.

Introduction: The Problem of Global Justice

conclusion that the relevant relations now also occur on a global scale. As there is no world state, this claim is implausible. Globalization may have increased global interactions and interdependence, but it is certainly far from having generated a global society mirroring domestic ones.

To conclude, statists appear to neglect the normative relevance of global interdependence, thereby downplaying liberal societies' responsibilities towards the world's poor. Relational cosmopolitans seem to overemphasize the systemic, integrated, character of world politics, thereby exaggerating liberal societies' responsibilities for world poverty. Finally, non-relational cosmopolitans problematically move from the general principle of the moral equality of persons to a global egalitarian account of justice.

1.4.2 Practical Difficulties

Parallel to the theoretical difficulties affecting cosmopolitanism and statism are several 'practical' difficulties. Both of these outlooks are in fact often charged with failing to guide action in the real world. From a guidance viewpoint, statist approaches are accused of being too realistic and subservient to the *status quo*. This is a direct consequence of their peoples-centred framework, and assistance-based account of liberal societies' duties towards poor nations.

By failing to appreciate the systemic causes of global poverty, so the argument goes, statists not only mischaracterize the moral relations between liberal and developing countries, but are also unable to offer an effective remedy to the problem of global poverty. If the causes of world poverty are at least partly systemic, focusing on 'interactional' duties of assistance will certainly not suffice to eradicate them. By insisting that liberal societies should help the poor, without realizing that they should first stop harming them, statists' practical recommendations are likely to perpetuate, rather than eliminate, global poverty.[30]

Far from being accused of *status-quo* bias, cosmopolitans' accounts of global justice are instead dismissed as implausibly idealistic and utopian. Critics worry that the cosmopolitan ideal will fail to motivate agents, if anything because the institutional reforms needed to realize it are so radical that one does not know where to begin. Even more troublingly, the critics warn us that attempting to realize the cosmopolitan ideal is likely to be dangerous and counterproductive in at least two ways. First, it might attract the hostility of non-liberal societies, thus threatening international peace and security. Second, it might require the establishment of world-large state-like

---

[30] See Pogge, '"Assisting" the Global Poor'.

institutions, and these would either be unstable (in the best-case scenario) or degenerate into global despotism.[31]

In short, while statist principles are unable effectively to guide action because they are too subservient to the *status quo*, cosmopolitan principles fail because the ideal world they advocate is too detached from the *status quo*. Given that a capacity to guide action is a necessary attribute of any plausible normative theory (or at least so most normative theorists, including myself, think), these practical difficulties further undermine the tenability of cosmopolitans' and statists' respective accounts of global justice.

1.5 MY PROPOSED WAY OUT OF THE IMPASSE

Given the theoretical and practical difficulties discussed in the previous section, the debate between cosmopolitanism and statism appears to have reached an impasse. Genuine progress in theorizing about global justice seems possible only by 'mediating' between these two positions. In light of this, more conciliatory, less divisive approaches to global justice have started to emerge in recent years, and the aim of the present book is to lay out and defend one such approach in particular. More specifically, I ask *whether there can be a coherent liberal answer to the question of extension capable of overcoming the theoretical and practical difficulties with cosmopolitanism and statism*. As I briefly mentioned in the opening section, my answer is articulated in a three-part argument. In Parts I and II of the book, I analyse the most prominent accounts of cosmopolitanism and statism, and trace their theoretical and practical difficulties to methodological flaws. In Part III, building on the conclusions reached in Parts I and II, I develop a methodologically sound normative framework for constructing principles of justice, and consider its implications for the question of justice beyond borders.

Central to this framework is a particular account of the normative and empirical grounds of duties of justice. From a normative viewpoint, I argue that both duties of justice and duties of humanity are generated by the principle of equal respect for persons. While duties of justice are fundamentally duties not to infringe persons' right to lead their lives in accordance with their conceptions of the good (what I call their right to freedom), duties of humanitarian assistance are duties to help those in need when this is not too costly to oneself.

From an empirical viewpoint, while duties of humanity apply whenever there are persons in need who could be helped at reasonable costs, duties of

---

[31] See Rawls's *The Law of Peoples*.

justice are activated by coercive relations. Coercive relations are necessary and sufficient triggers of concerns of justice. Specifically, the role of duties of justice is to place limits on permissible coercion, where coercion is understood broadly, as always involving non-trivial restrictions of freedom.[32] I distinguish between two types of coercion: interactional and systemic. The former is coercion exercised by an agent (be it a collective or an individual), the latter is coercion exercised through a system of rules supported by a large enough number of agents. On this view, what duties of justice apply beyond borders depends on what forms of coercion are present or possible at the international level. Since, plausibly, the world at large is marked by systemic as well as interactional coercion, I conclude that a theory of global justice should contain both interactional principles evaluating the justness of interstate coercion, and systemic principles placing constraints on the way states and their citizens coerce one another indirectly, through supporting world-large practices and systems of rules.

I argue that this coercion-based normative framework offers a plausible liberal answer to the question of extension, steering a middle course between cosmopolitanism and statism, and laying the foundations for an approach to global justice capable of overcoming the theoretical and practical difficulties affecting these competing views.

Before providing a more detailed outline of the book's contents, one aspect of it is worth emphasizing, namely its modularity. The arguments offered in the book, and the outlook on global justice they support, can be accepted or rejected in a piecemeal fashion. For instance, some readers may agree with my methodological criticisms of cosmopolitanism and statism, and yet find the particular framework I offer unconvincing (or vice versa). Other readers might instead think that my account of the role and conditions of applicability of justice is correct, and yet doubt that the notion of coercion appropriately captures them. If so, these readers can simply choose a different label for it. Or else, readers might agree with my account of both justice and coercion, but find the particular conception of freedom I employ to define them unsatisfactory. In this case, they can keep much of my framework, and simply replace my notion of freedom with whichever one they favour.

In short, even though the different parts of this book mutually support one another, the views presented in it are meant to be flexible. Of course, this is of little consolation for readers (hopefully not too many!) who find *all* of my claims implausible. However, it is good news for those who are at least somewhat sympathetic to my proposal, but not entirely convinced by it. Given the proposal's modularity and flexibility, these readers can follow me

---

[32] Some will find this initial definition of coercion implausibly broad. I shall explain in Chapter 6 why I do not think it is.

'part of the way', and then take the framework I offer in the direction they find most congenial.

1.6 DETAILED CONTENTS

In Part I of the book, I examine different versions of cosmopolitanism and show that while the practical objection of inability to guide action is inconclusive, the theoretical objection of lack of consistency with liberal values points to significant shortcomings in (at least some versions of) the cosmopolitan outlook.

In Chapter 2, 'Assessing the Cosmopolitan Ideal', I explore the *practical implications* of the cosmopolitan conception of a just world order, and discuss what I call 'the guidance critique' of such a conception. According to this critique, cosmopolitan principles are either likely to be counterproductive, leading to global conflict if not global despotism, or altogether unable to guide action in the world in which we live. I argue that those who advance this critique either misapply cosmopolitan principles, or have unreasonable expectations about the sort of guidance a theory of justice can plausibly deliver. Theories of justice do not answer questions such as 'What ought we to do, here and now?' Instead, they offer normative frameworks for guiding our thinking about such questions. As cosmopolitanism does provide a distinctive normative framework, one that supports duties of *egalitarian justice* with global reach, I conclude that it fulfils those guidance requirements that can be plausibly placed on any theory of justice.

In Chapter 3, 'Justifying Cosmopolitanism: A Methodological Critique', I consider the different methodologies grounding the *justification* of cosmopolitan principles, and argue that they are affected by significant difficulties. In the case of non-relational cosmopolitanism, such difficulties are serious enough to warrant rejection. I argue that non-relational cosmopolitans' defence of global equality as a demand of justice gives excessive weight to intuitions about highly counterfactual scenarios, which should be largely discounted when designing a theory of justice for the world in which we live. Because of this methodologically dubious reliance on intuitions about unfamiliar scenarios, non-relational cosmopolitans fail appropriately to capture what distinguishes duties of justice from demands of humanitarian assistance.

My critique of relational cosmopolitanism is more nuanced. I argue that its empirical claim that there exists a global basic structure of society, identical to the domestic basic structure, is poorly supported. Even though it cannot be conclusively refuted, it cannot be convincingly established either, because of both empirical complexities and the vagueness of the (widely invoked) Rawlsian idea of the basic structure of society. For this reason, I suggest that we should suspend judgement on 'strong' cosmopolitan views – that is, those advocating the direct extension of principles of domestic egalitarian justice to the global realm – and provisionally endorse a 'weak' cosmopolitan approach: one that places limits on permissible global socio-economic inequalities without insisting that they should coincide with those placed on domestic ones. This concludes my analysis of cosmopolitanism.

In Part II of the book, I discuss statism. My conclusions about this position are almost the exact reverse of my conclusions about cosmopolitanism. I argue that statists' rejection of egalitarian socio-economic justice at the global level is fully consistent with liberal values but that their overall normative framework is unable successfully to guide action in real-world circumstances.

In Chapter 4, 'Assessing the Statist Ideal', I consider the complaint that the statist ideal is excessively biased in favour of the *status quo*, and argue that this critique is only partly successful. While statists' refusal to extend egalitarian socio-economic justice to the global realm does not in itself indicate subservience to the *status quo*, statist principles have unduly conservative implications because they are insufficiently sensitive to the main causes of international injustice. Cosmopolitan critics are right in charging statists' accounts of justice with neglecting forms of international interdependence which significantly affect poor countries' prosperity. Although statists rightly identify peoples (states) as important subjects of international justice in virtue of the particular forms of coercive power they exercise by directly interfering in one another's affairs, they fail to appreciate that these are not the only forms of international coercion standing in need of justification. The more the world becomes interdependent, the more international coercion gains a systemic dimension. Individuals and communities may constrain and affect one another's fate not only through direct intervention but also through participating in global informal practices and formal institutional arrangements. Since the normative outlook underpinning statism is blind to these potential sources of injustice, its principles may very well turn out to be *status-quo* biased, and thus rightly criticized on guidance grounds.

In Chapter 5, 'Justifying Statism: A Methodological Critique', I identify and discuss the methodological flaws that make statism excessively subservient to the *status quo* from a guidance point of view. In particular, I focus on three methodological commitments on the basis of which statist conclusions have been advocated. These are (*a*) the view that principles of justice are constructed by interpreting the values informing the specific practices they aim to regulate; (*b*) the view that principles of justice can only guide the conduct of authoritative agents, such as the state; and (*c*) the view that principles of justice only apply in the presence of specific cooperative or coercive relations. Since (*a*) the values underpinning global practices differ from domestic ones, (*b*) there exists no global authoritative agent, and (*c*) domestic coercive and cooperative relations are not replicated at the global level, advocates of statism contend that principles of domestic justice cannot be coherently extended beyond the nation-state.

This threefold methodological defence of statism reinforces, rather than discredits, the charge of *status-quo* bias advanced in the previous chapter. I argue that by (*a*) relying on already moralized understandings of existing practices, (*b*) placing overly demanding agency requirements on normative principles, and (*c*) adopting excessively narrow accounts of the conditions under which principles of justice apply, statists by and large limit the reach of justice to those activities we already submit to justice-based assessment. Their methodology lacks sufficient critical capacity, and should therefore be rejected. This concludes my analysis of statism and marks the beginning of Part III of the book, where I develop a normative framework for understanding the function, content, and scope of principles of justice.

In Chapter 6, 'The Function of Justice: Assessing Coercion', I develop a new and nuanced account of the types of social relations that trigger demands of justice. I argue that the function of justice is to limit the ways we may permissibly restrict others' freedom, that is, to limit the ways we may permissibly coerce them. Even though my outlook is centred on the familiar idea of coercion, it departs from standard treatments of this notion in important respects. In particular, standard views implicitly assume what I call a *narrow* account of coercion – that is, coercion exercised by an agent (typically the state) through commands backed by the threat of sanctions – whereas I distinguish between two types of coercion, *interactional* and *systemic*, and show that they both appropriately capture those constraints on freedom that, from a liberal viewpoint, stand in need of justice-based assessment.

Two key insights underpin my coercion-based normative framework. First, from a liberal perspective, certain restrictions of freedom – those I define as coercive – need special justification. The principles articulating the required justification are those we should call principles of justice. Second, the relevant restrictions of freedom need not be direct, perpetrated by an agent – collective or individual – against other agents. Instead, they can also be indirect, resulting from formal and informal social rules, supported by a large enough number of agents. This conclusion has important implications for our thinking about justice in the global realm, where there clearly are pervasive systems of formal and informal social rules but no overarching, state-like, group agent.

In Chapter 7, 'The Content of Justice: Freedom and Equality', I discuss how to move from a general concern with the justification of coercion, to particular substantive principles of justice. I argue that a social system is just only so long as it respects its subjects' right to freedom, namely their right to the necessary social conditions to lead autonomous lives, pursuing their ends and goals. For this to be the case, the distribution of freedom engendered by the system has to be justifiable in the eyes of all those who are subject to it. Focusing on domestic societies in particular (before turning to the global realm in the following chapter), I conclude that a multiplicity of distributive criteria might instantiate mutually justifiable distributions of freedom. This means that, if we wish to appeal to liberal mutual justifiability, we have to abandon the aspiration of offering a complete and conclusive theory of justice. Instead of identifying what justice positively requires, we are on firmer grounds simply pointing out what it must exclude.

More specifically, I argue that a domestic social system cannot be regarded as protecting its subjects' right to freedom unless it gives them (*a*) equal civil and political rights, (*b*) equal opportunities, and (*c*) adequate economic rights allowing them to take meaningful advantage of their civil and political guarantees. As there is bound to be reasonable disagreement about what (*c*) specifically entails, I only posit meeting persons' basic needs as a condition any society must satisfy in order to qualify as *reasonably* just or legitimate. What economic inequalities are permissible beyond this basic-needs threshold is a question to be answered on a case-by-case basis, and which should be ultimately decided through the democratic decision procedures of each political community. Contrary to most mainstream liberal accounts of justice, then, on my view, economic equality is *not a fundamental* demand of domestic justice.

In Chapter 8, 'The Scope of Justice: Global', I consider the implications of the normative framework developed in the previous two chapters for the question of justice beyond borders. According to this framework, both duties of justice and duties of humanitarian assistance are grounded in the principle of equal respect for persons. The former place limits on permissible coercion, while the latter require that we help those in need when this is not unreasonably costly to us. As the mere presence of need is sufficient to trigger duties of humanity, on the view I defend, citizens of wealthy liberal societies certainly have duties of humanitarian assistance to help the inhabitants of poorer nations. But what about duties of justice?

In this respect, thanks to its double focus – on systemic and interactional coercion – my normative framework steers a coherent middle course between cosmopolitanism and statism, and explains why each seems to get only part of the 'global justice picture' right. While statists typically concentrate on the moral evaluation of interactional coercion between states – setting out conditions for domestic sovereignty and international intervention – cosmopolitans are concerned with the justification of global systemic coercion. But a closer look at our world reveals that both types of coercion exist at the international level.

Interstate interactional coercion is a familiar phenomenon. States routinely act in ways that place constraints on one another's freedom, and hence on the freedom of their citizens. Moreover, the freedom of states and of their citizens is seriously constrained by systems of formal and informal social rules, stretching beyond national borders: think, for instance, of the global economy. States and their citizens are thus also subject to systemic coercion.

In light of this, I argue that a plausible liberal approach to global justice should contain principles assessing both interactional and systemic coercion. Statist principles of internal legitimacy and just interstate conduct need to be supplemented by cosmopolitan principles of global justice, assessing the justifiability of global systemic coercion. Even though there is (once again) bound to be reasonable disagreement about what justifying global systemic coercion requires, I argue that we can still plausibly identify what a just world order must exclude. For example, a system such as the one in which we live, where powerful actors can enhance their prosperity at the expense of weaker ones, is incompatible with the demands of justice. I bring the chapter to a close by sketching what a just world order would look like, suggesting that it would contain a plurality of states and supranational institutions, the latter in charge of regulating global systemic coercion (especially of an economic nature) so as to make it compatible with everyone's right to freedom.

Finally, in Chapter 9, 'Conclusion', I show that the view I defend successfully overcomes the theoretical and practical difficulties affecting cosmopolitanism and statism, and allows us to offer a principled answer to the question of extension. While the *concept* of justice, which indicates a broad category of principles placing limits on the legitimate exercise of coercion, can be extended from the domestic context to the world at large, different *conceptions* (i.e. different substantive principles) will apply to these two domains, in light of the different forms of coercion existing within them.[33] From a substantive viewpoint, this brings me to conclude that global justice requires more than statist assistance, but less than full-blown cosmopolitan equality. The chapter illustrates how my view helps us reframe the debate on global justice, steers a fruitful middle course between cosmopolitanism and statism, and offers unified grounds for talk of justice in the international arena.

Of course, once a coherent foundation for thinking about (global) justice has been developed, there remains the complex task of establishing what exactly global justice requires of us here and now. In this book, I shall have relatively little to say about this. While I argue that the coercion-based normative framework I defend may offer a plausible starting point for reasoning about our real-world duties and obligations, what the content of such duties and obligations actually is remains, to a significant extent, an open question. Moreover, it is an implication of my approach that this question can only be answered with the aid of specialists other than political philosophers, encompassing disciplines such as law, sociology, political science, and economics. Finally, the question 'What ought I to do?' is one for each of us to ask and for each of us to answer. In my capacity as a political philosopher, I can only offer an account of the fundamental principles that I believe should guide deliberation: the rest is up to you.

---

[33] For the distinction between concepts and conceptions, see Rawls, *A Theory of Justice*, p. 5; Rawls follows H. L. A. Hart, *The Concept of Law* (Oxford: Clarendon Press, 1961), pp. 155–9.

Part I

Cosmopolitanism

2

Assessing the Cosmopolitan Ideal

2.1 INTRODUCTION

Conceiving of the world at large as a unified polis, a *cosmopolis*, cosmopolitan theories hold that liberal-egalitarian principles of (domestic) justice are global in scope.[1] In a cosmopolitan world order, 'people everywhere stand to one another roughly as citizens of a liberal state stand to one another today. They have the same rights and the same opportunities, so that their life-chances depend only on individual characteristics', such as choice and hard work.[2] For the cosmopolitan, a child born in London's district of Mayfair, and one born in Kitwe, Zambia, ought to have roughly equal life prospects.[3] Inequalities between them should be condemned as unjust.

Even though it is unclear what the world would look like if cosmopolitan global equality were realized, it is clear enough that it would look radically different from the *status quo*. The distribution of social goods and resources would be completely reorganized, and so would the world's political and geographical boundaries. It is in fact doubtful that cosmopolitan justice could be realized in a politically and culturally fragmented system of states. The cosmopolitan ideal of a just global order is thus highly progressive, inviting us to envisage a world in which all human beings relate to each other as equals.

This radically progressive ideal has been challenged at both the level of its normative foundations and that of its practical implications. Foundational challenges focus on the different justifications offered in support of the claim that egalitarian principles of justice should apply globally. Practical challenges focus on the ability of cosmopolitan principles (or lack thereof) to criticize

---

[1] Cf. David Miller, *National Responsibility and Global Justice* (Oxford: Oxford University Press, 2007), pp. 23ff.
[2] David Miller, 'Caney's "International Distributive Justice": A Response', *Political Studies*, 50 (5) (2002), 974–7, p. 976. See also Simon Caney, 'International Distributive Justice', *Political Studies*, 49 (5) (2001), 974–97.
[3] For a similar example, see Darrel Moellendorf, *Cosmopolitan Justice* (Boulder, CO: Westview Press, 2002), p. 49.

existing practices and offer meaningful guidance towards institutional reform. Since a valid justification and a capacity to guide action are both widely regarded as necessary features of a plausible normative theory, failing to meet either requirement would seriously damage the credibility of cosmopolitan approaches.

In this chapter, I discuss only the second family of criticisms, and address a common set of worries about the 'downstream' practical consequences of cosmopolitan principles – what I shall call the 'guidance critique'. In the next one, I turn to the theoretical underpinnings of such principles and analyse the different justifications on which they may rest.

What, then, is so allegedly problematic about the real-world implications of cosmopolitan principles? Simply put, critics charge cosmopolitan justice with being so detached from existing social conditions that, as a guide for action, it is either useless or altogether counterproductive. Since this charge affects cosmopolitanism independently of the particular justification one might invoke in its defence (more than one is available), it has to be taken particularly seriously. Does it succeed in providing a decisive objection to cosmopolitanism? I argue that it does not.

My argument is structured as follows. In Section 2.2, I excavate the theoretical underpinnings of the guidance critique. I distinguish between two fundamentally different approaches to normative inquiry: embedded and transcendent. I consider John Rawls as a paradigmatic example of the former, and G. A. Cohen as a representative of the latter. I argue that only embedded approaches are moved by the guidance critique and suggest that, by their very nature, cosmopolitan theories cannot but be of an embedded kind. In Sections 2.3, 2.4, and 2.5, I look into such a critique more in detail and suggest three possible readings of it. I argue that none of them poses a serious threat to the cosmopolitan ideal, indeed to *any* normative ideal. I conclude that, even though the guidance critique does not suffice to refute cosmopolitanism, it draws attention to the incompleteness of cosmopolitan theories, and reveals that any answer to the question of whether the cosmopolitan ideal is realizable is bound to rest on speculative grounds, at least for the time being.

2.2 EMBEDDED AND TRANSCENDENT APPROACHES TO JUSTICE

Implicit in the definition of a normative theory is the idea that the principles constituting such a theory should be, in some sense (to be specified later), capable of guiding action. At the very least, this requirement entails meeting the 'ought implies can' proviso. If a theory of morally just action grounds commands that creatures like us, or institutions like the ones we can reasonably hope to create, would never be able to follow, the theory is for that very reason misguided.[4] At the basis of this guidance requirement lies a certain understanding of the point of normative theories in general, and of theories of justice in particular. A capacity to guide action is a constitutive feature of valid theories of justice only on a particular understanding of the function and subject of such theories.

Let me thus distinguish between two overall approaches to justice: embedded and transcendent.[5] I take John Rawls to be the most eminent contemporary proponent of the former, and G. A. Cohen of the latter. These approaches understand the question of justice in very different ways. On the one hand, the embedded approach sees justice as a matter of conferring rights on individuals competing over scarce resources, *given certain relevant natural and social facts*. These facts may include, for instance, moderate scarcity, limited altruism, and disagreement about both justice and the good.[6] Although the question of which facts are relevant is a matter of debate among advocates of the embedded approach – for example, solely general facts about the human condition, or also more specific facts about existing societies? – they all understand justice as offering a response to normative problems generated by those facts.

On the other hand, the transcendent approach sees justice as a fundamental value whose meaning is independent of any natural or social facts. On this view, justice is entirely 'disembedded', and it is conceptually independent of the facts that characterize the human condition in general, or existing human societies in particular. For proponents of the transcendent approach, the very same principles of justice would still hold true even if such facts about the human condition were drastically to change. To make better sense of

---

[4] See Harry Brighouse, *Justice* (Cambridge: Polity Press, 2004), ch. 2.

[5] This distinction should not be confused with Amartya Sen's recent distinction between transcendental and comparative approaches to justice. See Sen, 'What Do We Want from a Theory of Justice?', *Journal of Philosophy*, 103 (5) (2006), 215–38, and *The Idea of Justice* (Cambridge, MA: Harvard University Press, 2009). On Sen's view, while proponents of the former approach think of justice in categorical terms (for them, something is either just or unjust), proponents of the latter think of it in comparative terms (for them, something can be more or less just). On my view, by contrast, a transcendent approach to justice is one that *transcends* the circumstances of human existence, quite independently of its comparative or non-comparative nature. For a critique of Sen, see Laura Valentini, 'A Paradigm Shift in Theorizing about Justice? A Critique of Sen', *Economics and Philosophy*, 27 (3) (2011), 297–315.

[6] These conditions are the Humean 'circumstances of justice' discussed by John Rawls in *A Theory of Justice* (Oxford: Oxford University Press, 1999 rev. ed.), pp. 109–12. Rawls discusses disagreement about what is of value in life in *Political Liberalism* (New York: Columbia University Press, 1996).

2.2.1 The Embedded Approach

The embedded approach sees theories of justice as offering principles for fairly adjudicating competing claims over valued goods or resources. In so doing, these principles determine 'who has a right to what' within any given social system. For those who subscribe to this approach, justice is inextricably tied to the social dimension of the human condition; at the very least, it is *a response to the human problem* of living together in circumstances of moderate scarcity, limited altruism, and disagreement about what is of value in life.

Human beings are, to some extent, self-interested creatures: they strive to realize their ends and goals, their plans of life. As Rawls says, '[i]n an association of saints, agreeing on a common ideal... disputes about justice would not occur',[8] but they do occur among imperfect beings like us. To pursue their different ends and goals, human beings need material resources. When these are scarce, an agent's consumption of a certain resource inevitably results in others' being deprived of the opportunity to use it in pursuit of their own ends. Conflicts over resources are therefore bound to arise among agents living in close connection with one another – for example, within the same social system – that is, conflicts that will require the elaboration and implementation of criteria for adjudicating their competing claims, and establishing who has a right to what.[9] These are what Rawlsians call principles of justice.

In particular, justice demands that such conflicts be solved fairly, in a way that is true to the core liberal idea that each human being is, impartially speaking, equally an object of moral concern. As one scholar puts it, the problem of justice 'is part of the problem of how people are to pursue good lives for themselves, with every person attaching special importance to her own success, in a way that yet takes account of the equal importance of all their striving'.[10]

---

[7] This distinction broadly models the differences between G. A. Cohen's and John Rawls's approaches to justice. See Thomas W. Pogge, 'Cohen to the Rescue!', *Ratio*, 21 (4) (2008), 454–75; and David Miller, 'Political Philosophy for Earthlings', in David Leopold and Marc Stears (eds.), *Political Theory: Methods and Approaches* (Oxford: Oxford University Press, 2008), 29–48, for further discussion.

[8] Rawls, *A Theory of Justice*, p. 112. See also Rawls's 'Justice as Fairness', *Philosophical Review*, 67 (2) (1958), 164–94, p. 173.

[9] Here, I have benefited from Jeremy Waldron's description and interpretation of Kant's account of the state of nature. See Waldron, 'Special Ties and Natural Duties', *Philosophy and Public Affairs*, 22 (1) (1993), 3–30, pp. 14–15.

[10] A. J. Julius, 'Basic Structure and the Value of Equality', *Philosophy and Public Affairs*, 31 (4) (2003), 321–55, p. 326.

Principles of justice are meant to offer a solution to this problem. When they are respected, each person is in a position to pursue her/his plans of life without unduly limiting others' possibility to do the same. Justice thereby places constraints on action and urges us to respect others' spheres of agency, defined by their rights and entitlements to liberties, resources, and opportunities. A just society is one in which citizens relate to one another as equals: no one's agency is unduly constrained and no one is oppressed.

So understood, justice is an 'embedded' virtue, one that does not transcend the circumstances of human social existence but is inherently tied to them. Moreover, given that, for proponents of the embedded approach, principles of justice play a social function, their design must be informed not only by normative but also by empirical assumptions about the particular social system they are meant to regulate. To illustrate this point, consider once again Rawls's work.

As I briefly mentioned in Chapter 1, Rawls's principles of justice are arrived at through a hypothetical consent test, known as the original position, where representatives of citizens are asked to select the principles that should govern their society. The original position contains three types of constraints: (*a*) normative; (*b*) factual; and (*c*) formal (or, as I shall call them, 'functional'). The *normative* component of the original position embodies the idea of a *fair* agreement between parties concerned to further their interests. The fairness of such an agreement is ensured by placing the parties under a 'veil of ignorance', which leaves them in the dark about their natural talents, social position, specific conception of the good, and the characteristics of the society in which they live.[11] While prevented from accessing particular, contingent information about themselves and their society, the parties are not prevented from knowing 'general facts'. These correspond to what I called the *factual component* of the original position. In Rawls's own words:

> [t]here are no limitations on general information, that is on general laws and theories, since conceptions of justice must be adjusted to the characteristics of the systems of social cooperation which they are to regulate, and there is no reason to rule out these facts.[12]

The availability of this considerable factual knowledge to the parties is justified on the basis of the specific role that principles of justice are meant to play. Since this role is to regulate the basic structure of society in such a way as to ensure that 'each gets her/his due' (i.e. that citizens' conflicting claims over social goods are justly settled), such principles must be applicable to 'ongoing political arrangements' and generate sufficient support on the part of citizens to endure over time.[13] Hence, the parties in the original position deliberate

---

[11] Rawls, *A Theory of Justice*, pp. 118–19.   [12] Rawls, *A Theory of Justice*, p. 119.
[13] John Rawls, 'The Independence of Moral Theory', *Proceedings and Addresses of The American Philosophical Association*, 48 (1974–1975), 5–22, p. 13.

over competing principles in the light of 'general facts about the world, including basic psychological principles'.[14] As Rawls says, 'the principles of justice *presuppose* a certain theory of social institutions' and human psychology.[15]

Finally, in addition to normative and factual stipulations, the parties in the original position deliberate taking into account what Rawls calls 'formal constraints on the concept of right'.[16] As one commentator has suggested, however, the terminology of 'formal constraints' seems somewhat misplaced. Instead, most of the constraints Rawls has in mind would seem to be better labelled as 'pragmatic' or, as I would call them, 'functional'.[17] It is the social role of principles of justice, namely that of reaching 'a common conception of justice' that justifies such constraints. Rawls nicely summarizes these constraints by saying that principles must 'be general in form and universal in application, that is to be publicly recognized as a final court of appeal for ordering the conflicting claims of moral persons'.[18]

Rawls's theory is thus premised on a practical understanding of justice. On this understanding, principles of justice are inherently tied to the human condition, and have a social function that they can perform only by meeting certain guidance requirements. Crucially, the guidance critique only makes sense against conceptions of justice so understood.[19] This point is worth making because, even if, at first sight, one might be tempted to consider 'embedded' approaches as indisputably dominant in contemporary theorizing about justice, they are not. Diametrically opposed to embedded approaches are what I call transcendent approaches to justice.

2.2.2 The Transcendent Approach

Proponents of the transcendent approach see justice as a fundamental moral value insensitive to existing facts, including general facts about the human condition.[20] Justice, on this view, is not responsive to the sorts of creatures that

---

[14] Rawls, *A Theory of Justice*, p. 399.
[15] Rawls, *A Theory of Justice*, p. 138, emphasis added.
[16] Rawls, *A Theory of Justice*, pp. 112ff.
[17] See Fred D'Agostino, 'The Legacies of John Rawls', in Thom Brooks and Fabian Freyenhagen (eds.), *The Legacy of John Rawls* (London: Continuum, 2005), 195–212, p. 207.
[18] Rawls, *A Theory of Justice*, p. 117.
[19] On this, see Laura Valentini, 'On the Apparent Paradox of Ideal Theory', *Journal of Political Philosophy*, 17 (3) (2009), 332–55.
[20] See G. A. Cohen, 'Facts and Principles', *Philosophy and Public Affairs*, 31 (3) (2003), 211–45 and *Rescuing Justice and Equality* (Cambridge, MA: Harvard University Press, 2008). For a detailed analysis of Cohen's argument on the *logical relations* between facts and principles, see Miriam Ronzoni and Laura Valentini, 'On the Meta-Ethical Status of Constructivism: Reflections on G. A. Cohen's "Facts and Principles"', *Politics, Philosophy & Economics*, 7 (4) (2008), 403–22.

we are or the circumstances in which we live. Transcendent theorists thus think of justice in the same way in which Plato famously thought of it: as belonging to an order of ideas transcending the circumstances of human existence.

To gain a more concrete understanding of what form a transcendent outlook on justice might take, consider the principles of justice defended by G. A. Cohen, the most prominent contemporary advocate of this approach. Cohen holds the view – labelled 'luck-egalitarianism' – that inequalities in agents' life prospects are justified so long as they are traceable to their genuine choices but unjustified if they are due to circumstances that lie outside their control.[21] Justice is about the choice-sensitive equal distribution of life prospects across different agents, regardless of the specific natural and social circumstances in which they live. On Cohen's view, the range of principles of justice is thus maximally extensive. In Thomas Pogge's words, these principles are meant to 'cover all possible combinations of facts and hence all possible worlds'.[22]

It is also important to note that, although Cohen sees luck-equality as a fundamental demand of justice, his commitment to equality is not of an exclusive nature.[23] For him, and others in sympathy with his view, distributive equality is only one among several values that ought to be optimally realized.[24] This is why Cohen calls himself a 'weak egalitarian', namely an egalitarian who thinks that the achievement of equality should be made compatible, or suitably balanced, with the pursuit of other values. As he says, 'there is something that justice requires people to have equal amounts of, not no matter what, but to whatever extent is allowed by values which compete with distributive equality'.[25]

Since Cohen thinks of justice as one of a wider set of morally worthy goals to be promoted, on his view, the specific task of theories of justice is to offer the best interpretation of the value of equality in particular, and not the best account of the principles grounding the rights and duties that apply to existing

---

[21] The label luck-egalitarianism was coined by Elizabeth Anderson in 'What is the Point of Equality?', *Ethics*, 109 (2) (1999), 287–337. In particular, Cohen's favoured version of luck-egalitarianism is equality of access to advantage.

[22] Pogge, 'Cohen to the Rescue!', p. 469.

[23] Specifically, Cohen sees it as a fundamental demand of distributive justice. See his distinction between a just society and a just distribution in *Rescuing Justice and Equality*, pp. 127–8. Since Cohen is mostly concerned with criticizing Rawls's approach to justice, it is particularly hard to form an accurate picture of his own views on justice. For discussion, see Patrick Tomlin, 'Survey Article: Internal Doubts about Cohen's Rescue of Justice', *Journal of Political Philosophy*, 18 (2) (2010), 228–47.

[24] For somewhat similar views, see Richard J. Arneson, 'Luck Egalitarianism and Prioritarianism', *Ethics*, 110 (2) (2000), 339–49, p. 345; and Andrew Mason, 'Just Constraints', *British Journal of Political Science*, 34 (3) (2004), 251–68.

[25] See G. A. Cohen, 'On the Currency of Egalitarian Justice', *Ethics*, 99 (4) (1989), 906–44.

agents. His work gives us tools to answer the *evaluative* question of what counts as a just state of affairs (tools that are meant to be valid across all possible worlds), but does not directly address the *normative* question of what principles (Cohen would say what 'rules of regulation') apply to us. The two questions are clearly related, but how exactly they relate to each other – for example, what weight justice should be given in our moral reasoning – is something Cohen does not explore.

This lack of engagement with normative questions is fully in line with the transcendent theorist's understanding of the task of political philosophy. For advocates of 'transcendentalism', political philosophy is not primarily concerned with guiding our actions in the world. It is not a fundamentally practical project. Instead, it is a matter of discovering what justice and other values are, quite independently of the implications that these values have for what we ought to do. If justice had no implications for action, for the transcendent theorist, political philosophy would still make sense as an intellectual enterprise. How does this view compare to Rawls's embedded approach?

2.2.3 The Two Approaches *vis-à-vis* One Another

It should be clear that, for embedded and transcendent approaches, the question of justice starkly differs.[26]

1. Transcendent theories ask: 'What is the value of justice in its pure form?'
2. Embedded theories ask: 'What principles should govern the assignment of rights and duties within a social system, given certain natural and social facts?'[27]

While question (2) assumes that principles of justice should perform a certain function, namely that of governing people's relations within different social systems by establishing 'who has a right to what', question (1) has no such functional connotation. Consequently, while plausible candidate answers to question (2) must display *some* capacity for guidance, no such guidance requirement applies to possible answers to question (1). As Cohen says, justice might 'not [be] something that the state, or, indeed, any other agent, is in a position to deliver'.[28] Rather than telling us 'what we should do', principles of

---

[26] See Valentini, 'On the Apparent Paradox of Ideal Theory', pp. 335–6, for a similar distinction.

[27] This can be taken as a generalized description of what Cohen calls 'rules of regulation'; see 'Facts and Principles', p. 241.

[28] G. A. Cohen, 'Expensive Taste Rides Again', in Justine Burley (ed.), *Dworkin and His Critics* (Oxford: Blackwell, 2004), 3–29, p. 18.

justice express 'what we should think even when what we should think makes *no* practical difference'.[29] They answer an evaluative question, but need not answer a normative one.

In light of this, whatever the merits of transcendent approaches, the particular line of critique I am considering in this chapter has no bite on them. If justice *need not* make any practical difference – if, indeed, fundamental principles of justice need not even respect the 'ought implies can' proviso – no argument pointing to its practical deficiencies can cause trouble to the transcendent theorist.[30]

This being the case, before proceeding in the discussion, we need to ask whether cosmopolitan (and statist) theories can be meaningfully taken to instantiate the transcendent paradigm or whether they are instead an expression of the embedded one. So far as I can see, no proponent of the transcendent paradigm could possibly be interested in the issue of global justice at the level of fundamental principle. Since advocates of transcendentalism believe that the same fundamental principles of justice (e.g. luck-equality) are valid across different contexts, in fact across all possible worlds, they have little reason to ask about the extensibility of justice to the global realm. The answer to this question is obvious: 'If the range of principles of justice includes all possible contexts and all possible worlds, then it also includes the global realm.'

For the transcendent theorist, this conclusion is not only trivial but also separate from the issue of how we ought to act. On her/his view, it is one thing to inquire into the nature of justice, and affirm its timelessness and fact-insensitivity, while it is quite another to ask about the grounds for our duties and obligations. As we have seen, the transcendent theorist typically has a lot to say in answer to the former question, but very little in answer to the latter.

By contrast, those who operate in the field of international ethics (including cosmopolitans) see the issue of global justice as being fundamentally connected with the *normative* project of defining the principles that apply beyond state borders. In their views, the point of theorizing about justice is to help us find coherent guidance in solving the moral dilemmas arising in *this* (evermore globalized) *world*, no matter what might be the case in parallel worlds or possible ones.

What is more, if what we are interested in is guidance in this world, trying to construct a theory that aims to be valid across all possible worlds, including very remote ones, will come at serious costs. As Pogge puts it, in so doing, 'we are likely to achieve less unity and likely also to trade off fit with our considered judgments about this world (which matters greatly) against fit with our judgments about very different worlds (which matters little)'.[31] The

---

[29] Cohen, 'Facts and Principles', p. 243, emphasis added.
[30] Cohen, *Rescuing Justice and Equality*, pp. 250ff.
[31] Pogge, 'Cohen to the Rescue!', p. 475.

point is a fairly simple one: if we are looking for guidance and orientation in this world, then we better stick to it. It is therefore unlikely that theorists engaged in the debate on global justice deliberately subscribe to the transcendent approach.

Moreover, to the extent that cosmopolitan and statist proposals (as understood in this book) have been developed from within the Rawlsian tradition broadly construed, such proposals are plausibly thought to share the fundamental guidance aspirations of Rawls's own theorizing. True, the need for a theory to be action-guiding is seldom explicitly affirmed by cosmopolitan theorists, but this only shows that it is so widely accepted that no one feels the need to make it explicit.

In light of the above, in this chapter, in fact throughout the rest of this book, I shall proceed by assuming that cosmopolitan and statist theories instantiate, or at least *intend to* instantiate, the embedded paradigm and are therefore in principle troubled by the guidance critique.

2.3 THE GUIDANCE CRITIQUE (I)

The guidance critique says that a sound theory of justice must be, in some sense, action-guiding. But what is the sense in question? I suggest that we can distinguish between at least three different senses of guidance, each corresponding to a distinct interpretation of the guidance critique (GC): GC1, GC2, and GC3.[32] GC1 focuses on the alleged incapacity of cosmopolitan principles to motivate people; GC2 accuses cosmopolitan principles of being either unhelpful or counterproductive; GC3 contends that the ideal described by such principles is altogether infeasible. In what follows, I devote one section to each critique and argue that none of them conclusively disproves cosmopolitanism, beginning with GC1.

As anticipated, proponents of this critique argue that cosmopolitan theories lack a capacity for guidance because they fail to *motivate* existing agents: in practice, cosmopolitanism is doomed to fail because no one is willing to follow its prescriptions. Even though this line of argument is seldom invoked as a crucial charge against cosmopolitanism, it is often mentioned in support of the anti-cosmopolitan case. For instance, David Miller suggests that 'making equality our aim at the global level will push justice so far out of reach that

---

[32] This distinction is broadly drawn from Valentini, 'On the Apparent Paradox of Ideal Theory'. While the article briefly discusses different versions of the guidance critique in general, this chapter looks at them in greater detail, and in relation to cosmopolitan outlooks on justice in particular.

most people would abandon the effort to achieve it'.[33] Cosmopolitanism, so understood, would propose a motivationally idle, if not counterproductive, social ideal. How could a cosmopolitan respond to this challenge?

It is true that, as Joseph Carens has pointed out, an *effective* morality, one capable of having immediate purchase on people's motivations, has to take into account a number of psychological, political, and sociological constraints. As he puts it, an effective morality should not 'place greater moral demands on people in any given context than their degree of emotional identification with others in that context will enable them to fulfil'.[34] In addition, a morality in line with individual self-interest stands a better chance of being followed than a morality that evidently clashes with it. If we want morality to be 'realistic and effective', which in turn requires a capacity to motivate agents to comply with its prescriptions, the proposed moral 'oughts' should not be too far from the existing 'is'.[35]

Having said that, Carens, however, also warns us against the risk for a realistic morality to be biased in favour of the *status quo* and incapable of condemning fundamental injustices. Consider, for instance, the case of slavery: a deep-rooted practice in eighteenth-century America.[36] At the time, a realistic approach to morality could not have required the abolition of slavery. For those participating in that institution, a world without slavery would have been almost unimaginable, and few would have taken such an injunction seriously. On the other hand, a morality recommending that slaves should be treated humanely would have had much better chances of being acted upon. Does this fact *per se* invalidate the normative ideal of a slavery-free society? Obviously not.

Radical normative proposals are unlikely to have immediate motivational purchase: because they are radical, they often challenge deeply held habits (or convictions) and tend to run against settled expectations and individual self-interest. But the fact that they fail to motivate agents here and now does not count against their moral soundness.

People's lack of political will to act in accordance with principles of justice is certainly regrettable, but it hardly undermines the validity of a conception of justice. The point of a theory of justice is precisely to give us a conceptual framework from within which to criticize agents and practices when they do not conform to it. If we were to judge its validity exclusively by reference to its actual impact, then the best theory of justice would be one that acritically vindicates the *status quo*, which is absurd.

---

[33] David Miller, 'Against Global Egalitarianism', *The Journal of Ethics*, 9 (1/2) (2005), 55–79, p. 57.
[34] Joseph H. Carens, 'Realistic and Idealistic Approaches to the Ethics of Migration', *International Migration Review*, 30 (1) (1996), 156–70, p. 161.
[35] Carens, 'Realistic and Idealistic Approaches to the Ethics of Migration', p. 164.
[36] Carens, 'Realistic and Idealistic Approaches to the Ethics of Migration', pp. 164–6.

Things would look different if a conception of justice were to demand actions that, for all we know, are beyond human possibility. For instance, a theory of justice that required human beings to act selflessly and altruistically in all circumstances would indeed be objectionable, since it would assume away the very problem it seeks to tackle. As we have seen, on an embedded approach, certain features of the human condition, such as moderate scarcity and limited altruism, must be taken seriously and factored into the design of principles of justice. But this is not the point made by GC1.[37] GC1 simply complains that the cosmopolitan ideal fails to motivate existing agents because it is too radically detached from the *status quo*. This, however, poses no challenge to the cosmopolitan ideal as such.

Of course, in arguing that GC1 does not disprove cosmopolitanism, I am not suggesting that there is nothing we should learn from it. GC1 has the merit of bringing our attention to the fact that implementing the cosmopolitan ideal would certainly require making strategic compromises with individual self-interest and existing political forces. It is a matter of slow, perhaps painful, political change. But, as Carens points out, 'it is essential to distinguish between a regrettable but useful tactical concession to powerful political forces pursuing a morally objectionable path and a legitimate defense of an important and honorable value'.[38] The fact that, unless tactical concessions are made, the cosmopolitan ideal fails to motivate existing agents does not by itself speak against that ideal.

2.4 THE GUIDANCE CRITIQUE (II)

A second sense in which cosmopolitan principles might be said to lack a capacity for guidance focuses on their applicability. Critics complain that such principles fail to be *immediately applicable* to day-to-day political decisions. It is indeed undeniable that the cosmopolitan approach leaves answers to questions, such as how citizens and officials should act in this or that particular situation largely indeterminate. Even worse, critics insist, applying cosmopolitan principles to real-world circumstances might be self-defeating, rendering the achievement of any form of international justice even more remote. Do these charges undermine the cosmopolitan ideal? I doubt so. The first 'immediacy' charge presupposes unreasonable expectations as to what any plausible

---

[37] As we will see, this is the point made by GC3.
[38] Carens, 'Realistic and Idealistic Approaches to the Ethics of Migration', p. 166.

normative theory can offer, while the second mistakes a failure in the application of a normative theory for a failure in its design.[39]

Regarding the alleged lack of immediate applicability of the cosmopolitan ideal, as Immanuel Kant noted, 'no matter how complete the theory may be, a middle term is required between theory and practice, providing a link and a transition from one to the other'.[40] That is, in order to become practically relevant, a theory needs to be brought to bear on specific cases through judgement, which involves a careful assessment of the facts of the matter. As suggested by Onora O'Neill, the role of principles is to help us identify the relevant facts and evaluate their implications for action – implications that cannot be already contained in the principles themselves. Again in Kant's words, principles 'are abstracted from numerous conditions which, nonetheless, necessarily influence their practical application'.[41] Cosmopolitan theories are, of course, no exception. Accusing them to fail to do what they cannot reasonably be expected to do is no serious accusation at all.

With regard to the claim that applying the cosmopolitan ideal to the real world might lead to counterproductive results, this is true only when we replace 'directly applying' with 'misapplying'.[42] Let me elaborate on this, beginning with some examples of misapplication.[43]

It is often lamented that directly pursuing the cosmopolitan ideal, that is, promoting civil and political liberties worldwide and imposing a global egalitarian distributive scheme, would appear to express disrespect for those political cultures that reject liberal values. As a result, it would in all likelihood generate tensions and increase the potential for conflicts between liberal societies and non-liberal political communities. Given that peace and stability are a necessary precondition for the realization of justice, it seems that the direct pursuit of the cosmopolitan ideal would bring the real world even further away from its achievement.[44]

In a similar vein, one might also worry that the creation of the institutions needed to implement global justice might, at least in the beginning, exacerbate

---

[39] A similar point is made by Onora O'Neill in 'Abstraction, Idealization and Ideology in Ethics', in J. D. G. Evans (ed.), *Moral Philosophy and Contemporary Problems* (Cambridge: Cambridge University Press, 1988), 55–69.

[40] Immanuel Kant, 'On the Common Saying: This May be True in Theory, but It Does Not Apply in Practice' (1793), in Hans Reiss (ed.), *Kant's Political Writings* (Cambridge: Cambridge University Press, 1970), 61–92, p. 61.

[41] Kant, 'On the Common Saying', p. 61.

[42] See O'Neill, 'Abstraction, Idealization and Ideology in Ethics'.

[43] The following discussion partly draws on Christian Barry and Laura Valentini, 'Egalitarian Challenges to Global Egalitarianism: A Critique', *Review of International Studies*, 35 (3) (2009), 485–512, Section VIII. Section VIII of the paper in turn partly draws on Chapter 2 of my PhD thesis, *Global Justice: Cosmopolitanism, Social Liberalism, and the Coercion View* (London: UCL, 2008).

[44] See, for instance, John Rawls's remarks in *The Law of Peoples* (Cambridge, MA: Harvard University Press, 1999), p. 62.

the hegemonic tendencies displayed by some members of the present international system. '[G]iven the nature of politics', says Chandran Kukathas, 'the institutions or rules that are adopted will reflect not the demands of justice, but the balance of power.'[45] To avoid this scenario, Kukathas defends an analogue of the Westphalian model, placing great emphasis on the sovereignty and independence of individual communities. Permitting the powerful to intervene in other, weaker, societies 'in the name of justice' would be equal to allowing them either to impose their beliefs on others, or to pursue their self-interest at the cost of that of others, or both. After all, notes Kukathas, '[b]etter to have many petty tyrants than a few great ones'.[46]

Similar worries animate Thomas Nagel's reflections on the moral costs of bringing about global justice. Since, in Nagel's view, justice can only exist in the presence of a sovereign agent, global justice requires full-blown global *sovereignty*. However, Nagel observes, it is doubtful whether the creation of a global sovereign authority is a goal we should want to pursue. He reminds us that, historically, the establishment of legitimate states has typically been preceded by unjust concentrations of power, against which demands of justice were pressed at a later stage. Applying this historical regularity to the international case, Nagel envisages a process of transition towards 'some version of global justice' occurring 'through the creation of patently unjust and illegitimate global structures of power that are tolerable to the interests of the most powerful current nation-states'.[47] With the abuses of power that are likely to be perpetrated within these regimes, it is an open question whether we should want to speed up the process leading to global sovereignty, and ultimately, global justice.

All of these arguments point to the moral costs of transition from the world as it is to the world as it would be under cosmopolitan principles. To use Allen Buchanan's phrase, they claim that the ideal of a cosmopolitan world is *morally inaccessible* from where we are.[48] This sceptical conclusion implies that the imperialistic, aggressive imposition of liberal values is the only way in which a cosmopolitan global order could be brought about. But this claim is a very difficult one to establish. In fact, on its face, it is rather implausible. Processes of democratization and liberalization can occur both 'top-down' and 'bottom-up', and there is nothing necessitating the former rather than the latter in the global case. It might be true that the most straightforward way of

---

[45] Chandran Kukathas, 'The Mirage of Global Justice', *Social Philosophy and Policy*, 23 (1) (2006), 1–28, p. 20.
[46] Kukathas, 'The Mirage of Global Justice', p. 6.
[47] Thomas Nagel, 'The Problem of Global Justice', *Philosophy and Public Affairs*, 33 (2) (2005), 113–47, p. 146.
[48] Allen Buchanan, *Justice, Legitimacy, and Self-Determination* (Oxford: Oxford University Press, 2004), p. 61. See also Juha Räikkä, 'The Feasibility Condition in Political Theory', *Journal of Political Philosophy*, 6 (1) (1998), 27–40.

achieving global justice would be through the creation of a (temporarily unjust) global empire or through the imposition of liberal values, but there is no reason – and certainly none is dictated by cosmopolitan principles – why we should opt for such morally problematic strategies.

A softer approach to the realization of the cosmopolitan ideal is equally, if not more, plausible. Instead of direct armed intervention, arguably less invasive measures such as economic sanctions against oppressive regimes, and incentives in favour of democratization, might be adopted.[49] This suggestion is compatible with tolerating those regimes that, in spite of being non-liberal, are sufficiently respectful of basic human rights and attentive to the well-being of their populations to qualify as members of the international community. Such a community might, with the passing of time, move closer to a full-blown cosmopolitan ideal of global justice, but this is something we simply cannot know in advance.[50] Moreover, there is no conclusive reason to believe that only the creation of a global Leviathan could ensure the realization of cosmopolitan justice. A multiplicity of well-coordinated supranational institutions might also be able to deliver what cosmopolitanism demands.

The issue of the relation between the cosmopolitan ideal and its application to existing conditions is just an instance of the broader question of the relation between so-called 'ideal theory' and 'non-ideal circumstances'. Rawls briefly considers this question, suggesting that principles of ideal theory are meant to offer conceptual tools through which to make sense of, and assess, our social world from the viewpoint of justice. So understood, the main function of ideal theory is one of orientation of our normative thinking as well as our actions within social reality.[51]

By constructing an ideal picture of a just society, namely a society where all agents conform to the requirements of justice, the philosopher elaborates the standards through which meaningfully to see our world from the perspective of what is just and what is not. As Rawls puts it, '[t]he reason for beginning with ideal theory is that it provides . . . the only basis for the systematic grasp of [the] more pressing problems [of nonideal theory]'.[52] Indeed, '[e]xisting institutions are to be judged in the light of this [i.e. the ideal] conception and

---

[49] For further discussion, see Charles R. Beitz, 'Justice and International Relations', *Philosophy and Public Affairs*, 4 (4) (1975), 360–89, esp. pp. 383–9. Of course, economic sanctions might also turn out to be morally problematic, for instance when they place excessive burdens on innocent people.

[50] Rawls, *The Law of Peoples*, p. 62.

[51] See John Rawls, *Justice as Fairness: A Restatement* (Cambridge, MA: Harvard University Press, 2001), p. 3. See also the discussion in A. John Simmons, 'Ideal and Nonideal Theory', *Philosophy and Public Affairs*, 38 (1) (2010), 5–36.

[52] Rawls, *A Theory of Justice*, p. 8.

held to be unjust to the extent that they depart from it without sufficient reason'.[53]

Moreover, political ideals 'should also provide some guidance in thinking about nonideal theory, and so about difficult cases of how to deal with existing injustices. [They] should also help to clarify the goal of reform and to identify which wrongs are more grievous and hence more urgent to correct'.[54] To put it metaphorically, ideal theory furnishes a criterion for moral judgement as well as a 'compass' for action. I say 'a compass' because ideal theory is too general to tell us *which* courses of action we ought to undertake in the face of actual injustices, but rather it provides a regulative end at which our actions should aim. For this reason, cosmopolitan principles simply cannot be expected to issue *specific* recommendations as to how to move from the world as it is to the world as it should be. They can only indicate where we should ultimately want to be, and on what grounds we should act.

If we look at the cosmopolitan vision of a just world order through the lens of this account of the role of ideal theory, we are better placed to understand the sense in which it is action-guiding. By insisting that distributive inequalities in the current international scenario are a concern of *justice*, cosmopolitanism suggests that the duties to redress such inequalities are particularly stringent: they are *owed* to their recipients. Instead of primarily recommending development aid and resource transfers, the cosmopolitan plea for global justice directs action towards global institutional reform. For cosmopolitans, what is morally problematic is the overall system of entitlements distributing opportunities and resources on a global scale. This is why they think that global justice can only be achieved by modifying the institutional structures supporting it.[55] Which particular reform avenues are most likely to succeed in furthering the cosmopolitan ideal, however, is a question that can only be answered in context.

Moreover, by arguing for the extension of principles of domestic egalitarian justice to the global arena, cosmopolitans focus on relative, as opposed to absolute, deprivation. In practice, their recommendations go beyond the fulfilment of persons' basic needs.[56] Of course, basic-needs fulfilment is also a priority of cosmopolitan justice. Both supporters of global egalitarian justice (i.e. cosmopolitans) and supporters of sufficientarian assistance (i.e. statists) have reason to want policies aimed at reaching a threshold of basic-needs

---

[53] Rawls, *A Theory of Justice*, p. 216.
[54] Rawls, *Justice as Fairness*, p. 13.
[55] Kok-Chor Tan, *Justice without Borders: Cosmopolitanism, Nationalism and Patriotism* (Cambridge: Cambridge University Press, 2004), pp. 66ff.
[56] Notice that principles of assistance may demand more than basic-needs fulfilment. For instance, in Rawls's view, assistance requires helping burdened societies become well ordered. See Rawls, *The Law of Peoples*, pp. 105–13. The important point is that principles of assistance always focus on meeting an absolute, as opposed to a relative, threshold.

satisfaction. What is distinctive of cosmopolitans is that, for them, (at least some) inequalities are *still* problematic even once the relevant threshold of sufficiency has been met.[57]

In short, once the relationship between normative principles and political reality is correctly understood, cosmopolitanism is far from unable to guide action. As we have seen, no normative principle can be *immediately* action-guiding in the sense of providing a blueprint for action: to have bearing on existing practice, normative ideals have to be applied through context-sensitive judgement. Similarly, the cosmopolitan ideal becomes counterproductive when judgement about its application is misdirected. Nothing makes such an ideal doomed to be unable to guide action successfully, other than a bad use of it. Finally, and more constructively, I have suggested that the cosmopolitan ideal has characteristic guidance implications: the stringency, form, and content of cosmopolitan obligations differ from those of the obligations defended by their statist opponents.

Does this completely shield cosmopolitanism from the guidance critique? Not quite, for there is a third, potentially more problematic interpretation of such a critique, to which I now turn.

2.5 THE GUIDANCE CRITIQUE (III)

The third formulation of the guidance critique, GC3, holds that the cosmopolitan ideal is misguided because it is infeasible: it violates the 'ought implies can' proviso.[58] Of course, one has to be clear about the sense of 'ought implies can' one has in mind. One option we can immediately discount, given the arguments of the previous section, is the expectation that the cosmopolitan ideal should be *immediately* capable of being fully implemented. In this case, the 'can' in 'ought implies can' is interpreted as immediate feasibility. However, immediate feasibility – technical, political, psychological – is too narrow a requirement on a valid normative theory, one that, as we have seen, dangerously pushes it in the direction of a defence of the *status quo*.

The charge of infeasibility must thus take a different form to pose a serious challenge to the cosmopolitan ideal. In particular, it must amount to the rather radical claim that given our best understanding of human nature and its operation under different institutional arrangements, the cosmopolitan ideal is simply unrealizable. This argument differs from the 'moral inaccessibility' accusation examined in the previous section. While the former claimed that

---

[57] Cf. Miller, 'Against Global Egalitarianism'.
[58] See e.g. Menno Kamminga, 'Why Global Distributive Justice Cannot Work', *Acta Politica*, 41 (1) (2006), 21–40.

the moral costs of bringing about the cosmopolitan ideal were too high to make it worth pursuing, the latter simply argues that the cosmopolitan ideal is a chimera. Judging existing global relations against that ideal is like judging existing societies against the ideal of a society of angels: a normative mistake.

A version of this argument is offered by John Rawls in his defence of *The Law of Peoples*. Anticipating the objections of those who have read his theory of international justice as setting out a second-best, because of its inclusion of some non-liberal societies in a just Society of Peoples, Rawls states '[t]hough we can imagine what we sometimes think would be a happier world – one in which everyone, or all peoples, have the same faith that we do – this is *not the question*, excluded as it is by the nature and culture of free institutions'.[59] That is, given the fact of pluralism and its status as an inevitable by-product of liberal institutions, a solution to the problem of international justice that did not take seriously this fact would be hopelessly utopian, failing to offer a plausible answer to the problem it aims to solve.

Of course, Rawls is prepared to admit that

> there are questions about how the limits of the practicably possible are discerned and what the conditions of our social world in fact are. The problem here is that the limits of the possible are not given by the actual, for we can to a greater or lesser extent change political and social institutions and much else. Hence we have to rely on conjecture and speculation, arguing as best we can that the social world we envision is feasible and might actually exist, if not now then at some future time under happier circumstances ... To show that reasonable pluralism is not to be regretted, we must show that, given the socially feasible alternatives, the existence of reasonable pluralism allows for a society of greater political justice and liberty.[60]

Nonetheless, if it is true that liberalism and pluralism are inseparable, a fully liberal world order, one populated with liberal states alone, or indeed one governed by a liberal supranational authority, would only be the fruit of a philosopher's imagination. In reality, the achievement of such an order, if at all possible, would be gained through the establishment of a global, despotic sovereign, namely by denying the very freedom that constitutes the hallmark of liberal institutions.[61] Such a world would be practically impossible because it would be self-contradictory. Paradoxically, a fully liberal world order would turn into an authoritarian regime.

What can a cosmopolitan reply to this challenge? Very little by way of rigorous argumentation, because testing the limits of what is practically possible is, to a certain extent, beyond our epistemic possibilities. This consideration applies to the fact of pluralism and to almost any – not obviously

---

[59] Rawls, *The Law of Peoples*, p. 12, emphasis added.
[60] Rawls, *The Law of Peoples*, p. 12.
[61] Rawls, *The Law of Peoples*, p. 36.

false – social fact one might invoke against cosmopolitanism. Whether the fact of pluralism is a persistent, ineliminable fact of free human existence, and whether a fully liberal world order could only be established through the imposition of despotic global institutions, is something we cannot establish with any reasonable degree of certainty. Human nature is (to some extent) malleable, and the future unpredictable. As David Reidy nicely puts it, 'the fact of reasonable pluralism itself, taken as a permanent, trans-historical fact about the human condition but restricted to morality, religion, and philosophy, may be reasonably rejected'.[62] This being the case, whether a cosmopolitan world order could *ever* exist, and how exactly to get there, are questions we are ill-equipped to answer.

Similar considerations apply to the (related) argument that it would be impossible for persons across the world to develop the necessary fellow-feelings and attachments to sustain a global redistributive scheme of the kind defended by cosmopolitans. There is no way in which we can conclusively establish whether this is the case or not. Our knowledge of human nature is insufficient at this point to allow us to vindicate such claims.

Because they rest on highly speculative assumptions, these objections offer no valid grounds for accepting or rejecting the cosmopolitan ideal. Charles Beitz is thus right when he says that

> Unless international cooperation according to the principles of justice can be shown to be infeasible, limiting the scope of the principles to national societies on the grounds that international cooperation does not exist today... would arbitrarily favour the status quo.[63]

Since we cannot prove such infeasibility, we can conclude that GC3 speaks neither in favour nor against cosmopolitanism. Even if GC3 does not suffice to refute cosmopolitanism, it has the merit of drawing attention to the tentative nature of the cosmopolitan ideal. In particular, although on Rawls's political approach 'principles of justice *presuppose* a certain theory of social institutions',[64] no such robust theory has been provided in the case of cosmopolitanism.[65] This suggests that, instead of being misguided, cosmopolitanism is incomplete. For now and the foreseeable future, cosmopolitan theorists are

---

[62] David A. Reidy, 'Rawls on International Justice: A Defense', *Political Theory*, 32 (3) (2004), 291–319, p. 307.
[63] Charles R. Beitz, 'Cosmopolitan Ideals and National Sentiment', *Journal of Philosophy*, 80 (10) (1983), 591–600, p. 595.
[64] Rawls, *A Theory of Justice*, p. 138, emphasis added.
[65] For an account of the institutional arrangements which might support the cosmopolitan ideal, see Thomas W. Pogge, 'Cosmopolitanism and Sovereignty', *Ethics*, 103 (1) (1992), 48–75; and Andrew Kuper, 'Rawlsian Global Justice: Beyond the Law of Peoples to a Cosmopolitan Law of Persons', *Political Theory*, 28 (5) (2000), 640–74.

unlikely to be able to offer a complete description of the institutional arrangements needed in order to realize their favoured ideal fully.

Notice, however, that until such an ideal is proven infeasible, cosmopolitans need not worry too much about this incompleteness. Their principles will still make sense as standards against which to assess *feasible* alternative social arrangements.[66] In order to rank different feasible institutional structures, we need not know whether the cosmopolitan ideal is fully realizable.[67] Cosmopolitans can be open-ended about the ultimate shape of their ideal world order, and its realizability. They can simply limit themselves to judging which one of a set of feasible reforms of the current world structure would best approximate such an ideal, and criticize the *status quo* as unjust by reference to that feasible alternative.[68]

Of course, it would be desirable if cosmopolitans said more about the sorts of institutional reforms that would allow us to bring the world closer to that ideal.[69] But, however regrettable, their relative silence on this matter cannot be used as a reason to reject their overall normative approach.

2.6 CONCLUSION

In this chapter, I have analysed the guidance critique of cosmopolitanism, namely the charge that cosmopolitan theories are doomed to fail to guide action in real-world circumstances. After distinguishing between embedded and transcendent approaches to justice, I have examined three different understandings of this critique, and argued that none of them undermines the cosmopolitan ideal. By insisting that principles of justice should apply to the world at large, cosmopolitan theories do possess distinctive guidance implications. Whether their overall ideal world order can be *fully* realized, or whether it falls within the limits of human possibility, is something we cannot establish with certainty (at least for the time being), and thus offers no evidence in favour of, or against, the ideal itself.

---

[66] This way of understanding how cosmopolitan principles allow us to assess the global order is defended by Thomas W. Pogge in *Realizing Rawls* (Ithaca, NY: Cornell University Press, 1989), Part III.

[67] I am grateful to Christian Barry for bringing this point to my attention. In our joint paper, 'Egalitarian Challenges to Global Egalitarianism', we offer a short discussion of the alleged infeasibility of cosmopolitan principles broadly in line with the one offered in this chapter, together with other six critiques of global egalitarianism.

[68] This, of course, will also require a metric enabling us to measure how far the existing world is from our ideal. See Sen, *The Idea of Justice*, for discussion.

[69] For discussion of several such reforms, see Simon Caney, 'Global Justice: From Theory to Practice', *Globalizations*, 3 (2) (2006), 121–37.

The *positive* lesson to learn from this discussion concerns the type of guidance we can reasonably expect from theories of justice. The aim of theories of justice is not to motivate existing agents, or to offer immediate guidance for day-to-day political decisions, but to provide a *comprehensive framework for thinking about* the duties and obligations that apply to us. Their task is to help us establish what types of conduct are morally problematic and on what grounds. The question of how to remedy existing injustices is not one for political philosophy *alone* to address. Instead of answering such a question, the primary role of a theory of justice is to enable us to formulate it, by identifying what counts as unjust. Crucially, political philosophers are encouraged to collaborate with other social scientists in an attempt to provide solutions to the moral problems they identify. All I have shown is that a theory of justice cannot be deemed implausible because it does not directly tell us how to solve them. (Readers who worry that this might cast doubt on the distinction between embedded and transcendent approaches are invited to read this note.[70])

---

[70] At this point, someone might object that I have overstated the distinction between embedded and transcendent approaches. After all, if no normative theory can offer immediate guidance for action, then the distinction between transcendent and embedded approaches is not a categorical one, but a matter of degree. The guidance provided by the transcendent approach is simply less direct than the guidance provided by the embedded one. Would it then make sense to reformulate the earlier distinction in these terms? I believe not. This is because the difference in 'directness of guidance' between the two approaches rests on a much deeper difference concerning their understandings of the task of political philosophy. While proponents of the embedded approach see the task of political philosophy as that of responding to real-world practical problems, for the proponents of the transcendent approach political philosophy is fundamentally about the discovery of timeless values. The fact that such timeless values will also have some (however remote) implications for action does not make the difference between the two approaches a simple matter of degree. In addition, as I have noted in Section 2.2.3, the way we design principles of justice is bound to be very different depending on whether we subscribe to one approach or the other. It is one thing to try to come up with principles which aim to be valid across all possible worlds, and do not presuppose any natural or social facts, and it is quite another to try to construct moral theories which are meant to systematize our convictions about how we ought to act in this world.

3

Justifying Cosmopolitanism: A Methodological Critique

3.1 INTRODUCTION

In Chapter 2, I examined the 'downward effects' of cosmopolitan principles. That is, I examined their application to real-world circumstances. In this chapter, my analysis will move in the opposite direction: I will work my way 'upwards' and scrutinize the different *justifications* that might be offered in support of cosmopolitanism.

Cosmopolitanism is far from being an internally homogenous normative doctrine. On the basis of the specific role assigned to existing social relations in the *justification* of cosmopolitan principles, we can distinguish between two main strands of cosmopolitanism. Those who see existing social relations as constitutive of principles of justice are so-called 'relational cosmopolitans', those who oppose this view are termed 'non-relational cosmopolitans'.[1] In this chapter, I illustrate and critically discuss each position in turn, beginning with non-relational cosmopolitanism.

In Section 3.2, I lay out the core claims of this particular outlook on global justice. In Section 3.3, I test such claims against a hypothetical scenario and show that they have implausible moral implications. This is because, although non-relational cosmopolitans subscribe to what, in Chapter 2, I called 'the embedded approach' to justice, their methodology concedes too much to its transcendent counterpart.[2] In particular, by giving excessive weight to our moral intuitions in scenarios that are far removed from the world as we know it, non-relational cosmopolitans have difficulties building a unified and appealing normative outlook.

---

[1] For this distinction, see Andrea Sangiovanni, 'Global Justice, Reciprocity, and the State', *Philosophy and Public Affairs*, 35 (1) (2007), 3–39, pp. 5–8.
[2] For the distinction between embedded and transcendent approaches to justice, see Section 2.2.

In Section 3.4, I turn to relational cosmopolitanism and suggest that, thanks to its structure, it does not suffer from the shortcomings affecting the non-relational view. I then consider two versions of relational cosmopolitanism, each defending a specific account of the types of social relations that trigger principles of justice. While for all relational cosmopolitans the global applicability of principles of justice rests on the existence of a 'global basic structure of society' (i.e. a set of legal, political, and economic institutions such as those underpinning a domestic social order), some conceive of such a structure in moralized terms, others in non-moralized ones. In Section 3.6, I discuss the implications of the former view, and in Section 3.7 those of the latter. I argue that both are unsatisfactory and conclude that, although the general approach adopted by relational cosmopolitanism is promising, its claim that domestic liberal-egalitarian justice should apply to the global basic structure is poorly supported. Even if my argument does not provide a refutation of relational cosmopolitanism, it shows that, as it stands, the view is insufficiently robust to warrant endorsement.

3.2 NON-RELATIONAL COSMOPOLITANISM: AN OVERVIEW

Non-relational cosmopolitanism holds that, since liberal-egalitarian principles of domestic justice rest on inherently universalistic grounds, they ought to apply globally.[3] In particular, non-relational cosmopolitans share a distinctive understanding of both the grounds and the content of principles of (global) justice.

In their view, the grounds of such principles are non-relational in kind: our obligations of justice do not rest on the existence of particular types of social relations or institutions, but are entirely grounded on a certain *conception of the person*. As argued by Simon Caney, 'persons throughout the world share some morally relevant properties and hence if some moral values apply to some persons then they should, as a matter of consistency, also apply to all'.[4] For Caney, these values are those typically protected by liberal principles of domestic justice.

---

[3] Prominent advocates of this view are Simon Caney, *Justice beyond Borders: A Global Political Theory* (Oxford: Oxford University Press, 2005); Kok-Chor Tan, *Justice without Borders: Cosmopolitanism, Nationalism and Patriotism* (Cambridge: Cambridge University Press, 2004); and Charles R. Beitz, 'Cosmopolitan Ideals and National Sentiment', *The Journal of Philosophy*, 80 (10) (1983), 591–600.

[4] Caney, *Justice beyond Borders*, p. 265.

In a similar vein, Charles Beitz argues that Rawls's principles of domestic justice should apply globally because of the universal validity of the conception of moral personality on which they are premised.[5] Given that 'a capacity for a sense of justice' and 'a capacity to form, to revise and rationally to pursue a conception of the good' are common to all human beings, Beitz claims, the principles delivered by the original position have an inherently global reach.

In terms of content, non-relational principles require civil, political, and socio-economic equality across all humans.[6] Typically, these principles either closely resemble, or coincide with, those defended in Rawls's theory of domestic justice – that is, they demand that people across the globe should enjoy equal civil and political liberties, as well as equal opportunities, and that income and wealth should be distributed with special concern for the global worse-off people.[7] The idea behind extending Rawlsian justice to the world at large is that '[i]f one thinks, as egalitarian liberals do, that it is unjust if persons fare worse because of their class or ethnic identity one should surely also think that it is unjust if persons fare worse because of their nationality'.[8] This being so, limiting the scope of principles of justice to the domestic arena would be inconsistent with liberals' own fundamental commitments.

Non-relational cosmopolitanism thus instantiates what Mathias Risse and Michael Blake call *direct* theories of distributive equality, that is, theories that defend distributive equality without the mediation of particular social relations. For such theories, 'it is an ideal of equality of persons, most plausibly equal respect and concern for persons, that calls for the equalization of the distributive goods identified by the theory as relevant for the purposes of justice. Distributive equality is not stipulated, but derived from a normative account of personhood'.[9]

Schematically put, the train of thought underpinning non-relational cosmopolitanism takes the following shape:

---

[5] Beitz, 'Cosmopolitan Ideals and National Sentiment', pp. 594–5. Notice that, in his earlier work, Beitz used to defend a relational cosmopolitan approach, which will be discussed in the second part of this chapter.

[6] 'Socio-economic equality' is here, and throughout the book, broadly construed, also encompassing principles, such as Rawls's difference principle, which do not demand perfect equality but place limits on permissible inequalities.

[7] Recall, Rawls's 'difference principle' holds that inequalities in income and wealth are justified only if they benefit the worse-off people in absolute terms. See John Rawls, *A Theory of Justice* (Oxford: Oxford University Press, 1999 rev. ed.), 65–73.

[8] Caney, *Justice beyond Borders*, p. 123; see also Simon Caney, 'Cosmopolitan Justice and Equalizing Opportunities', *Metaphilosophy*, 32 (1/2) (2001), 113–34, p. 124.

[9] Michael Blake and Mathias Risse, 'Two Models of Equality and Responsibility', *Canadian Journal of Philosophy*, 38 (2) (2008), 165–99, p. 170.

1. All human beings are owed equal respect *qua* moral persons.[10]
2. There are goods that all human beings have reason to value: civil and political liberties, opportunities, income, and wealth.
3. Equal respect demands that human beings should not be worse off in the relevant respects (see 2 above) due to morally arbitrary (unchosen) factors.
4. A person's place of birth is a morally arbitrary factor.
5. Equal respect demands that rights, opportunities, income, and wealth should be equally – or roughly equally – distributed across the world's population.

Claim (1) states the fundamental liberal commitment to equal respect for persons. Claim (2) specifies the 'currency' or metric of non-relational cosmopolitan justice, and is broadly in line with Rawlsian social primary goods, or resources more generally. Claim (3) articulates non-relational cosmopolitans' preferred interpretation of equal respect for persons, and expresses what in Chapter 2 was termed a luck-egalitarian view of justice. This is the view that people's life prospects ought not to be determined by morally arbitrary factors, namely unchosen factors for which they cannot plausibly be held responsible. Claim (4) identifies one's place of birth as a morally arbitrary factor. Finally, claim (5) states non-relational cosmopolitans' *substantive* account of the demands of international justice: global equality. This train of thought shows that institutions and existing social relations play no role in the justification of non-relational principles of justice. As stated at (5), justice demands a global (roughly) equal distribution of liberties, opportunities, income, and wealth, independently of whether there exist worldwide social practices. For non-relational cosmopolitans, worldwide social practices are mere instruments through which justice may be realized.[11]

Non-relational cosmopolitanism has been attacked on many fronts. Some, for instance, have challenged claim (2) accusing it of being an expression of Western imperialism. Not all human beings have reason to value the goods that are deemed to be valuable within liberal democratic societies. To think otherwise, so the objection goes, is to attribute universal validity to a parochial conception of the good and of moral personality. Others have argued that there can be no plausible metric for measuring inequalities in a culturally plural world. On this view, as it is simply impossible to establish what global equality of opportunities or resources means, global egalitarian justice is doomed to fail as a normative ideal.[12] In addition, critics have also objected to claim (4), arguing that it overlooks national responsibility and

---

[10] Following most participants in the debate on global justice, I am here simplifying matters, and bracketing off difficult cases involving children and the severely mentally disabled.
[11] Caney, *Justice beyond Borders*, pp. 120–1.
[12] David Miller, 'Against Global Egalitarianism', *The Journal of Ethics*, 9 (1/2) (2005), 55–79.

self-determination. Nationality, they argue, need not always be a morally arbitrary factor: under appropriate circumstances, it makes sense to take special responsibility for one's nation's domestic and international conduct.[13]

These are important challenges, but they do not target non-relational cosmopolitanism as such. So formulated, the challenges apply to any cosmopolitan outlook. Since I here want to focus on non-relational cosmopolitanism specifically, I leave these challenges to one side (I will return to some of them later) and concentrate on the distinctive feature of this particular view: its non-relational grounds.

Looked at from this perspective, non-relational cosmopolitanism can be interpreted as offering a particularly thin version of the embedded approach to justice. It is a version of the *embedded* approach because non-relational cosmopolitans are clearly interested in their theories being action-guiding in the world as we know it. They embrace the 'ought implies can' proviso and affirm that a theory of justice that exceeds the limits of human possibility is, for this reason alone, an inadequate theory.[14] That said, their version of the embedded approach is particularly *thin* because the facts they consider relevant to the elaboration of a theory of justice are only those that characterize the human condition as such. More specific facts about existing social relations and institutions have no bearing on the justification of principles of justice.

In light of this, it seems appropriate to say that the non-relational cosmopolitan version of the embedded approach comes closest to the transcendent approach. This appears clear also looking at the substantive principles advocated by non-relational cosmopolitans, which, as we have seen, have much in common with Cohen's luck-egalitarianism. Despite this, we should not conflate the two views. Non-relational cosmopolitans do not consider the applicability of justice to the global realm a trivial matter. The way they come to defend such applicability is not by meta-ethical *fiat* (because it is in the nature of fundamental principles of justice – whatever they are – to hold true across all contexts) but rather through first-order moral reasoning. They look at arguments in favour of egalitarian justice in the domestic context, arguments appealing to the arbitrariness of features outside persons' control, such as race and gender, and see those arguments as naturally extending beyond that context.

With a clearer picture of the methodological underpinnings of non-relational cosmopolitanism in hand, we can now turn to its evaluation.[15]

---

[13] David Miller, *National Responsibility and Global Justice* (Oxford: Oxford University Press, 2007), chs. 2 and 5.

[14] See Beitz, 'Cosmopolitan Ideals and National Sentiment', p. 595.

[15] Christian Schemmel offers an insightful discussion of why global luck-egalitarianism is incapable of accounting for the special nature of duties of justice in his 'On the Usefulness of

3.3 TESTING NON-RELATIONAL COSMOPOLITANISM

To test non-relational cosmopolitanism, I consider a hypothetical two-society scenario. This is in fact the kind of scenario non-relational cosmopolitans invite us to consider, by claiming that existing social ties and institutions have no impact on the question of the scope of justice. One of our societies, Well-off-land (W) – the name says it – is prosperous and wealthy, while the other, Badly-off-land (B), is – predictably – in conditions of gruelling poverty. In order to focus on the distinctive features of non-relational cosmopolitanism, the two societies are assumed to be self-contained and fully independent of one another: no stable relations exist, or ever existed, between them.

One day, a group of explorers from W, venturing in a remote corner of the world, come into contact with B. Understanding the life-threatening seriousness of B's inhabitants' conditions, they immediately return to their homeland and report on what they have seen. What moral duties would fall on the people of W once they learn about B?[16] Would they be duties of humanitarian assistance, or duties of egalitarian justice?[17]

At first sight, W's duties to B look like a matter of humanity. There seems to be no relevant difference between the case at hand, and Peter Singer's paradigmatic example of a humanitarian duty to save a child drowning in a shallow pond.[18] Any bystander who could rescue the child at reasonable costs to herself/himself would have a duty to do so. Similarly, if W could help B at reasonable costs, W would have a duty to do so. On this telling of the story, by acting on this duty, W would be generously using its *own* resources to relieve the suffering of B's inhabitants.

For the non-relational cosmopolitan, this diagnosis of the moral duties applying in our scenario is too quick and superficial because it surreptitiously assumes that W's inhabitants are *entitled* to the resources they currently possess. Whether W's inhabitants are entitled to those resources or not, the non-relational cosmopolitan would argue, depends on the causes of B's poverty. Two alternatives are possible.

One is that B's poverty results from its people's wasteful behaviour. They have been irresponsible, and adopted a collectively unsustainable lifestyle. After centuries of reckless use of their resources, they have found themselves destitute. In this first scenario, the non-relational cosmopolitan would say,

---

Luck Egalitarian Arguments for Global Justice', *Global Justice: Theory Practice Rhetoric*, 1 (2007), 54–67. I am grateful to Christian for helpful conversations on this issue.

[16] Examples of this sort are often used to test non-relational cosmopolitanism. See e.g. Sangiovanni, 'Global Justice, Reciprocity, and the State', pp. 24ff.; and Schemmel, 'On the Usefulness of Luck-Egalitarian Arguments to Global Justice', p. 59.

[17] For this distinction, see Section 1.3.

[18] Peter Singer, 'Famine, Affluence, and Morality', *Philosophy and Public Affairs*, 1 (3) (1972), 229–43.

W's duty would indeed be one of humanitarian assistance. W's inhabitants ought to donate their *own* resources to help those of B. If they refused to do so, they would be committing a moral wrong against humanity as such, but would not violate the rights of B's inhabitants in particular.

Things, however, look different in the second scenario, where B's destitution is the consequence of bad brute luck. B's inhabitants are an industrious and hard-working people, but they have been hit by a natural catastrophe, which has damaged their agriculture and urban infrastructure.[19] In such circumstances, non-relational cosmopolitans would continue, it would make sense for W to have a justice-based duty to transfer resources to B. After all, why should the inhabitants of W be exclusively entitled to the better resources present on their territory? On this telling of the story, by holding on to its resources, W would be violating B's rights. Failing to transfer such resources would amount to infringing on the legitimate spheres of agency to which B's inhabitants are entitled.

If this conclusion proves convincing, then non-relational cosmopolitans' account of justice is vindicated. In what follows, I show that it is not. In particular, I argue that, on reflection, it is wrong to take W to be bound by a duty of egalitarian justice when B's poverty is due to bad brute luck: this duty both misconstrues the moral position of W *vis-à-vis* B, and ignores the strongest reasons in support of egalitarianism.

3.3.1 The Moral Position of W *vis-à-vis* B

As we have seen, non-relational cosmopolitans contend that the nature of W's duties towards B depends on whether B is morally responsible for its plight. If it is, W has duties of humanity, if it is not, W has duties of justice. The plausibility of this conclusion, and of the luck-egalitarian principle underpinning it, rests on how strong our intuitions about these two scenarios are. At least in my case, such intuitions are very unstable. Although I find the claim that W's duties towards B change across the two scenarios *prima facie* plausible, I am immediately thrown into doubt when reflecting on a case analogous to our scenarios, but less far-fetched.

---

[19] Charles Beitz has famously argued for a global natural-resource redistribution principle as a principle of justice for an international society of mutually independent states. See Beitz, 'Justice and International Relations', *Philosophy and Public Affairs*, 4 (4) (1975), 360–89, Section II, and *Political Theory and International Relations* with a new afterword (Princeton, NJ: Princeton University Press, 1999), pp. 136–43. For powerful critiques of natural-resource redistribution principles, see Miller, *National Responsibility and Global Justice*, ch. 3; and Thomas W. Pogge, *Realizing Rawls* (Ithaca, NY: Cornell University Press, 1989), pp. 250–2.

Let us consider a modified version of Singer's shallow pond example, in which the rescuee is no longer a child but an adult, Bob, who can therefore be held responsible for his choices. Again, there may be two construals of our scenario. On one construal, Bob-1 is consciously taking a risk. He knows he cannot swim, and yet he dangerously leans over the water to catch a beautiful autumn leaf floating on the surface, not too far from the shore. The result is predictable, Bob-1 loses balance and falls into the water. On another construal, Bob-2 is leisurely strolling in the pond's proximity. He is not taking any risks, he is just enjoying the beautiful day. All of a sudden, he slips onto a muddy patch, loses balance, and falls into the water. Assume that I am a bystander witnessing the scene: Does the *nature* of my duty to help Bob change across these two scenarios?

Following the normative rationale proposed by non-relational cosmopolitans, we would have to say that it does. My duty towards Bob-1 would be a matter of humanity, whereas my duty towards Bob-2 one of justice. On reflection, however, it is unclear why. After all, there is nothing *I* do that makes *my* moral position with respect to Bob change across the two scenarios. In both cases, I have a duty to respond to Bob's needs if this is not too costly to me, independently of whether his falling into the water is accidental, or attributable to his own agency.

What is more, it is not even clear that my duty towards unlucky Bob-2 is more stringent than my duty towards risk-taking Bob-1. To see this, consider a case in which both Bob-1 and Bob-2 are drowning, but only one of them can be saved at reasonable costs. Under these circumstances, I have a duty to save someone, but it is up to me to choose whom to save. People are likely reasonably to disagree about who should be rescued. For instance, some may believe that Bob-2 is more deserving to be saved than Bob-1 because the former fell into the pond because of bad brute luck. But others may equally legitimately believe that Bob-1's life is valuable, admire his love for nature, and decide to save him instead. Others still may instinctively decide to swim towards Bob-1 because he is closer to them than Bob-2.

All of these courses of action appear to be permissible. So long as I save someone, thus appropriately responding to human need, I do my duty. Of course, I should feel sorry for the death of the other Bob, but provided I rescue one, I cannot be accused of committing a moral wrong, let alone a rights violation. The fact that Bob-1 took a risk, and Bob-2 did not, does not *conclusively* tell in favour of saving the latter. It does not make Bob-2 the bearer of a right against me, which Bob-1 does not have.

By contrast, were I to push Bob-2 into the water, my moral position *vis-à-vis* him would indeed change, because of the involvement of my agency in his predicament. Under those circumstances, I would have a more stringent duty of justice to rescue him in particular: that is, he would have a *right* to be rescued by me.[20] Similarly, if the inhabitants of B were destitute due to unfair trade agreements with W, or to direct acts of aggression on W's part, then W would have a stringent duty of justice to compensate B in particular.[21]

Holding the content of the duties constant, duties of justice are more stringent than duties of humanity.[22] This proviso is a crucial one. If we did not make the special stringency of justice conditional upon the content of the duties remaining constant, we would run the risk of defending an implausible view. For instance, it would be problematic to claim that my duty of justice to return five pounds to Johnny is more stringent than my duty to assist Mary who is malnourished and could survive for several weeks with that small amount. Although I would be doing something wrong by not returning the five pounds to Johnny, I might be all-things-considered justified in giving the money to Mary. Judgements of relative stringency are bound to be controversial, and have to be made on a case-by-case basis. The important point here is that my duty to Mary would be all the more stringent had I originally stolen those five pounds from her. By the same token, my duty to Bob would be all the more stringent had I pushed him into the water, and W's duty to B would be all the more stringent were W culpably implicated in B's plight. But as the example of Bob shows, so long as W is not implicated in B's plight, its duties towards B are a matter of humanity, independently of how B's plight came about.

At this point, the non-relational cosmopolitan might come back and suggest that W's duties towards B, when B is the victim of bad brute luck (i.e. when B is in the position of Bob-2), cannot but be duties of justice, because they are obviously enforceable. Would it not be permissible for B's inhabitants forcibly to appropriate the resources they badly need? Most people, including myself, would answer in the affirmative. But doing so, the non-relational cosmopolitan continues, is tantamount to denying that W's duties are a matter of humanitarian assistance, as duties of humanity are paradigmatically non-enforceable. Enforceable duties are only duties of justice.[23]

This is a widely accepted dogma in contemporary political philosophy, but one whose grounds are hardly ever systematically explored. In particular, there are two possible readings of it. One implies that duties of humanity can *never*

---

[20] A similar example appears in David Zimmerman, 'Coercive Wage Offers', *Philosophy and Public Affairs*, 10 (2) (1981), 121–45, p. 135.

[21] See Thomas W. Pogge, *World Poverty and Human Rights: Cosmopolitan Responsibilities and Reforms* (Cambridge: Polity, 2002).

[22] I owe this proviso to Thomas W. Pogge, 'Severe Poverty as a Violation of Negative Duties', *Ethics and International Affairs*, 19 (1) (2005), 55–83, p. 76, who makes it in relation to the difference between negative and positive duties. Notice, however, that the distinction between negative and positive duties need not map on to that between justice and humanity.

[23] See the discussion in Pablo Gilabert, 'Kant and the Claims of the Poor', *Philosophy and Phenomenological Research*, 81 (2) (2010), 382–418; and in Laura Valentini, 'Justice, Charity and Misery: What, if Anything, Is Owed to Haiti?' (manuscript).

be permissibly enforced, the other that while duties of justice can be permissibly enforced *without wrongdoing*, duties of humanity may be permissibly enforced, but only at certain moral costs. The latter interpretation strikes me as more plausible.

Applied to our model scenario, this second interpretation allows us to conclude that B is all-things-considered justified to enforce W's duties. It would be morally implausible to ask the inhabitants of B, who are suffering through no fault of their own, to let themselves die for the sake of respecting W's entitlements. Even if B's lack of responsibility for its plight makes no difference to W's moral position towards it, it does make a difference to what B can permissibly do to W. Although it remains true that, by appropriating some of W's resources, B's inhabitants would commit an injustice (a rights violation), given B's innocence, this rights violation would be all-things-considered permissible.

B's situation is morally analogous to that involving an innocent victim and an innocent attacker: say someone who has lost control over a vehicle through no fault of his own, and is about to hit a pedestrian in the vicinity. In this case, neither of our agents can be said to have forfeited their right to life. Yet, it seems morally permissible for the victim to kill the driver, thereby violating his right to life, if this is the only way she/he has of defending her/his own life. Asking the innocent victim to accept to die for the driver's sake seems to be asking too much. Similarly, asking the inhabitants of B, who have no responsibility for their own plight, to accept a slow and painful death to respect W's entitlements appears to be too much to ask.[24] Some duties of humanity may be permissibly enforceable, but their enforcement, unlike the enforcement of duties of justice, always involves some wrongdoing.[25]

In sum, the general intuition that people should not be worse off through no fault of their own has some normative pull, but how much weight we should give it in designing a theory of justice depends on how reasonable its implications in specific cases are. In our discussion, we have seen that, even though this intuition seems *prima facie* plausible in the scenario involving W and B, it delivers counterintuitive conclusions once we move to that involving Bob-1 and Bob-2. In light of its rather shaky nature, how should we treat this intuition? If our aim is to design a normative framework that can help guide

---

[24] Cécile Fabre, 'Guns, Food and Liability to Attack in War', *Ethics*, 120 (1) (2009), 36–63, p. 62. Notice, however, that some dispute the view that it is ever morally permissible to kill an innocent, even if this is done to save one's own life. See Jeff McMahan, 'Self-Defense and the Problem of the Innocent Attacker', *Ethics*, 104 (2) (1994), 252–90.

[25] Things would look different if B's people were responsible for their own destitution (say they adopted predictably disastrous, wasteful policies). If that were the case, they would no longer be 'innocent' in the proper sense, and their attempt to appropriate W's resources would be *excusable*, because of duress, but *impermissible*.

our actions in the real world, we should not give it as much weight as non-relational cosmopolitans do.

The case of W and B – in which our intuition seems tenable – is a far-fetched one, involving societies that have developed independently from one another, and circumstances in which we can isolate brute luck as the only cause of B's plight. But our moral thinking is meant to apply to very different, more complex, scenarios. Under these more complex circumstances, societies interact with one another, and it is almost impossible to separate neatly between social and natural causes of poverty. Just consider the extent to which what counts as a valuable resource is determined by social facts. Two thousand years ago, a society sitting on copious quantities of oil would not have been considered resource rich, while it clearly is in our day and age.[26]

If we want to design a theory of justice that can help us in the world as we know it, we have much more reason to trust our considered convictions when these are developed against plausible real-world scenarios (such as the one involving Bob slipping into the lake) rather than intuitions that arise in scenarios that are far removed from situations we will ever encounter. As we saw in Chapter 2, by trying to account for our intuitions in improbable counterfactual cases, as proponents of the transcendent approach typically do, we undermine our chances of constructing a unified and parsimonious theory that can successfully guide our actions in the real world. As Thomas Pogge puts it, why should we want to 'trade off fit with our considered judgments about this world (which matters greatly) against fit with our judgments about very different worlds (which matters little)'?[27] Seeing no reason for wanting to do so, I conclude that the luck-egalitarian intuition driving non-relational cosmopolitanism should be, to a large extent, discounted. Even though it might plausibly play some role in our moral reasoning, it does not mark the dividing line between duties of justice and other types of moral concern.

Up to now, I have suggested that we should still consider W's duty towards B as a matter of humanity, even on the assumption that B's plight has been caused by something as morally arbitrary as a natural catastrophe. So long as differences in the causal chains of events leading to B's poverty do not involve W's responsible actions, the nature of its duties towards B remains unchanged. Although I find the methodological reasons offered for this conclusion compelling, some might still be sceptical. They might not be committed to the same methodological outlook, and be instead convinced that our intuitions in counterfactual scenarios, however unstable, are revelatory of deeper truths.

As I shall shortly argue, however, even *they* would find non-relational cosmopolitanism implausible as a theory that could help guide our actions in the real world. This is because, at the level of policy prescriptions,

---

[26] David Miller, *National Responsibility and Global Justice*, pp. 58ff.
[27] Thomas W. Pogge, 'Cohen to the Rescue!', *Ratio*, 21 (4) (2008), 454–75, p. 475.

non-relational cosmopolitans are *not* in a position genuinely to discriminate between the case in which B is destitute through no fault of its own, and the case in which it is responsible for its plight. Each newborn baby in B is owed equal opportunities as a matter of justice, *even if* B's poverty is simply a consequence of the earlier generations' wasteful behaviour. Arguably, every newborn in B can only enjoy equal opportunities for a decent life by making B, as a society, better off overall. It thus turns out that, *in practice* (although not in principle), there is no difference between W's duties towards B across our two scenarios. Justice is always owed either to all the inhabitants (if they have been unlucky), or to those inhabitants who have not yet reached the age of responsibility, no matter what the causes of their poverty are.[28]

3.3.2 Why Equality Matters

So far, we have seen that, with their focus on the neutralization of bad brute luck, non-relational cosmopolitans fail adequately to capture the special nature, and stringency, of duties of justice. I shall now argue that this focus also fails to vindicate non-relational cosmopolitans' egalitarian aspirations. As it turns out, the strongest arguments in support of equality presuppose the existence of a thick relational background.

Let me begin by asking: Why should W have duties to 'equalize' as opposed to duties to relieve B from absolute deprivation, and help it establish a viable social system? Non-relational cosmopolitans are committed to answering that W's egalitarian distributive duties stem from the fundamental liberal principle of *equal respect*. Respecting persons as rational and autonomous agents, so the argument goes, requires rectifying unchosen inequalities. Does this account of equal respect adequately capture the reasons why most of us believe that inequalities attached to morally arbitrary factors are problematic? It seems not. To fully appreciate what is wrong with these inequalities we need to put them into context.

Violations of equal respect occur when some agents *treat* other agents as inferiors.[29] Consider, for instance, the predicament of members of a racial minority in a racist society. Most of us would want to argue that they suffer injustice. But what explains this judgement? The non-relational cosmopolitan would invoke the by-now familiar luck-egalitarian intuition. She/he would suggest that what makes the minority's situation unjust is the fact that they are

---

[28] Cf. Miller, *National Responsibility and Global Justice*, pp. 70ff.
[29] This point about treatment is also made by Christian Schemmel in 'On the Usefulness of Luck Egalitarian Arguments', pp. 60ff. In this discussion, I am indebted to Andrea Sangiovanni, 'Global Justice, Reciprocity, and the State', pp. 25–6.

worse off because of a morally arbitrary (unchosen) factor: their race. In other words, they are unlucky.

I find this response not only unconvincing but possibly even offensive. Members of racial minorities in racist societies are not simply 'unlucky'. What makes them underprivileged is not a natural or genetic fact, but a social one.[30] They are *placed* in a position of inferiority by their fellow citizens; they are the victims of social stigma and domination. In short, they are not respected as equals.[31] If their disadvantage did not stem from these asymmetric social relations, we would not regard it as morally outrageous.[32]

To see this, consider the inequalities existing between two independent and well-ordered societies – call them Mediocria and Ingenia – one of which is better off than the other simply because of the greater intelligence of its inhabitants. Are the inequalities between these two societies as morally troublesome as those between members of different races within the same social system? They are not. In fact, it is not even clear to me that the inequalities between Ingenia and Mediocria are troublesome at all. There is no obvious sense in which, by failing to transfer resources to Mediocria, Ingenians thereby treat its inhabitants disrespectfully. Perhaps one could even argue that transferring resources would express disrespect towards Mediocrians, treating them as inferiors, suggesting that what their society has achieved is not 'good enough'. As this example shows, in the absence of a thick relational background, the reasons that motivate our concern for distributive equality apparently cease to exist.

This is further confirmed by looking at the case of W and B. Once again, it is unclear why equal respect would demand egalitarian transfers between these two societies. W and B are fully independent of each other, so there is no sense in which W might be treating B's inhabitants as inferiors by refusing to pursue inter-societal equality. Moreover if, *ex hypothesi*, W and B have no shared status norms, or social relations, how could inequalities between their inhabitants count as stigmatizing? How could they possibly lead to, or be caused by, domination? Of course, in our globalized world, cross-country comparisons between people's levels of well-being are almost unavoidable, and opportunities for domination abound.[33] But our world is conspicuously different from the idealized scenario we are considering.

In this scenario, W would express disrespect towards B if it ignored the needs of its people. Respect for persons *qua* human beings requires an

---

[30] Pogge, *Realizing Rawls*, pp. 251–2.

[31] On this, see Martin O'Neill, 'What Should Egalitarians Believe?', *Philosophy and Public Affairs*, 36 (2) (2008), 119–56, pp. 126ff.

[32] For this line of argument, and its articulation in the following paragraphs, see Elizabeth Anderson's famous piece: 'What is the Point of Equality?', *Ethics*, 109 (2) (1999), 287–337. See also Samuel Scheffler, 'What Is Egalitarianism?', *Philosophy and Public Affairs*, 31 (1) (2003), 5–39.

[33] See Cécile Laborde, 'Republicanism and Global Justice: A Sketch', *European Journal of Political Theory*, 9 (1) (2010), 48–69.

appropriate response to their neediness and suffering, a response that is offered by the morality of humanity, not by that of egalitarian distributive justice.

In light of our discussion, the non-relational cosmopolitan conclusion that a world containing W and B would be characterized by *injustice* until the life prospects of the inhabitants of these two countries are equalized, provided B is badly off through no fault of its own, seems poorly substantiated. Perhaps, once it has fulfilled its duties of humanitarian assistance, W could donate some extra resources to B as a matter of generosity. But the claim that such transfers would be required by duty, in fact by a stringent duty of justice, unduly impoverishes our moral vocabulary. To say that justice is about helping those who are already well off, but not lucky enough to be as well off as we are, robs justice of its privileged moral status.

Before closing my discussion, let me briefly respond to a complaint that non-relational cosmopolitans might voice against my analysis. The complaint consists in pointing out that the example I have focused on to criticize their outlook is implausibly fictional. They might insist that we do not live in a two-society world, and that their theories are meant to capture our duties and obligations in the world as it is. Hence, objecting to such theories by appeal to some fancy example is a theoretically unfair move.

I am sympathetic to this reply. Indeed, I myself am sceptical about imaginary scenarios that are nominally used to illustrate existing cases, but very often distort them. Despite this, I think it is legitimate to use such hypothetical examples when discussing non-relational cosmopolitanism. First, an analogue of our two-society scenario is suggested by Caney himself as a possible test for his view. Instead of resorting to examples involving aliens and Martians, says Caney, critics should consider 'a remote people living in gruelling poverty on an island with no trade, or political or environmental links to the rest of the world'.[34] For reasons of simplicity, I have replaced the island and 'the rest of the world' with two societies, but otherwise the example is equivalent to Caney's.

There is also a more general reason why fictional scenarios are appropriate when assessing non-relational cosmopolitanism. If we were to refer to the world as it is – with its intense interdependence – we would be unable to appreciate what is distinctive about this normative position. As I noted in the beginning of this chapter, and as we will shortly see in more detail, relational and non-relational cosmopolitans defend roughly the same substantive principles of global justice. Considered with respect to the world as it is – namely a deeply interconnected and interdependent world – these two theories reach

---

[34] Simon Caney, 'Global Poverty and Human Rights: The Case for Positive Duties', in Thomas W. Pogge (ed.), *Freedom from Poverty as a Human Right: Who Owes What to the Very Poor?* (Oxford: Oxford University Press, 2007), 275–302, p. 288.

very similar normative conclusions. To examine non-relational cosmopolitanism, we therefore need to look at cases that this view would handle differently from its relational counterpart. If, once we do so, non-relational cosmopolitans complain that we would not reach equally counterintuitive conclusions were we to test their theories in real-world scenarios, we can immediately infer that their claims make more sense against a certain relational background. This lends credibility only to relational cosmopolitanism, to which I now turn.

3.4 RELATIONAL COSMOPOLITANISM: AN OVERVIEW

Predictably, relational cosmopolitans hold that the content and applicability of moral principles depends on the particular relations they are meant to govern. When it comes to socio-economic justice in particular, the relevant relations are those holding between fellow citizens within the same political community, supported by a common set of political, economic, and legal institutions: a basic structure. For relational cosmopolitans, principles of justice are meant to govern persons' relations within, and as part of, such a structure.[35] In their view, social justice sets limits to what participants in a basic structure can do to one another, through the operation of their common institutions.

From a relational cosmopolitan perspective, the possibility of extending principles of justice from the domestic to the international realm therefore depends on whether there exists a 'global basic structure' similar enough to the domestic one to warrant the application of liberal-egalitarian principles of justice. Schematically put, their argument develops as follows.

1. All human beings are owed equal respect *qua* moral persons.
2. In the presence of a basic structure, equal respect requires substantive equality: that is, an equal (or roughly equal) distribution of civil and political liberties, opportunities, income, and wealth.
3. There exists a global basic structure.
4. Liberties, opportunities, income, and wealth should be equally – or roughly equally – distributed across the world's population.

One preliminary consideration to be made before proceeding further is that, from a structural viewpoint, relational cosmopolitanism seems to be better placed than its non-relational counterpart to make sense of the specificity of justice. For the relational cosmopolitan, socio-economic justice applies only between people who stand in particular kinds of relations *vis-à-vis* one

---

[35] Beitz, *Political Theory and International Relations*; Pogge, *Realizing Rawls*; and Darrel Moellendorf, *Cosmopolitan Justice* (Boulder, CO: Westview Press, 2002).

another. The mere presence of undeserved need, in the absence of special relations, is a sufficient trigger of duties of humanity, but not of stringent demands of justice.

Even though much more would have to be said to show that relational cosmopolitans are able to offer a fully satisfactory account of the distinction between justice and humanity, their overall approach looks promising in this respect. Therefore, relational cosmopolitanism and particularly its claim that there exists a global basic structure are at least worth exploring. Problematically, though, once we learn that the key to answering the question of extension is whether there exists a global basic structure, we still do not know what to look for. In its most simplistic understanding, the basic structure denotes the complex set of institutions – legal, political, and economic – typically found within a state. Since there is no global state, those who claim that there exists a global basic structure must have something else in mind.

As is well known, the basic structure may be described in a plurality of different ways.[36] Going through all potential interpretations would take us too far from the topic of the present discussion. I shall thus limit myself to two prominent interpretations: one understands the basic structure in partly moralized terms, the other in non-moralized ones.

3.5 MUTUALLY ADVANTAGEOUS OR FAIR COOPERATION

Some have suggested that Rawls's criteria of domestic justice should be extended to the world at large in virtue of the existence of a global basic structure understood as a system of *cooperation for mutual advantage*.[37] Given the degree of contemporary international interdependence, especially economic and financial, the world may plausibly be regarded as a close cooperative scheme from which all participants benefit. Like domestic cooperative schemes, then, the world at large should be placed under moral scrutiny and evaluated from the viewpoint of justice and injustice.

Does it make sense to consider the global basic structure as a system of cooperation for mutual advantage? It would seem not. As Brian Barry has

---

[36] See e.g. Arash Abizadeh, 'Cooperation, Pervasive Impact, and Coercion: On the Scope (not Site) of Distributive Justice', *Philosophy and Public Affairs*, 35 (4) (2007), 318–58.

[37] This line of argument has been famously (and in my view somewhat unfairly) attributed to Charles Beitz by Brian Barry in 'Humanity and Justice in Global Perspective', in Brian Barry, *Liberty and Justice: Essays in Political Theory 2* (Oxford: Clarendon Press, 1991), 182–210, pp. 193ff.

pointed out, the problem with the globalization of this 'mutual advantage' account of the basic structure is that it is hard to see how we could possibly regard the world economy as a *mutually advantageous* cooperative system.[38] If we take mutual advantage as the constitutive feature of the basic structure, we end up with a conception of justice whereby oppressive relations (which are advantageous for one party only) are in principle beyond justice-based assessment, which is absurd.

Notice that this problem with justice as mutual advantage arises not only in the international but also in the domestic context. This means that this characterization of the basic structure is implausible as a starting point for a theory of justice in general.[39] In Charles Beitz's words, '[t]o say that a society is "a cooperative venture for mutual advantage" is to add certain elements of a social ideal to a description of the circumstances to which justice applies ... [which] ... unnecessarily narrow the description of these circumstances'.[40]

To see this, consider the even more obvious implausibility of a 'fair cooperation' account of the basic structure – which is particularly popular among Rawlsian scholars.[41] If a condition for the applicability of principles of justice were the existence of systems of *fair* cooperation, justice would only apply to contexts in which it is, in some sense, not needed because it is already in place. While it makes moral sense to think that duties of justice apply only to certain kinds of relations, it makes no moral sense to conceive of those relations in already moralized terms.[42]

What we need to ask is whether there exist *de facto* global relations such that the principles of justice applying to domestic relations should also apply to the world at large. Before asking whether X is just, we need to ask whether X is the sort of thing to which justice applies. We can thus safely conclude that a moralized understanding of the basic structure – both in terms of cooperation for mutual advantage, and in terms of fair cooperation – is unsuitable as a basis for a relational account of justice, both domestically and globally.

---

[38] Barry, 'Humanity and Justice', pp. 193ff.
[39] Beitz, *Political Theory and International Relations*, pp. 131, 203.
[40] Beitz, *Political Theory and International Relations*, p. 131.
[41] See Samuel Freeman, 'The Law of Peoples, Social Cooperation, Human Rights, and Distributive Justice', *Social Philosophy and Policy*, 23 (1) (2006), 29–68, p. 37. For a similar criticism, see Abizadeh, 'Cooperation, Pervasive Impact, and Coercion', pp. 330–1; and Christian Barry and Laura Valentini, 'Egalitarian Challenges to Global Egalitarianism: A Critique', *Review of International Studies*, 35 (3) (2009), 485–512.
[42] As we will see in Part II of this book, this is one of the main methodological difficulties characterizing statist accounts of international justice.

3.6 A RULE-GOVERNED SOCIAL SYSTEM

A number of theorists have understood the basic structure to indicate a rule-governed social system with a profound impact on people's life prospects. Since the world at large might be regarded as a system of this kind, Rawls's criteria of justice, many have argued, should be global in scope.[43]

The claim that the international arena is a rule-governed, closed social system with a deep and pervasive impact on people's lives is undisputable. The rules governing the state system – those defining the powers and prerogatives of states – as well as those regulating international organizations and institutions all contribute to shaping our opportunities and life prospects. If this is what a basic structure is, namely a pervasive system of rules placing constraints on people's actions, then clearly there is a global basic structure. This, however, does not mean that relational cosmopolitans can bring the point home. To do so, they would have to show that this global basic structure is sufficiently similar to domestic basic structures to warrant extending domestic principles of justice to the international arena. If we do not want the dispute between cosmopolitans and statists to hinge on mere terminology, we have to ask whether those particular basic structural features that make it plausible to apply Rawlsian justice to the domestic context also exist globally.

After all, there are many rule-governed social systems with a deep impact on persons' lives. Consider, for instance, families, churches, universities and, finally, society itself. All of these institutions have a 'basic structure', which should be governed by moral principles of some kind. But most of us would find the suggestion that families, churches, universities, and states should all be governed by the same principles rather implausible. It would seem that, as Rawls's constructivist methodology recommends, each of these institutions and associations should be governed by different moral standards, reflecting the particular aim they are meant to foster (consistently with the principle of equal respect).[44]

In other words, different rule-governed social practices seem to require different types of regulatory principles and the mere fact that they are rule governed and have a deep and pervasive impact on people's lives does not settle the question of *what* principles should govern them. Unless we say more about the kinds of practices they are, the content of the principles that should govern them remains underdetermined.

To vindicate the claim that liberal-egalitarian principles of justice should apply to the world at large, cosmopolitans cannot simply insist that the world

---

[43] This view can be primarily attributed to Thomas Pogge. Versions of it are also defended by Beitz, *Political Theory and International Relations*; and Moellendorf, *Cosmopolitan Justice*.

[44] See John Rawls, 'The Basic Structure as Subject' in *Political Liberalism* (New York: Columbia University Press, 1996), 257–88.

at large is a rule-governed social system that significantly shapes people's life prospects. Instead, they must also prove that the way in which it shapes life prospects is the same as the way in which domestic basic structures shape citizens' life prospects. This claim is a hard one to establish.

As critics have argued, contrary to those who insist that nowadays we are all citizens of a global society, the international institutions constituting the global order are unlike domestic ones in at least four respects: (*i*) they are not supported by the same sense of community typically underpinning domestic politics; (*ii*) they are not unitary authorities like the state;[45] (*iii*) they preside over a different range of activities;[46] and (*iv*) they are usually marked by deep value pluralism. In what follows, I consider each of these differences in turn.

(i) Absence of a Sense of Community[47]

Some contend that there now exists a global civil society, and that the number of those exhibiting cosmopolitan attitudes is constantly growing.[48] This may be partly true, but it is also certainly true that those who really feel strong bonds to the rest of humanity, as opposed to their near and dear (however defined), are still a very small percentage.[49] The empirical claim that there exists no global sense of community comparable to the sense of community bringing together citizens of the same country is hard to dispute. What we need to ask is whether such a disanalogy between our *current* domestic and global affections should make a difference to the applicability of principles of justice.

The answer seems to be no. Tying the applicability of principles of justice to the existence of a sense of community would be as implausible as adopting a moralized conception of the basic structure. Making the appropriateness of principles of justice depend on entirely subjective feelings may easily lead to arbitrary discrimination. For instance, such a stance might legitimize denying the existence of duties of justice towards women and African-Americans in sexist and racist societies because they are not perceived as being part of the community.

Of course, fellow feelings are likely to facilitate the realization of justice. People are much more likely to accept and abide by principles of justice when

---

[45] A similar thought is expressed in A. J. Julius, 'Nagel's Atlas', *Philosophy and Public Affairs*, 34 (2) (2006), 176–92, p. 190.
[46] On range-limited principles, see Jeremy Waldron, 'Special Ties and Natural Duties', *Philosophy and Public Affairs*, 22 (1) (1993), 3–30.
[47] This point is discussed by Beitz in *Political Theory and International Relations*, pp. 155–7.
[48] See e.g. Jeremy Waldron, 'Minority Cultures and the Cosmopolitan Alternative', in Will Kymlicka (ed.), *The Rights of Minority Cultures* (Oxford: Oxford University Press, 1995), 93–119.
[49] On this, see Miller, *National Responsibility and Global Justice*, ch. 2.

these are perceived as applying to their associates. This, however, is a purely instrumental consideration: the existence of a sense of community should not affect the normative applicability of principles of justice as such but only their prospects of success.[50]

(ii) Absence of a State-like Agent

Critics of cosmopolitanism have often pointed out that '[t]he difference principle... presupposes a single political agent or agency with authority over economic relations at the most basic level... In the domestic case, there is such an agent or agency; it is the people and its authorized government. In the international case there is no such agent or agency, and there could be none without the near total eclipse of the political autonomy and independence of peoples.'[51] The most articulate statement of this line of argument is offered by Saladin Meckled-Garcia, who contends that, in order for Rawls's principles to apply to a particular domain of human action, there needs to be an authoritative agent capable of carrying out the function of 'background adjustment', that is, of addressing the distributive inequalities which would otherwise result from the combined effects of individuals' transactions.[52]

No agent other than the state has the capacity and the authority to carry out this kind of adjustment; therefore, no agent other than the state can reasonably be held responsible for it. As there exists no global state, so the critique goes, the claim that, judged by Rawls's standards of justice, the global order is unjust, is morally implausible. What can we make of this criticism?

The observation that principles of justice should apply to appropriate agents is valid and important. But, as I argued in Chapter 2 and will argue at greater length in Chapter 5, the contingent fact that there exists no state-like agent that can apply Rawls's principles to the global realm does not prove that there ought not to be one.[53] For instance, we can easily imagine a domestic state that, here and now, *cannot* implement liberal-egalitarian principles of justice, say because it lacks the necessary institutional structures: it is a minimal state with no agencies regulating the economy. Surely, we do not want to say that liberal-egalitarian justice does not apply to the society in question. Rather, we

---

[50] Of course, one could say that a sense of community could never exist on a global scale. As I argued in Chapter 2, this is too speculative a claim to refute cosmopolitanism.

[51] David A. Reidy, 'A Just Global Economy: In Defense of Rawls', *The Journal of Ethics*, 11 (2) (2007), 193–236, p. 213.

[52] Saladin Meckled-Garcia, 'On the Very Idea of Cosmopolitan Justice: Constructivism and International Agency', *Journal of Political Philosophy*, 16 (3) (2008), 245–71.

[53] I am grateful to Cécile Laborde for bringing this point to my attention. See Beitz, *Political Theory and International Relations*, pp. 154–7, for discussion.

want to say that the said society should strive to build a stronger state, capable of meeting the demands of justice.

By the same token, it is perfectly consistent for cosmopolitans to argue that there exists a global basic structure – a set of legal, political, and economic relations extending to the world at large – and that such a basic structure can only be justly governed through the creation of a functional equivalent of a global state. On this view, there is a global basic structure, but because of the lack of regulation, it is an unjust one. As we cannot discount the possibility that a just global regulatory institution might one day exist, the 'state-like agency' argument against relational cosmopolitanism proves inconclusive. All it shows is that, under existing circumstances, justice requires us to work towards the creation of appropriate global (state-like) institutions.[54]

(iii) Different Domain

Some might argue that there exists a global basic structure *only partly* like the domestic one. This is because, even though people's lives are increasingly affected by decisions made outside their borders, and even if the body of rules governing global markets, labour, and finance is growing, the activities regulated by these international rules do not fully coincide with those regulated by the domestic basic structure. This objection acknowledges the existence of a global basic structure more and more similar to the basic structure of domestic societies, but it also recognizes that we are 'not quite there yet'.[55] In the face of this, there are three possible responses open to cosmopolitans.

The first consists in insisting that, in spite of first appearances, the global basic structure is exactly the same as the domestic basic structure. This reply is bound to be unconvincing though. Critics of cosmopolitanism will always be able to point to *factual* disanalogies between domestic and international realms putting this cosmopolitan claim into question. So long as we do not live in a global state, the empirical claim that domestic and global basic structures are 'exactly the same' lacks even *prima facie* plausibility.

Second, cosmopolitans might more credibly acknowledge the existence of empirical differences but argue that, ultimately, such differences are of no moral relevance. This reply echoes my earlier response to the 'state-like agency' critique. The idea is that, even though, as it stands, the global basic structure governs a different range of activities than the domestic one, the reforms needed to make it fully just would turn it into a *de facto* global version

---

[54] I have already discussed worries about global despotism arising in connection with the idea of a global state in Section 2.4.
[55] This seems to be the position taken by Julius in 'Nagel's Atlas'.

of the domestic basic structure.[56] On this view, the reason why the global basic structure is unjust is that its purview is too narrow: it regulates certain activities, but not others.[57] So, for instance, it might be argued that the rules governing international finance and trade lead to injustice because they cover only some sectors, but not others. Or it might be suggested that the way to ensure the justness of humanitarian intervention would be to create a global UN army or police force, that is a globalized, state-like coercive apparatus.[58] In short, the reply argues that, taken together, the various reforms necessary to make the institutions we already have just would lead to the creation of a *de facto* global analogue of the domestic basic structure, to which principles of domestic justice would then apply.

This is an interesting line of argument; however, once again it seems too speculative to merit theoretical warrant. Whether making existing international/global institutions just would require turning them into worldwide versions of our domestic institutions is something we are unlikely to be able to establish now and in the foreseeable future. Why should international regulatory institutions look *just like* domestic ones? Why would global justice demand the construction of a global state, and not the establishment of a multiplicity of supranational authorities?[59]

Third, cosmopolitans might acknowledge that, in light of this uncertainty, it is best to put their arguments in favour of a global extension of liberal-egalitarian (Rawls-like) principles of justice to one side (without necessarily abandoning them), and opt for a more moderate version of the cosmopolitan view. Doing so would correspond to following Beitz's (not so well known but interesting) proposal for a 'weak' cosmopolitan thesis. Such a thesis 'is agnostic about the content of international distributive justice, holding only that international justice should be regarded as an extension of a corresponding doctrine of distributive justice for domestic society'.[60] In other words, the weak cosmopolitan view holds that the *concept* of justice that liberals use for the evaluation of domestic political communities (particularly in socio-economic matters) should also apply to the world at large, but that different *conceptions* of justice are suitable for these different spheres. For example, a weak cosmopolitan view may place permissible limits on global inequalities,

---

[56] I am grateful to Miriam Ronzoni for discussion. See also her 'Two Concepts of the Basic Structure and their Relevance to Global Justice', *Global Justice: Theory Practice Rhetoric*, 1 (2008), 68–85.

[57] This is a point a Rawlsian liberal could make in relation to the basic structure of a Nozickian minimal state.

[58] See e.g. James Pattison, 'Humanitarian Intervention and a Cosmopolitan UN Force', *Journal of International Political Theory*, 4 (1) (2008), 126–45.

[59] Cf. the arguments offered in Elisa Orrù and Miriam Ronzoni, 'Which Supranational Sovereignty: Global Criminal and Socio-economic Justice Compared', *Review of International Studies*, 37 (5) (2011).

[60] Beitz, *Political Theory and International Relations*, p. 199.

but these limits might differ from those we place on domestic inequalities, given the different social facts characterizing the domestic and the global context.[61] Even though considerable theoretical work is needed to substantiate such a claim, this seems a viable alternative for those relational theorists inclined towards cosmopolitanism. Interestingly, the alternative appears all the more plausible when considered in connection with our fourth disanalogy.

(iv) Deep Value Pluralism

The last challenge to relational cosmopolitanism does not focus on the empirical basis of the relational cosmopolitan thesis – it does not question the claim that there exists a global basic structure – but it focuses on the *values* that may be legitimately invoked when constructing principles applying to the world at large. In particular, this challenge disputes the claim, stated under (2) above, that 'in the presence of a basic structure, equal respect requires substantive equality: i.e., an equal (or roughly equal) distribution of civil and political rights, opportunities, income and wealth'. This claim, so the objection goes, is unqualified: the presence of a domestic basic structure is insufficient to warrant the application of liberal-egalitarian principles of justice; what is needed is a *liberal-egalitarian* basic structure, a basic structure already informed by liberal-egalitarian values. In a context such as the international arena, where the value pluralism already present within domestic societies is all the more pervasive, defending liberal-egalitarian principles of justice would be an unwarranted act of imperialism.

What can we make of this charge? Of course, the claim would be implausible if interpreted as a defence of what might be referred to as an 'agreement approach' to justification. On this view, something is justified so long as it is agreed upon. Because we cannot have agreement on liberal principles at the international level, such principles turn out to be unjustified. This view is clearly susceptible to the charges of conservatism and *status-quo* bias already levelled against the 'sense of community' and 'state-like agency' objections.

A more plausible interpretation of the claim suggests that it is unwarranted to assume that a *liberal-egalitarian* political morality, such as the political

---

[61] See e.g. Joshua Cohen and Charles Sabel, 'Extra Rempublicam Nulla Justitia?', *Philosophy and Public Affairs*, 34 (2) (2006), 147–75; Miriam Ronzoni, 'The Global Order: A Case of Background Injustice? A Practice-dependent Account', *Philosophy and Public Affairs*, 37 (3) (2009), 229–56; Laura Valentini, 'Global Justice and Practice-Dependence: Conventionalism, Institutionalism, Functionalism', *Journal of Political Philosophy*, 19 (4) (2011), 399–418; and Andrew Altman and Christopher Heath Wellman, *A Liberal Theory of International Justice* (Oxford: Oxford University Press, 2009), ch. 6.

morality Rawls defends in the domestic context, is the only one capable of expressing respect for persons. The reason why it would be illiberal to globalize Rawls's principles of domestic justice, the critics say, is that, contrary to some liberals' arrogant assumption, there *can* be political cultures that are respectful of their members' moral personality and yet do not implement the full schedule of liberal-egalitarian rights. So long as this is possible, liberals should hesitate in claiming the universal validity, hence the global applicability, of their domestic conceptions of justice.[62]

How should we respond to this challenge? Here, I will say very little about this matter, as I will explore the topic at greater length in Chapter 4. For the time being, let me just note that, so phrased, this challenge is not altogether implausible. While there is little doubt that the violation of a person's right to life, food, shelter, or freedom of movement constitutes an affront to her/his moral status as a person, whether such a status can only be expressed through liberal-egalitarian justice is something not straightforwardly obvious. Can a society plausibly qualify as one expressing equal respect for its citizens only if it implements Rawls's difference principle? Frankly, I am not sure. This consideration, of course, is relevant not only to the international arena but also to those domestic contexts in which there exists deep value pluralism. In this book, I focus only on questions of international political morality, and it seems true to say that, if we have reasons to worry about domestic pluralism, *a fortiori* we have reasons to worry about its international counterpart.

In light of the arguments advanced in this section, I conclude that, although relational cosmopolitanism cannot be conclusively refuted, some of its core claims are insufficiently argued for. In particular, the fact that the global basic structure seems to encompass different domains of human activity from the domestic one, and the presence of deep value pluralism at the global level, suggests caution in advancing the claim that liberal-egalitarian domestic justice should apply globally. Even though, as I said, none of the arguments offered against such a claim seems fully successful, they at least show that the relational cosmopolitan thesis is not *obviously right*. In fact, they suggest that, for now and the foreseeable future, it is unlikely that cosmopolitans will come up with a convincing defence of such a thesis in its strong form. Since the evidence in support of relational cosmopolitanism is neither sufficient for us to endorse it, nor poor enough to warrant refutation, the most theoretically justified stance to take towards this outlook is, I believe, a healthy agnosticism.

---

[62] See David Reidy, 'Rawls on International Justice: A Defense', *Political Theory*, 32 (3) (2004), 291–319, p. 313.

3.7 CONCLUSION

In this chapter, I have explored different justificatory avenues in defence of the cosmopolitan claim that Rawls's liberal-egalitarian principles of justice (or their analogues) should apply to the world at large. In particular, I have focused on two versions of cosmopolitanism: relational and non-relational. I have rejected non-relational cosmopolitanism on the grounds that its theoretical apparatus generates implausible moral demands, obscuring what is distinctive about duties of justice (as opposed to duties of humanity). With respect to relational cosmopolitanism, I have argued that, even though its overall theoretical framework is *prima facie* well suited to capture what is special about justice, its strong claim that the global basic structure should be regulated by liberal-egalitarian principles of domestic justice remains partly unsupported. This form of relational cosmopolitanism cannot be proven wrong, but it also lacks solid enough foundations to be proven right. In light of this, I have suggested that cosmopolitans are probably on firmer ground taking a more moderate ('weaker') stance. This would involve extending the *concept* of justice to the international arena, without necessarily claiming that domestic *conceptions* of justice should also apply to the world at large.

Of course, as it stands, this is just a suggestion, and more work needs to be done in order to show what it is that makes the same concept (but different conceptions) apply to both domains. Before doing the required argumentative work, however, we should investigate the view of cosmopolitans' direct opponents: statists. If they turn out to offer a plausible approach to global justice, there will be no need to explore the moderate cosmopolitan avenue, as I have just suggested.

Part II

Statism

4

Assessing the Statist Ideal

4.1 INTRODUCTION

As I noted in Chapter 1, like cosmopolitanism, statism is susceptible to two powerful critiques: one focuses on the justification of statist principles, the other on the cogency of the statist ideal, and its ability (or lack thereof) to guide action in real-world circumstances. In this chapter, I focus on the latter critique, and consider the complaint that the statist ideal is excessively biased in favour of the *status quo*.

But what, exactly, does the statist ideal amount to? In a nutshell, statists advocate a world of self-determining and internally diverse political communities, between which no principles of egalitarian socio-economic justice apply. In the words of David Miller, a prominent advocate of statism, theorists who share his convictions

> envisage a world of diversity in which the variety of national cultures finds expression in different sets of citizenship rights, and different schemes of social justice, in each community. In this vision we should aim to create a world that offers each community adequate scope to pursue its own distinctive values. States should work together to ensure that every community can protect its members' basic rights, but there should be no attempt to impose uniformity.[1]

The ideal world depicted by statists has much in common with the world in which we live, with its separate political communities, cultural differences, and lack of provisions for worldwide socio-economic equality. It is therefore no surprise that critics of statism have started to worry about this ideal being biased towards the *status quo*. The question before us is: Are these worries warranted after all?

In this chapter, I argue that they are only partly warranted. While statists' refusal to extend egalitarian justice to the global realm does not in itself

---

[1] David Miller, 'Caney's "International Distributive Justice": A Response', *Political Studies*, 50 (5) (2002), 974–7, p. 976. Recall, in this book I use the term 'statism' broadly, as also encompassing nationalism and social liberalism.

indicate subservience to the *status quo*, statist principles are ill-suited to guide action in real-world circumstances. They are insufficiently sensitive to the main causes of international injustice, and therefore unable to address them effectively. Surprisingly, this is not because statist principles take too many features of the existing state of affairs for granted, but because they assume too few. Statists appear to underestimate the level, and moral importance, of systemic international interdependence and power inequalities characterizing the world today.[2] Their principles would thus be appropriate for a world of relatively independent political communities, but are unsatisfactory as a guide for action under existing circumstances. My argument proceeds as follows.

In Section 4.2, I outline the key commitments of a statist view. In Section 4.3, I distinguish between two versions of the *status-quo* bias critique of statism: the static and the dynamic version. The former focuses on the moral desirability of the statist picture of a just world order; the latter focuses on the ability of statist principles to offer positive guidance for action. In Section 4.4, I argue that the static version of the critique is for the most part unsuccessful: the statist picture of a just world order is at least as morally appealing as – if not more morally appealing than – the cosmopolitan one. In Section 4.5, I move on to the dynamic version of the critique and show that it points to a serious shortcoming in statists' account of justice. I then conclude by introducing the topic of Chapter 5.

Before getting started, let me make one prefatory clarification. Although I refer to more than one author, my discussion in this chapter primarily focuses on Rawls's *The Law of Peoples*.[3] Rawls's monograph offers the most influential statement of statism to date, and it is against Rawls's position that most of the critiques I examine have been raised. That said, to the extent that contemporary statist theory is inspired by Rawls's outlook, the significance of (at least some of) my arguments need not be confined to Rawls's own views. What, then, is statism?

4.2 STATISM: AN OVERVIEW

The view I here call statism has been most comprehensively advocated by John Rawls and David Miller. More recently, aspects of it have also been defended by other theorists including Thomas Nagel, Michael Blake, and

---

[2] As will appear clear, from an empirical point of view, this complaint applies primarily to Rawls. Thomas Nagel and other statists show greater awareness of existing global interdependence. See e.g. Nagel, 'The Problem of Global Justice', *Philosophy and Public Affairs*, 33 (2) (2005), 113–47. Nevertheless, they still downplay its moral relevance.

[3] John Rawls, *The Law of Peoples* (Cambridge, MA: Harvard University Press, 1999).

Andrea Sangiovanni.[4] Although there are differences between the views proposed by these authors, and the arguments they deploy to defend them, they all broadly subscribe to the following four claims:

a. Legitimate political communities ought to respect one another's self-determination and ought not to interfere in one another's affairs.
b. Political communities have duties to assist one another when they are in need.
c. Political communities ought to be internally legitimate, that is, they ought to comply with certain (more or less demanding) domestic moral standards.
d. Stringent criteria of egalitarian justice do not apply beyond state borders.[5]

To substantiate this characterization of statism, let me briefly look at the accounts of international morality proposed by the authors I have mentioned.

In *The Law of Peoples*, Rawls famously develops 'the ideals and principles of the *foreign policy* of a reasonably just *liberal* people'.[6] By a people Rawls means a territorially organized political unit, whose population is united by common sympathies and upholds a reasonable or 'common good' idea of justice. Broadly speaking, a people may be regarded as an idealized version of a state, a form of political community that differs from states traditionally conceived primarily in virtue of its moral – as opposed to merely self-interested – nature.[7] Rawls holds that, in their mutual relations, peoples so understood should follow eight 'familiar principles' of international conduct:[8]

1. Peoples are free and independent, and their freedom and independence are to be respected by other peoples.
2. Peoples are to observe treaties and undertakings.
3. Peoples are equal and are parties to the agreements that bind them.
4. Peoples are to observe a duty of non-intervention.
5. Peoples have the right of self-defense but no right to instigate war for reasons other than self-defense.

---

[4] Rawls, *The Law of Peoples*; David Miller, *On Nationality* (Oxford: Clarendon Press, 1995); Nagel, 'The Problem of Global Justice'; Michael Blake, 'Distributive Justice, State Coercion, and Autonomy', *Philosophy and Public Affairs*, 30 (3) (2001), 257–96; and Andrea Sangiovanni, 'Global Justice, Reciprocity, and the State', *Philosophy and Public Affairs*, 35 (1) (2007), 3–39. In his more recent work, David Miller places greater emphasis on power inequalities between societies, and on the justice-based responsibilities these trigger. See David Miller, *National Responsibility and Global Justice* (Oxford: Oxford University Press, 2007), p. 74. Since this renders his recent views not entirely in line with statism as I define it, I focus only on his earlier work.
[5] In this chapter too, by 'egalitarian principles of justice' I mean any stringent principles focusing on agents' relative, as opposed to absolute, shares.
[6] Rawls, *The Law of Peoples*, p. 10, emphasis original.
[7] Cf. Allen Buchanan, 'Rawls's Law of Peoples: Rules for a Vanished Westphalian World', *Ethics*, 110 (4) (2000), 697–721, pp. 698–9.
[8] Rawls, *The Law of Peoples*, p. 37.

6. Peoples are to honor human rights.
7. Peoples are to observe certain specified restrictions in the conduct of war.
8. Peoples have a duty to assist other peoples living under unfavourable conditions that prevent their having a just or decent political and social regime.

Principles 1–4 protect peoples' self-determination and ground duties of non-interference; Principle 6 posits minimal domestic moral standards (human rights) that, in Rawls's view, fall short of liberal principles of justice; Principles 5 and 7 specify the rules of just war; and, finally, Principle 8 places a duty of *assistance* on peoples, according to which societies 'burdened by unfavourable conditions' should be helped to become well ordered. As anticipated, in Rawls's ideal of a just world, no principles of egalitarian distributive justice apply, but only duties of humanity aimed at assisting needy societies.[9]

In a similar vein, Miller envisages a world of autonomous and justly organized nation-states which, in their mutual relations, ought to respect the following obligations:

1. The duty to abstain from materially harming another state.
2. The duty not to exploit states that are one-sidedly vulnerable to your actions.
3. The duty to comply with whatever international agreements have been made.
4. Obligations of reciprocity, arising from practices of mutual aid whereby states come to one another's assistance in moments of need.
5. [O]bligation[s] on the part of resource-rich states to aid those that are resource poor.[10]

---

[9] Some might complain that I am misstating Rawls's position because his duty of assistance is in fact a duty of justice, not a duty of humanity. See e.g. Gillian Brock, *Global Justice: A Cosmopolitan Account* (Oxford: Oxford University Press, 2009), ch. 2. In the present context, by a duty of humanity I mean a duty whose sole aim is to respond to others' neediness (however this is defined). The duty of assistance Rawls proposes is a duty of this kind, triggered by the simple fact that a particular society is burdened by unfavourable conditions. Had internally legitimate societies attacked and pillaged burdened ones, their duties towards them would be all the more stringent (in my view, they would not be duties of humanity but duties of justice). This is all I mean when I say that Rawls's duty of assistance is a duty of humanity rather than a duty of justice. Notice, moreover, that almost nothing in what follows hinges on the particular label we assign to Rawls's duty of assistance. For an insightful critical discussion of this duty, see Chris Armstrong, 'Defending the Duty of Assistance', *Social Theory and Practice*, 35 (3) (2009), 461–82.

[10] Miller, *On Nationality*, pp. 104–5. Notice that, in the original text, each principle is followed by an informal discussion.

Duties 1–3 defend the territorial integrity and self-determination of nation-states, while Obligations 4 and 5 posit demands of mutual help ensuring that each political community possesses the necessary means to sustaining itself.[11] Finally, although Miller does not explicitly invoke criteria of domestic justice in this passage, elsewhere he makes it clear that a nation-state can only have moral status if it complies with basic human-rights standards.[12] In short, like Rawls's, Miller's picture of international justice 'portrays a world in which nation-states are self-determining, but respect the self-determination of others through obligations of non-interference and in some cases of aid'.[13] Once again, no egalitarian distributive principles apply to the world at large.

Finally, Thomas Nagel, Michael Blake, and Andrea Sangiovanni have recently added their voices to the statist choir. Even though, unlike Rawls and Miller, they have not (yet) offered a comprehensive account of international morality, they too have argued that 'the presumption against arbitrary inequalities' liberals defend domestically has no place in the international arena. In this context, only duties aimed at relieving absolute deprivation apply.

Although our authors offer different accounts both of the specific level of well-being below which assistance is needed,[14] and of the domestic moral standards each political community ought to respect,[15] their pictures of what a just world order would look like have one crucial element in common: they all deny that egalitarian justice should operate within such an order. Is this outlook on international justice as implausibly biased in favour of the *status quo* as critics of statism claim?

4.3 THE CHARGE(S) OF *STATUS-QUO* BIAS

To answer this question, we first need to distinguish between two versions of the *status-quo* bias critique. I shall call them the 'static' and 'dynamic' versions.

The static version: the statist ideal takes for granted too much of the *status quo*.

I call this version of the critique 'static' insofar as it focuses on the picture of a just world order statists defend, rather than on how their principles guide

---

[11] Miller's Obligations 4 and 5 could actually be merged into one principle of aid. Indeed, the duties he has in mind regarding natural resources involve transfers 'made so as to allow each national community to reach a threshold of viability'. *On Nationality*, p. 106.

[12] Miller, *On Nationality*, pp. 74ff.

[13] Miller, *On Nationality*, p. 107.

[14] Nagel focuses on desperate need, while Rawls and Miller on the ability of a society to become well ordered and pursue the values it holds dear.

[15] Nagel explicitly advocates liberal principles, while Miller and Rawls settle for a more parsimonious list of basic human rights.

action in the real world. In particular, this critique claims that the ideal proposed by statists is 'insufficiently idealized', because it takes too much of the existing geopolitical state of affairs for granted in two main respects. First, statists presuppose a world of separate states, but this international set-up is certainly not carved in stone. Why not envisage a more dense network of worldwide institutions to which principles of egalitarian distributive justice could apply instead? Wouldn't this world order be much more in tune with the fundamental commitments of liberalism?

Second, statists – especially Rawls – problematically allow non-liberal societies to be part of a just global order. Surely, critics complain, a liberal theory of international justice should be liberal all the way down. The only reason for admitting non-liberal societies within a just world order, critics say, is to render the theory more realistic and 'practical'. This may be a worthy policy goal, but it is a mistake to lower the ambitions of one's ideal theory in order to achieve it.

In line with these reflections, Henry Shue, for instance, suggests that while 'cosmopolitans are busy working out the best set of principles for the international arena...Rawls [*qua* statist] seems to have confronted what might reasonably be considered the more practical (because more immediate) question: according to what principles shall states conduct themselves in the interim while the debates about the best principles continue?'[16] On this view, the statist ideal, what Rawls calls his 'realistic utopia', is not a genuine liberal *ideal*. Instead, it is a second-best solution, a compromise with less-than-optimal existing political realities.

> **The dynamic version**: statist principles fail successfully to guide action because they are insufficiently sensitive to important facts characterizing the international arena.

This version of the critique is dynamic insofar as it focuses on the ability of statist principles to guide action in real-world circumstances. Interestingly, contrary to the static version of the critique, its dynamic counterpart claims that statist principles, and again Rawls's in particular, fail to deliver appropriate guidance for action *because they are too idealized*. They are designed against a background that does not take the *status quo* sufficiently seriously, and specifically the systemic power dynamics existing in the international order. There is much greater morally relevant interdependence and integration in this order than statists seem to presume. By failing to appreciate many of the empirical complexities shaping the global order and their normative importance, so the argument goes, statist principles are systematically blind to

---

[16] See Henry Shue, 'Rawls and the Outlaws', *Politics, Philosophy & Economics*, 1 (3) (2002), 307–23, p. 311.

the main sources of international injustice, and therefore lack the conceptual tools to address them.

Having outlined the two versions of the *status-quo* bias charge, in what follows I discuss each of them in turn.

4.4 ASSESSING THE STATIC VERSION OF THE *STATUS-QUO* BIAS CHARGE

4.4.1 Why Not Global Egalitarianism?

The first complaint advanced by proponents of the static version of the *status-quo* bias charge is that, by presupposing the state system more or less as we know it, statists are compromising their moral ideals, conceding too much to existing political realities. For those who put forward this critique, there is a reasonably feasible global scenario in which the state system no longer exists and liberal principles, that is, global egalitarian principles, can be fully realized on a global scale.

From this perspective, the reason why statists – particularly Rawls and Nagel – refuse to extend liberal-egalitarian principles of justice to the world at large lies in perceived feasibility constraints. In order for such redistributive principles to become viable, a great deal of international institution building would be necessary, and we can be almost certain that, at least for now and the near future, such institution building is unlikely to occur. Moreover, as we saw in Chapter 2, (at least some) statists worry that, if this kind of institution building were to occur, we might end up with a global despotic state, which would be too high a risk to run.[17] Faced with this possibility, statists prefer to compromise their highest ideals to accommodate existing political realities. Is this move at all warranted?

As I noticed in Chapter 2, what would or would not happen were we to implement the cosmopolitan egalitarian project is a largely speculative question. What exactly would be needed to realize global egalitarianism, and what risks this would involve, is something I and, I suspect, most political theorists are unable to determine with precision. The limits of long-term practical political possibility are by and large inscrutable.

Setting this issue aside, I will focus on the claim, central to the static version of the *status-quo* bias critique, that a world in which egalitarian principles of domestic justice apply globally is a *better world* from a liberal point of view. That is, I will test the idea that, from the perspective of a liberal morality,

---

[17] Rawls, *The Law of Peoples*, p. 36; and Nagel, 'The Problem of Global Justice', p. 146.

a world governed by cosmopolitan principles is *obviously* superior to one governed by statist ones. It is indeed on the basis of this assumption that cosmopolitans perceive statism as striking a suboptimal compromise between liberal ideals and regrettable real-world constraints.

To test the validity of the cosmopolitan complaint, we need to consider whether a statist world would be inimical to the foundational liberal principle of equal respect. According to this principle, everyone's life has equal worth from an impartial point of view, yet each person has a special responsibility for her or his own life going well.[18] If cosmopolitans are right, the statist ideal must fall short of this principle. Does it? I believe not.

In the ideal statist world, each society is internally well ordered according to some relevant normative criterion (more on this later); societies are largely independent, and respect one another's self-determination; moreover, they help each other when they are in need. How is this a bad world from a liberal point of view? In what sense would citizens across these societies fail to be true to the liberal principle of equal respect?

To be sure, within a statist world, there can be steep resource inequalities between societies. Part of these will be the product of societies' own policy decisions, but part will also result from factors outside societies' control, such as natural catastrophes. What presumably strikes (some) cosmopolitans as problematic is that, so long as the targeted societies do not fall below some relevant threshold of prosperity, these inequalities do not trigger *any* distributive duties. This conclusion is said to breach the principle of equal respect. Isn't it unfair, and therefore disrespectful, that some end up being not as well off as others are through no fault of their own? Surely, so the argument goes, a global order designed to rectify such inequalities would be better, more just, from a liberal point of view.

In Chapter 3, I have already offered a number of arguments, mostly methodological, against placing as much moral weight on the luck-egalitarian rationale as this cosmopolitan view does.[19] Here, I want to strengthen my case by appeal to some further substantive moral considerations. In particular, I argue that although the cosmopolitan and statist ideals can be both regarded as *prima facie* consistent with the principle of equal respect, on reflection, the latter appears more psychologically plausible, and in line with common-sense morality.

According to the principle of equal respect, we should act in a way that (*a*) responds to the intrinsic worth of everyone's life and yet (*b*) leaves us enough time and resources to pursue our own ends and goals.[20] That is, equal respect

---

[18] See Ronald Dworkin, *Sovereign Virtue* (Cambridge, MA: Harvard University Press, 2000); and Thomas Nagel, *Equality and Partiality* (Oxford: Oxford University Press, 1991).

[19] See Section 3.3.

[20] See also Barbara Herman, 'Mutual Aid and Respect for Persons', *Ethics*, 94 (4) (1984), 577–602, p. 598.

demands impartial concern, while allowing a measure of partiality towards oneself and one's near and dear. The cosmopolitan and statist interpretations of this principle strike different balances between its impartial and partial components. On the cosmopolitan interpretation, the concerns of impartiality can only be satisfied by rectifying all arbitrary (unchosen) inequalities. This, in turn, places important constraints on permissible partiality, on the extent to which we may legitimately privilege our own goals in the face of others' disadvantage.

By contrast, according to the statist interpretation, what equal respect requires varies across different contexts, and when it comes to distant others, respect can be expressed simply by helping those in need. Doing more than this may be praiseworthy but not a matter of duty. As a result, the statist interpretation of equal respect leaves more space for individual partiality.

At first sight, there does not seem to be a decisive argument in favour of one or the other interpretation. Recall that, for liberals, 'all aspects of the social should either be made acceptable or be capable of being made acceptable to every last individual'.[21] But by running such a hypothetical consent test we cannot immediately pick out the cosmopolitan or the statist ideal as the correct one. Both pictures of what a just world would look like seem to be in principle acceptable to rational and autonomous agents concerned with pursuing their ends and goals. After all, in neither of our envisaged world orders individuals would be left in dire straights. In both of them, each would have enough to lead a decent life, and would inhabit a well-ordered society. The difference between cosmopolitan and statist arrangements would manifest itself through different patterns of advantage and disadvantage. The cosmopolitan world would be more egalitarian than the statist one, but at the cost of placing greater constraints on individuals' permissible partiality, and *vice versa*.

From the viewpoint of hypothetical consent among rational agents, the cosmopolitan and statist world orders seem roughly equivalent. They both have their advantages and disadvantages, so that choosing one over the other does not appear to be rationally required. In short, they both presuppose suitable interpretations of the demands of equal respect.

This conclusion suffices to rebut the cosmopolitan claim that the reason why statists reject global egalitarianism, thereby compromising liberal values, is to make their theories more practical (i.e. less removed from the *status quo*). But before moving on to the next point, I wish to make a few remarks to help us see why, even though the cosmopolitan and statist ideals are *prima facie* equivalent, on reflection, the statist one has greater moral as well as psychological plausibility and should be preferred all things considered.

---

[21] Jeremy Waldron, 'Theoretical Foundations of Liberalism', *The Philosophical Quarterly*, 37 (147) (1987), 127–50, p. 128.

To see this, suppose you and your family live in a prosperous society: Fortunia. All of a sudden an equally prosperous neighbouring society, Disgratia, is hit by a natural catastrophe that leaves its people destitute and desperate. Following statist principles, your society embarks onto a large-scale aid operation. After months of efforts, it looks like Disgratia is recovering, its economy is picking up, basic services are again available, and each citizen is finally in a position to rebuild her/his life. Even though Disgratians are no longer destitute and desperate, they are also no longer as prosperous as Fortunians. On the statist interpretation of equal respect, this state of affairs is not morally troublesome. Fortunians have done their duty.[22]

This, it seems to me, is the conclusion that most ordinary people would also reach. Disgratians have been unlucky, but Fortunians have come to their aid. They have given them considerable help, and allowed them to rebuild a well-ordered society. Any further help would be beyond the call of duty. For instance, most people – I take it – would think that it would be supererogatory for Fortunia to lower the quality of welfare provisions for its citizens in order to make it 'more equal to' that of Disgratia. This form of partiality towards one's fellow associates seems entirely permissible.[23] And indeed, as I have argued in Chapter 3, it is.

By the same token, we would not be inclined to condemn a father who buys some extra toys for his daughter, when his neighbour's daughter has less to play with (but enough) because her family is reasonably well off but not in as good a financial situation. This type of partiality is not self-serving in a morally repugnant way, and the fact that it seems to reflect ordinary people's moral sensitivities is perhaps a point in favour of the statist interpretation of what equal respect requires. To put it in Richard Miller's words:

> I am not equally concerned for the girl who lives across the street and for my daughter; for example, I am not inclined to do as much for this neighbor when she is just as needy as my daughter, even if her parents have reached their limit. But I do not regard this neighbour's life as less valuable than the life of my daughter; my unequal concern reflects a proper valuing of my special relationship to my daughter, not unequal respect.[24]

In short, statists' interpretation of equal respect has the advantage of being more in tune with people's moral sensitivities, and seems to presuppose a

---

[22] Cf. John Rawls, *The Law of Peoples*, pp. 117–18; David Miller, 'Justice and Global Inequality', in Andrew Hurrell and Ngaire Woods (eds.), *Inequality, Globalization, and World Politics* (Oxford: Oxford University Press, 1999), 187–210, esp. pp. 193–5; and Blake, 'Distributive Justice, State Coercion, and Autonomy', pp. 289–94.

[23] Of course, this would not be Peter Singer's view. See his 'Famine, Affluence, and Morality', *Philosophy and Public Affairs*, 1 (3) (1972), 229–43.

[24] Richard W. Miller, *Globalizing Justice: The Ethics of Poverty and Power* (Oxford: Oxford University Press, 2010), p. 18.

more realistic picture of human psychology. After all, human beings are not impartiality machines, equally concerned for everybody else in the world. Their altruism is limited. If we want to take this fact seriously when designing our theories of justice – as I believe we should – we have reason to favour the statist interpretation of equal respect.

So far, I have discussed and refuted the cosmopolitan complaint that, by denying the applicability of egalitarian justice to the world at large, the statist ideal represents a compromise between liberal principles and real-world constraints. This complaint was directed against claim (d) in our definition of the statist ideal. I now move on to a second cosmopolitan worry, which is particularly salient in the case of Rawls, namely that the domestic moral standards advocated by statists (claim c) are too permissive.

4.4.2 Why not Domestic Liberalism All the Way Down?

Before discussing this worry, let me briefly explain its grounds, focusing on Rawls's account of international justice. As we already know, Rawls's just world order features not only liberal peoples but also non-liberal yet *decent* political communities. Specifically, Rawls discusses the hypothetical case of what he calls 'decent hierarchical societies'. These societies do not qualify as liberal: they only give their members some rights and opportunities, rather than granting them equal rights and opportunities as well as an equal say in political matters. From a liberal viewpoint, decent societies are therefore less than just.

Despite that, the distinctly short list of human rights Rawls advocates in the international realm allows them to count as members in good standing of his society of well-ordered peoples. The human rights referred to in Principle 6 of Rawls's list do not encompass the entire set of liberal-democratic rights defended in contemporary Human Rights Charters and Covenants, but only a portion of it, compatible with some forms of non-democratic politics. Rawls defines human rights as 'a special class of urgent rights, such as freedom from slavery and serfdom, liberty (but not equal liberty) of conscience, and security of ethnic groups from mass murder and genocide'.[25] These are a 'subset of the rights possessed by the citizens in a liberal constitutional democratic regime',[26] which define minimal conditions without which a genuine political community cannot exist. Whenever these rights are persistently infringed, instead of a true society we have 'command by force, a slave system, and no cooperation of any kind'.[27] It is because Rawls advocates such a thin list of human rights that non-liberal societies can be recognized as internationally legitimate forms of

---

[25] Rawls, *The Law of Peoples*, p. 79.   [26] Rawls, *The Law of Peoples*, p. 81.
[27] Rawls, *The Law of Peoples*, p. 68.

political organization.[28] But why, one may plausibly ask, would a liberal defend such a minimalist account of human rights?

In Rawls's view, such an accommodation of non-liberal societies follows directly from a commitment to the value of toleration that should inform any credible liberal political morality under circumstances of pluralism. Seeing international pluralism as a consequence of the workings of human nature under conditions of freedom – hence something that could only be eradicated by establishing a despotic world government – Rawls sets himself the task of elaborating a social ideal showing that such a pluralism is compatible with the realization of justice and therefore 'not to be regretted'.[29] This type of social ideal is what he calls a 'realistic utopia'.[30] That is, an ideal world order compatible with the laws of nature and the conditions of our historical epoch – first and foremost with the fact of pluralism.[31] Just as liberal *citizens* should acknowledge the 'burdens of judgment'[32] and tolerate conceptions of the good that differ from their own, liberal *peoples* should also refrain from interfering with, in fact they should show respect for, societies governed by non-liberal political principles.

Critics of Rawls, however, complain that this analogy is invalid. Rawls's standards of international toleration are much more demanding than his domestic ones.[33] As Rawls says, 'whenever the scope of toleration is extended:

---

[28] Rawls's list of human rights is even thinner than the list of guarantees offered within decent societies. To count as members in good standing of the society of peoples, political communities need to respect human rights, but also be either reasonably just (like liberal peoples) or governed by a 'common good' idea of justice (like decent societies). For Rawls, there can be societies that respect human rights and yet do not count as full members in good standing of a society of peoples: benevolent absolutisms. These are fragile communities where respect for human rights is due to the benevolence of the ruling class, as opposed to being guaranteed by stable institutional constraints. In light of this, is it plausible to say that respect for human rights is what determines whether a country is fit for membership in a just society of peoples? I believe it is, if what we have in mind is *robust* respect for human rights. For it seems that only liberal and decent societies (but not benevolent absolutisms) can ensure *this kind* of respect for human-rights guarantees.

[29] Rawls, *The Law of Peoples*, p. 12.

[30] For an interesting discussion of the Rawlsian project, see Chris Brown, 'The Construction of a "Realistic Utopia": John Rawls and International Political Theory', *Review of International Studies*, 28 (1) (2002), 5–21.

[31] Rawls, *The Law of Peoples*, pp. 127–8.

[32] John Rawls, *Political Liberalism* (New York: Columbia University Press, 1996), pp. 54–8.

[33] This critique has been most comprehensively stated by Kok-Chor Tan, 'Liberal Toleration in Rawls's Law of Peoples', *Ethics*, 108 (2) (1998), 275–95, pp. 282ff. Other proponents of it are Andrew Kuper, 'Rawlsian Global Justice: Beyond the Law of Peoples to a Cosmopolitan Law of Persons', *Political Theory*, 28 (5) (2000), 640–74, pp. 648–53; Thomas W. Pogge, 'Critical Study: Rawls on International Justice', *The Philosophical Quarterly*, 51 (203) (2001), 246–53, p. 249 and 'An Egalitarian Law of Peoples', *Philosophy and Public Affairs*, 23 (3) (1994), 195–224, pp. 214–17. See also Simon Caney, 'Cosmopolitanism and the Law of Peoples', *Journal of Political Philosophy*, 10 (1) (2002), 95–123, pp. 100–3 and 105–6; Charles R. Beitz, 'Rawls's Law of Peoples', *Ethics*, 110 (4) (2000), 669–96, pp. 683–6; Allen Buchanan, 'Rawls's Law of Peoples: Rules for a Vanished Westphalian World', *Ethics*, 110 (4) (2000), 697–721, pp. 718–19; and Saladin Meckled-Garcia,

The criteria of reasonableness [which define admissible pluralism] are relaxed'.³⁴ But why should it be so? Is there a moral principle, consistent with liberal values, that justifies such a relaxation of the standards of reasonableness, of what sort of pluralism should be tolerated? If there is not, rather than principles of ideal theory, Rawls's international standards of toleration would be better described as a second best, the result of a compromise between liberal principles and the need to accommodate non-liberal societies.

These perplexities about the status of Rawls's theory are well expressed by Thomas Pogge, who wonders whether, in calling his society of peoples a 'realistic utopia', Rawls intends to propose liberalism's 'highest ideal for an indefinite future', or a 'stopgap model meant to accommodate, so long as they are still around, some slightly backward but basically passable societies'.³⁵

What can we make of this complaint? If it were true that a free world entirely populated with liberal societies is a utopia, then the cosmopolitan complaint would be unwarranted. As I have argued in Chapter 2, any plausible ideal theory must prescribe ideals and principles that do not clearly fall out of human reach. For instance, an ideal that could only be achieved by breaking the laws of physics would be, for that very reason, inadequate.

Unfortunately, when it comes to the fact of international pluralism, we are once again unable to make accurate predictions. Perhaps Rawls is right that a fully liberal world could only be brought about at the risk of global despotism; perhaps he is not. In fact, from what I can see, nothing in our history, or in Rawls's own work, rules out the possibility of the existence of a world populated by liberal societies alone. If critics of Rawls are correct in thinking that a world of this kind would be more in line with liberal values than the one described in his ideal theory, their critique would prove to have bite. And, this time, it does.

As I noted earlier, hypothetical-consent tests do not deliver one single determinate result. Nevertheless, they do rule out scenarios that agents concerned with pursuing their ends and goals could not all accept. From this perspective, a hypothetical-consent test would indeed rule out domestic principles of justice such as those upheld in decent hierarchical societies. Rawls's decent societies respect basic human rights, but their political system is undemocratic. Their decision-making process takes into consideration the interests of every social group, but to different degrees, and only members of the religious majority are allowed to hold public office.³⁶ Moreover, all citizens have

---

'International Justice, Human Rights, and Neutrality', *Res Publica*, 10 (2) (2004), 153–74, pp. 160–3.

³⁴ John Rawls, 'The Law of Peoples' (1993), in Samuel Freeman (ed.), *John Rawls: Collected Papers* (Cambridge, MA: Harvard University Press, 1999), 529–64, p. 561.

³⁵ Thomas W. Pogge, 'The Incoherence between Rawls's Theories of Justice', *Fordham Law Review*, 72 (5) (2004), 1739–59, p. 1758.

³⁶ Rawls, *The Law of Peoples*, pp. 71ff.

some rights and opportunities, but not equal rights and opportunities. Clearly, this is a political order that members of the disadvantaged minority have reason to reject. Their interests are given some consideration, but not equal consideration. *De facto*, they are constantly exposed to the possibility of being stigmatized and dominated by the ruling elite.[37] Of course, Rawls is keen to point out that decent societies are, as the name says it, decent, but the worry is that there can be no real-world society that is both hierarchical and yet decent in the way Rawls describes.

In sum, to show that a liberal world order is compatible with the fact of pluralism, Rawls has created an imaginary class of societies that look morally acceptable and yet fall short of liberal standards. But these artificially crafted societies do not serve the purpose Rawls wants them to. If we take their political structure seriously, this is too distant from what can be acceptable from a liberal perspective, no matter how open and tolerant the latter is. If we take Rawls's edulcorated description of these societies (where no oppression or abuses occur), they look too close to just liberal polities appropriately to represent the kind of pluralism Rawls is after.[38]

This, of course, does not mean that other forms of international pluralism, for example, between different, more or less egalitarian, liberal societies, would not be permissible. We may, for instance, plausibly argue that hypothetical consent, *per se*, does not single out one particular form of liberalism, for instance Rawls's liberalism, as the correct one. Rawls himself acknowledges that there may be different reasonably just liberal societies, some upholding strongly egalitarian principles of socio-economic justice, others allowing for greater socio-economic inequalities.[39] My point is rather that liberal equal civil and political rights are necessitated by hypothetical consent. A society that does not uphold such rights is not morally acceptable, from a liberal point of view. (I shall return to this in Section 7.5.)

To conclude, in this section I have looked at the static version of the *status-quo* bias critique. On the one hand, I have argued that statists' denial that principles of egalitarian socio-economic justice apply to the world at large (assuming a world of separate, independent states) is fully compatible with the liberal commitment to equal respect, and is not vulnerable to the charge of *status-quo* bias. On the other, I have suggested that statists who, like Rawls, include illiberal societies within their favoured world order, do indeed make compromises with the *status quo*, compromises that, for all we know, are not necessary. Unless we can prove that a world entirely populated by liberal states is impossible, we have little reason to compromise our highest ideals.

---

[37] For a critique of Rawls along these lines, with a specific focus on the position of women, see Martha Nussbaum, 'Women and the Law of Peoples', *Politics, Philosophy & Economics*, 1 (3) (2002), 283–306.

[38] Cf. Chris Naticchia, 'The Law of Peoples. The Old and the New', *Journal of Moral Philosophy*, 2 (3) (2005), 353–69.

[39] Rawls, *The Law of Peoples*, p. 14.

4.5 ASSESSING THE DYNAMIC VERSION OF THE *STATUS QUO* BIAS CHARGE

The dynamic version of the *status quo* bias charge holds that statist principles are unduly subservient to the *status quo*, and thus devoid of tools both for criticizing the existing international order and for guiding action towards its reform. This represents a shift in perspective, compared to the previous charge. We are no longer looking at the statist ideal, but rather at the principles underpinning such an ideal and which statists believe should guide the actions of real-world political communities, specifically of liberal societies. Once again, in outlining this critique, I will focus on Rawls's *The Law of Peoples*.

In this case too, the complaint is twofold. The first points to the *incompleteness* of Rawls's statist principles. Critics object that Rawls's monograph fails to discuss crucial international moral issues such as environmental justice, the regulation of global finance and trade,[40] reparations for past injustices, migration policies, and so forth. Because of these omissions, the critics contend, the book offers no guidance in those areas of real-world international politics where guidance is most needed.

The second, related, complaint focuses on the *conservatism* of *The Law of Peoples*. Critics argue that Rawls's monograph is unduly subservient to the *status quo*, because it fails to acknowledge the most important causes of global injustice and misery. Thomas Pogge figures prominently among the proponents of this objection. He has repeatedly attacked *The Law of Peoples* for its mischaracterization of the grounds and extent of the international distributive obligations of liberal democratic societies.[41] According to Rawls, liberals have no more than a duty to assist burdened societies, that is, societies that lack the necessary resources (including social capital and know-how) to become well ordered. This way of looking at the question of international socio-economic justice, Pogge argues, is misleading and ideological, given that liberal societies are partly responsible for the plight of the burdened. A past of depredations and colonial domination, and a present of unfair international property and trade rules have certainly contributed, and still contribute, to the suffering and the 'misfortunes' of the poor.[42]

---

[40] Caney, 'Cosmopolitanism and the Law of Peoples', pp. 118–19.
[41] See Pogge, 'An Egalitarian Law of Peoples'; 'Critical Study: Rawls on International Justice'; 'Moral Universalism and Global Economic Justice'; *Politics, Philosophy & Economics*, 1 (1) (2002), 29–58; and 'The Incoherence between Rawls's Theories of Justice'.
[42] Thomas W. Pogge, *World Poverty and Human Rights: Cosmopolitan Responsibilities and Reforms* (Cambridge: Polity, 2002), esp. Introduction and ch. 4. On the potentially ideological dimension of ideal theory more generally, see Charles W. Mills, '"Ideal Theory" as Ideology', *Hypatia: A Journal of Feminist Philosophy*, 20 (3) (2005), 165–84.

By overlooking these facts, so the argument goes, the real-world guidance offered by Rawls's statist principles ends up being problematic on both moral and pragmatic grounds. On the one hand, his principles mistakenly suggest that liberal political communities have a mere duty to 'help' unfortunate societies, when in fact their responsibilities towards the world's poor are more stringent and extensive than that. Their duties cannot be described solely in terms of aid, but are for the most part a matter of compensation for past and present injustice. On the other hand, Rawls seems to believe that assistance would suffice to relieve the plight of less developed nations, when what is needed is in fact extensive institutional reform.

What could Rawlsian statists say in response to these charges? Very little, I argue. The complaint that Rawls's principles have ideological connotations and fail appropriately to guide action in real-world politics rests on valid grounds. Unlike cosmopolitans, Rawls does not offer principles assessing feasible alternative global institutional arrangements. Instead, he provides a relatively well-defined picture of what a just world order would look like: a world of relatively independent, and well-ordered, states. The validity of the guidance offered by his principles is thus tied to this particular configuration of the international arena. Once the empirical assumptions (in fact, idealizations) of relative independence and just behaviour are dropped, Rawls's statist principles lose much of their relevance. As these assumptions clearly do not hold in our international scenario, I conclude that the statist principles outlined in Rawls's law of peoples give poor guidance in real-world circumstances. To substantiate these claims, let me discuss the incompleteness and conservatism charges in turn.

As we have seen in our discussion of cosmopolitanism, the incompleteness charge *per se* constitutes only a minor threat to the validity of a philosophical outlook. After all, no humanly devisable theory can ever hope to address all that is worthy of discussion within its specific area of concern – be it physics, geography, literature, or political morality. If the incompleteness critique were only stating that *The Law of Peoples* does not answer all the interesting questions one may ask in the field of international morality, it would amount to nothing more than the claim that there is still considerable work to be done by those who are broadly sympathetic to Rawls's views. By itself, this is hardly an objection.

The incompleteness charge gains greater critical bite once it is combined with the conservatism charge. From this perspective, the critique does not merely say that Rawls does too little; rather, it says that he does too little *in a way that introduces a systematic bias* in his answers to the questions he explicitly asks. For instance, Rawls's failure to discuss the issue of fair trade is tightly linked to his mischaracterization of the distributive duties of liberal societies denounced by Pogge. Lacking a discussion of what fair trade requires, Rawls's monograph provides no basis for criticizing existing liberal societies' behaviour in the international economy.⁴³ As a result, his treatment of global economic justice appears too conservative, seemingly defending the existing global economic order as legitimate. By the same token, Rawls's silence on questions of reparations drives attention away from the fact that, unlike his peoples, existing liberal societies do not avoid cooperation with 'outlaw states', and have not waged war only in self-defence.

The incompleteness and conservatism critiques both point to Rawls's failure to take seriously some morally relevant facts concerning how international politics is conducted. Rawls's portrayal of the international arena in general, and of liberal societies in particular, is distinctly idealized. Even a superficial look at international politics shows that existing liberal societies do *not* trade with others on fair terms, do *not* refuse to cooperate with outlaw states, have *not* consistently respected the territorial integrity of other countries, and so forth. Yet, even though existing liberal societies are far from well ordered, *The Law of Peoples* gives the impression that they are.⁴⁴ Instead of helping us identify what is morally problematic in the current state of affairs (beyond a failure to assist societies in need), it ideologically obscures the sources of existing injustice.

This conclusion may seem too harsh. After all, Rawls shows some awareness of the existence of a gap between his well-ordered peoples and existing liberal societies. For instance, he observes that 'a liberal society cannot justly require its citizens to fight in order to gain economic wealth and to acquire natural resources, much less to win power and empire. (When a society pursues these interests it no longer honors the Law of Peoples, and it becomes an outlaw state.)'⁴⁵ He then adds that 'so-called liberal societies sometimes do this, but that only shows they may act wrongly'.⁴⁶ True, it only shows they may act wrongly, but it follows from Rawls's own theory that this kind of wrongness is sufficient to turn such liberal societies into outlaw states. Similarly, Rawls notes that existing liberal states are marked by 'considerable injustice, oligarchic tendencies, and monopolistic interests',⁴⁷ and do not abide by his principles of foreign policy. But his references to the non-ideal conduct of real-world liberal states are sporadic, and never explicitly connected to his overall normative framework.

---

⁴³ Even though Rawls believes that well-ordered societies should conform with rules of fair trade, he does not make the content of these rules explicit, see Rawls, *The Law of Peoples*, p. 42, n. 52. As Pogge notes, this is a grave omission in his monograph, see Pogge, 'The Incoherence between Rawls's Theories of Justice', p. 1751.

⁴⁴ For further discussion of this point, see Laura Valentini, 'On the Apparent Paradox of Ideal Theory', *Journal of Political Philosophy*, 17 (3) (2009), 332–55.

⁴⁵ Rawls, *The Law of Peoples*, p. 91.

⁴⁶ Rawls, *The Law of Peoples*, p. 91, n. 3.

⁴⁷ Rawls, *The Law of Peoples*, p. 48.

Nonetheless, let us optimistically assume, for the sake of argument, that Rawls's readers are particularly careful, realize that his peoples do not represent existing societies, and conclude that it is precisely because no actual democracy conforms with the law of peoples that Rawls's monograph does not legitimize existing injustices, but can help us criticize them. Would it also offer a positive *solution* to the problem of international justice? Would Rawls's monograph be of assistance in guiding reform of the international order?

In this respect, Rawls seems convinced that, before they can be in a position successfully to solve the problem of international justice, a good number of societies must have achieved justice 'at home'. As he says, '[a]ny hope we have of reaching a realistic utopia rests on there being reasonable constitutional (and decent) regimes sufficiently established and effective to yield a viable Society of Peoples'.[48] Thus, given that no well-ordered societies exist at this point, following Rawls, the responsibility to bring the current world order closer to his ideal would fall upon the inhabitants of existing imperfect democracies, who should first promote just arrangements within their own borders and, subsequently, outside them.

The obvious difficulty with this one-way strategy, from domestic to international justice, is that it overlooks the plausible *empirical* hypothesis that the two problems – of domestic and international justice – are inextricably intertwined.[49] That is, the potential for a society to improve the justice of its domestic political system may be determined not only by endogenous but also by external factors, in which case not only Rawls's international project but also his domestic theory would seem to rest on fragile grounds.

More generally, Rawls's assumption that societies are (largely) self-sufficient and self-contained overlooks those forms of interdependence that ground the need for theoretical reflection on international justice in the first place.[50] If the question of justice arises in the domestic context, it is precisely because by participating in common social arrangements, people exercise power over one another and thereby mutually constrain their opportunities. In light of this *fact*, criteria need to be designed in order to prevent some from having access to a disproportionate amount of resources, thereby unfairly constraining the agency of others.

Similar considerations also hold in the global case: the basis for reflecting on international fairness should be the existence of mutually dependent international agents and agencies exercising power over one another, and affecting one another's prosperity. Sufficiently intense international interaction may

---

[48] Rawls, *The Law of Peoples*, pp. 29–30.
[49] On this, see Thomas W. Pogge, *Realizing Rawls* (Ithaca, NY: Cornell University Press, 1989), p. 255.
[50] I am grateful to Christian Schemmel for bringing this point to my attention. Many have criticized Rawls for making this assumption in relation to his domestic theory of justice as well. See e.g. Charles R. Beitz, 'Justice and International Relations', *Philosophy and Public Affairs*, 4 (4) (1975), 360–89; and Pogge, 'Moral Universalism and Global Economic Justice', p. 44.

give rise to precisely those problems of background justice that render redistributive measures appropriate in the domestic arena. As Rawls explains in the context of his domestic theory of justice, 'the overall result of separate and independent transactions is away from and not toward background justice'.[51] Under these circumstances, regulatory mechanisms become necessary in order to prevent the cumulative effects of individual interactions from generating harmful inequalities between people.

By the same token, the cumulative effects of international transactions between states may lead to problematic power inequalities and undermine the ability of individual societies to be genuinely self-determining and secure social justice at home.[52] In sum, without background justice – that is, without a fair background against which to interact – societies cannot be meaningfully seen as independent, as their fate is constantly affected by exogenous factors lying outside their control.

It would thus seem that any plausible account of global justice should address the question of what a fair international background requires. But instead of addressing this question, in *The Law of Peoples*, Rawls simply begs it, by assuming that a fair background is already in place.[53] In turn, this allows him to subscribe to what Pogge calls 'explanatory nationalism',[54] which traces the prosperity of a country almost entirely to the effectiveness of its political institutions, independently of its resource endowment and, crucially, of the wider global context in which it finds itself. In Rawls's words, 'the causes of the wealth of a people and the forms it takes lie in their political culture and in the religious, philosophical, and moral traditions that support the basic structure of their political and social institutions, as well as in the industriousness and cooperative talents of its members'.[55] Even if it is beyond doubt that domestic political institutions are a crucial determinant of a country's wealth, assuming that they constitute the exclusive determinant of the economic fate of a political community is questionable, especially when we cannot assume that a just background exists.

An accurate account of the causes of a country's prosperity or poverty would probably feature both endogenous and exogenous factors,[56] and a rigorous theory of justice would have to take such factual considerations extremely seriously and handle them with care. They are crucial not only to

---

[51] Rawls, *Political Liberalism*, p. 267.
[52] See Miriam Ronzoni, 'The Global Order: A Case of Background Injustice? A Practice-dependent Account', *Philosophy and Public Affairs*, 37 (3) (2009), 229–56.
[53] Rawls, *The Law of Peoples*, p. 52, n. 42. For discussion, see Valentini, 'On the Apparent Paradox of Ideal Theory', esp. pp. 351ff.
[54] Pogge defines and criticizes this position at length in his *World Poverty and Human Rights*, pp. 139ff.
[55] Rawls, *The Law of Peoples*, p. 108.
[56] Cf. Pogge, 'Critical Study: Rawls on International Justice', p. 253.

the assignment of moral responsibility but also to the identification of the best strategy to solve the problem of global justice in the first place. *If* the combined effects of international transactions, and the global economic system more generally, have a foreseeable impact on a country's prospects of economic growth, *then*, irrespective of the validity of its moral grounds, Rawls's duty of assistance will not be enough to grant burdened societies a prosperous future. By itself, the duty will not offer a successful solution to 'the problem' it aims to solve.

Of course, the search for an effective solution is an extremely complex task, especially given the high degree of uncertainty surrounding the phenomena under examination. As Charles Beitz puts it, 'as an empirical matter the question of the sources of economic backwardness is hardly settled'. He adds that the relative impact of factors such as resource endowments, political institutions, one's position in the global economy, and so on 'is a subject of dispute at the general level, and it certainly varies from one society to another'.[57] What does this imply for a liberal approach to international justice? If it turns out that there are certain *empirical facts* that cannot be fully ascertained, this epistemic limit should be taken into account in elaborating normative prescriptions.[58] Modesty and caution should be the philosopher's guiding values. Contrary to these recommendations, Rawls constructs his empirical case very hastily, assuming away some of the facts that give rise to the problem of global justice in the first place. As a result, his theory, which represents the most prominent statement of statism, ends up standing on shaky grounds.

4.6 CONCLUSION

In this chapter, I have turned to statism and specifically examined the plausibility of the cosmopolitan charge of *status-quo* bias. The outcome of this analysis is a nuanced one. In particular, three conclusions have been established. First, the statist ideal cannot be accused of being biased in favour of the *status quo* simply because it denies the applicability of principles of egalitarian distributive justice to the world at large. As we have seen, both global egalitarianism and the statist ideal are compatible with the fundamental liberal

---

[57] Beitz, 'Rawls's Law of Peoples', p. 690.
[58] Mathias Risse discusses the epistemic difficulties we are bound to encounter when attempting to make moral judgements about the global order in his 'Do We Owe the Global Poor Assistance or Rectification?', *Ethics and International Affairs*, 19 (1) (2005), sec. 2. See also David Miller, *National Responsibility and Global Justice*, ch. 9; and Sanjay Reddy, 'The Role of Apparent Constraints in Normative Reasoning: A Methodological Statement and Application to Global Justice', *The Journal of Ethics*, 9 (1/2) (2005), 119–25, pp. 122ff.

commitment to equal respect for persons. As David Miller puts it, 'cosmopolitans invite us to compare the shares of resources held by different people in different places, whereas their opponents focus on other aspects of the global order, typically on whether people's basic rights and interests are protected, and on the terms on which political communities interact with each other'.[59] Although both of these pictures, I have argued, are *prima facie* consistent with liberal normative individualism, the statist one is all-things-considered more morally and psychologically plausible than its cosmopolitan alternative.

Second, the statist ideal is problematic insofar as it includes societies whose internal organization falls short of liberal standards, and which therefore fail to honour the liberal commitment to equal respect for persons. The inclusion of such societies in a just liberal international order represents an instance of *status quo* bias.

Third, and finally, when we turn to the ability of statist principles to guide action in real-world circumstances, we reach disappointing conclusions. Statist principles, as articulated in Rawls's *The Law of Peoples*, surreptitiously presuppose a world of largely independent and well-ordered political communities. It is perhaps true that, in such a world, non-interference and assistance would suffice to ensure the freedom and self-determination of each political community, as well as the well-being of its members. This, however, is not the case in our highly interdependent world, which is marked by a history of depredation, and a present of power abuses. In such a world, societies cannot be appropriately self-determining, and realize domestic justice, unless a fair background is in place, preventing power imbalances from eroding their sovereign capacities. As Rawls's statist principles are largely blind to the systemic power-dynamics shaping and defining international interactions, they do not allow us to detect, and address, current international injustices.

This conclusion will be further substantiated in Chapter 5, where I will examine the different *justifications* offered in support of statism.

---

[59] Miller, 'Caney's "International Distributive Justice": A Response', p. 976.

5

Justifying Statism: A Methodological Critique

5.1 INTRODUCTION

In this chapter, I consider the justificatory strategies that lead statists to deny the applicability of liberal-egalitarian principles of justice to the world at large. My analysis will reveal that statist principles can be arrived at through three different justificatory avenues: interpretive, agency-based, and relational approaches. In what follows, I show that these approaches all contain a systematic conservative bias, and thus cannot provide a sound basis for designing principles of justice.

My argument is structured as follows. In Sections 5.2 and 5.3, I consider the interpretive approach. On this approach, moral principles are constructed by articulating and interpreting the values built into existing social practices. Since the values underpinning domestic social practices differ from those underpinning international ones, statists conclude that the right principles for one domain – including principles of egalitarian socio-economic justice – are not the same as those for the other. I argue that, despite its *prima facie* appeal, by grounding moral principles in existing practices, this approach makes them highly likely to be biased in favour of the *status quo*.

In Sections 5.4 and 5.5, I turn to the agency-based approach. On this view, any valid normative principle must apply to a particular agent or set of agents, with the capacity and the authority to act on it. Since at the global level there is no state-like authoritative agent capable of implementing principles of egalitarian justice, statists committed to the agency-based approach reject the applicability of such principles to the world at large. I argue that this view is also problematically biased in favour of the *status quo*, because it regards a capacity *immediately* to bring about egalitarian justice as a necessary condition for its moral relevance. This implausibly confines the applicability principles of justice to those contexts in which they are most likely to be already in place.

In Sections 5.6 and 5.7, I consider *relational* approaches to the justification of statist principles, specifically focusing on so-called cooperation- and coercion-based theories. The former contend that egalitarian justice only applies to fellow citizens by virtue of their cooperative relationships, the latter that it only applies to fellow citizens because they are subject to state coercion. I argue that both views are self-defeating. The grounds of justice they presuppose are either implausibly narrow, or so wide as to support the extension of liberal-egalitarian justice to the global realm.

5.2 THE INTERPRETIVE APPROACH[1]

On this approach, moral principles are constructed by articulating (interpreting) the values informing the specific practices they aim to regulate; hence, different principles apply to different practices – for example, principles regulating family life differ from principles regulating society's political life, and principles regulating the relations between friends differ from principles regulating the conduct of members of institutions such as universities and hospitals. As the values built into global practices are different from those of free and equal citizenship informing domestic ones, statists who adopt this approach conclude that principles of liberal-egalitarian justice in general, and of egalitarian socio-economic justice in particular, should not apply to the world at large.

Over the past few years, this line of justification for statism has gained increasing plausibility, and has been supplemented by a thorough defence of the interpretive methodology that lies behind it. One of the most important contributions to this methodological turn in the defence strategy for statism has been offered by Aaron James's exploration of the interpretive underpinnings of Rawls's *The Law of Peoples*.[2]

On James's account, Rawls's methodology combines the claim that different subjects of justice – that is different social practices such as society, the family, international relations, and so on – are governed by different principles with Ronald Dworkin's account of constructive interpretation.[3] Although Dworkin's account has been elaborated in the context of legal reasoning, it can be easily transferred to that of moral reasoning. On Dworkin's view, each exercise in interpretation comprises three phases: a pre-interpretive, interpretive,

---

[1] I have offered a detailed analysis and critique of the interpretive methodology in Laura Valentini, 'Global Justice and Practice-Dependence: Conventionalism, Institutionalism, Functionalism', *Journal of Political Philosophy*, 19 (4) (2011), 399–418. Although my conclusions in this chapter are similar to those advanced in the article, my argumentative strategy is, to a good extent, different.

[2] Aaron James, 'Constructing Justice for Existing Practice: Rawls and the Status Quo', *Philosophy and Public Affairs*, 33 (3) (2005), 281–316, pp. 298 and 308ff.

[3] John Rawls, *Political Liberalism* (New York: Columbia University Press, 1996), p. 258; and Ronald Dworkin, *Law's Empire* (Cambridge, MA: Harvard University Press, 1986), esp. ch. 2.

and post-interpretive phase. Each phase corresponds to a particular task performed by the interpreter.

1. *Pre-interpretive phase*: the identification of an already existing practice, call it 'X', which will constitute our object of interpretation.
2. *Interpretive phase*: an exercise in interpretation aimed at identifying the point of X and the goods produced within it – for example, social primary goods in the domestic case, peace, national self-determination, and cooperation between societies in the international one.
3. *Post-interpretive phase*: the elaboration of a set of principles that, if complied with by all participants in the practice, would best express the values built in X, and against which the *status quo* is to be evaluated.[4]

To make these observations more concrete, consider a relatively simple practice such as that of academic seminars in the (imaginary) University of Princeford. At the *pre-interpretive stage*, we focus on the following descriptive account of the practice. Students and academics gather in the seminar room to discuss a pre-circulated paper. The discussion is opened by a commentator, who is given forty-five minutes to summarize the paper and raise a few points for debate. Participants are then invited to take part in the discussion with priority given to faculty over students. The discussion continues for forty-five minutes, and then the seminar is brought to a close.

Assuming that this is an accurate description of the practice we are analysing, we now move on to the *interpretive stage*, and consider what the point of the practice exactly is. This is to discuss the paper, probe the author's arguments, and engage in an intellectually stimulating and constructive debate. Finally, at the *post-interpretive or reforming stage*, we ask whether the rules of seminar discussion as they currently are appropriately reflect the aims of the seminar. In this respect, we might suggest that a shorter presentation by the author herself/himself would be more conducive to a fruitful discussion – not everyone can be trusted to have read the paper, and commentators do not always do their job properly. Moreover, we might think that a commentator is needed, but that she/he should speak only for fifteen minutes rather than forty-five minutes, and urge to give priority to graduate students when they wish to ask a question. Students tend to be shy and should be therefore encouraged.

What I have just offered is a stylized example of what an exercise in constructive interpretation looks like, applied to the relatively straightforward practice of academic seminars. Political philosophers who subscribe to the interpretive approach believe it can also be used to construct moral rules for much more complex and elusive practices. In fact, as I have already

---

[4] James, 'Constructing Justice for Existing Practice', p. 301.

mentioned, Aaron James has convincingly argued that both Rawls's domestic and international theories of justice can be seen as resting on this particular methodological outlook.

On this reading of Rawls's methodology, the principles of *Political Liberalism* are arrived at by interpreting the point of social cooperation among free and equal citizens,[5] while *The Law of Peoples* is developed by reflecting upon the point of 'international law and practice', where participants are not individuals but political communities.[6] On this view, the content and applicability of principles of justice is determined by interpreting existing practices. Following this methodology, explaining the disanalogy between domestic and international morality is an easy task. Since domestic and international practices have different guiding values, the principles applying to them must also differ from one another. What can we make of this approach to the justification of moral principles?

5.3 THE INTERPRETIVE APPROACH: VIRTUES AND VICES

The interpretive approach is not without merit. In particular, it exhibits two highly desirable features for any normative methodology. First, it embodies the intuitively plausible idea that different normative principles apply to different domains of human action. It would indeed be extremely bizarre to claim that the principles that govern the conduct of governments should also govern the conduct of friends or family members, and *vice versa*. A private citizen has no duty to punish criminals, while the state has. A government official has no duty to be psychologically supportive of a tax evader, while a private person has a duty to be supportive of her/his friends. In short, the idea that different domains of life are governed by different principles seems correct.

Second, even though the interpretive methodology takes existing practices as a starting point, it has the potential for reforming them. If it turns out that the practices in question do not express the values that allegedly govern them, reform of those practices is in order. For instance, let us assume that the values underpinning family life are love, reciprocity, intimacy, and support. Let us further assume that the Smith family happens to be governed by rules of mutual non-interference. In all likelihood, the rules shaping the life of this family fail to express the values that ought to guide it. Of course, family

---

[5] Rawls, *Political Liberalism*.
[6] See also Saladin Meckled-Garcia, 'On the Very Idea of Cosmopolitan Justice: Constructivism and International Agency', *Journal of Political Philosophy*, 16 (3) (2008), 245–71.

members are entitled to some privacy, but to express love and support for one another they cannot simply leave each other alone. In short, given the values applying to family life, the rules currently structuring the relationships between members of the Smith family need reform.

Even though the interpretive methodology presents the aforementioned strengths, it also contains flaws that make it ultimately unviable, at least in its orthodox form. To appreciate them, we first need to notice that advocates of this methodology are somewhat unclear with respect to what counts as the relevant *object* of interpretation, identified at the pre-interpretive stage. Two possibilities are available.

1. The object of interpretation is the *actual* behaviour of the agents operating within the relevant domain.
2. The object of interpretation is the *normative, often legal, discourse* surrounding a particular domain of human action.

In what follows, I analyse each of these possibilities in turn, and argue that the interpretive methodology turns out to be flawed under both of them.

The first account of the object of interpretation points us towards the empirical regularities that characterize a particular domain of action, be it a household, a state, or the international realm. The 'thing' to be interpreted is the actual behaviour of the agents involved in the domain at hand: family members, public officials, states, and multinational corporations, depending on the particular social sphere we are focusing on. The idea of interpreting regularities in agents' behaviour is certainly a familiar one, moreover one that is easy to grasp. However, does it offer a solid basis for the development of moral principles? It does not.

The problem with this account of the relevant object of interpretation is that it may very well fail to lead us to the identification of any moral values at all. Consider, for instance, what conclusions we would probably have to draw were we to interpret the *actual* conduct of Robert Mugabe's public officials in today's Zimbabwe. The regularities in their corrupt and self-interested behaviour would not enable us to say that underpinning their practices is an ideal of freedom and equality, as well as respect for persons and societal cooperation. If what we are interpreting is their actual behaviour, the actual practices they engage in, we are unlikely to discover high moral ideals.

Similarly, consider the case of the Smith family mentioned earlier in the text. The members of this family simply leave each other alone. They do not share experiences, they do not help each other out, or talk to one another, unless this is strictly unavoidable. They live under the same roof, they use the same facilities, but all they care about is not being interfered with. If what we are interpreting is *this* practice, we can hardly conclude that the values underpinning it are love, affection, reciprocity, and mutual support. Of course, we may very well want to say that the Smiths are doing something wrong, or that they are not behaving like a real family, but this judgement will rest on independent moral standards and not on an *interpretation* of their behaviour, or their practices.

By the same token, if we look at the international realm, and gather evidence on the behaviour of major actors within it, we are unlikely to come to the conclusion that such behaviour is meant to express a commitment to peace, security, self-determination, and cooperation. Much of the conduct of states and transnational corporations is driven by self-interest. The recent US intervention in Iraq was arguably carried out to further national interests, and obtain control over the oil supply in the Middle East. Similar motivations were behind other cases of direct or indirect intervention on the part of the United States in Latin America.[7] If we go back only a few decades, we stumble into European colonial domination, hardly a practice expressing a commitment to peace, cooperation, and self-determination. Moreover, national and strategic interests are known to play a big part in shaping negotiations within the main existing international institutions such as the UN, the WTO, and the IMF.

Of course, this is not to say that moral considerations never influence international actors. But it is to say that self-interest is one of the driving forces behind the actions of states, international institutions, and transnational corporations. Interestingly, it is precisely for this reason that, in his theory of international justice, Rawls focuses on peoples rather than states. Peoples, Rawls says, are moral agents, while real-world states, which are the main object of study in International Relations, are not.[8] If statists were interpreting *actual* international practice, they would not be able neatly to identify peace, security, cooperation, and respect as its driving values. In summary, if they were to adopt the first account of the object of interpretation, statists would hardly be able to develop plausible moral principles. As the first account cannot be the one they have in mind, let me move on to the second.

This time, we are no longer dealing with agents' actual behaviour, but rather with the normative discourses and/or legal constraints defining a particular area of human action. On this account, domestically, the objects to be interpreted are first and foremost a society's constitution, body of legislation, and the discourses shaping its public political culture. Internationally, they are the key principles of international law, and the discourses surrounding them, involving ideas such as human rights, aid, self-determination, and sovereignty. What we are looking at, on this second account of the interpretive approach,

---

[7] Richard W. Miller, *Globalizing Justice: The Ethics of Poverty and Power* (Oxford: Oxford University Press, 2010), ch. 5.

[8] John Rawls, *The Law of Peoples* (Cambridge, MA: Harvard University Press, 1999), pp. 23–30.

are *normative, value-laden statements* explicitly embedded in positive legal documents and informal public discourse and practice.

This account of the object of interpretation seems to be more in line with what statists have in mind. Consider, for instance, Rawls's references to the constitutional tradition of a liberal democratic society in *Political Liberalism*, and to international law in *The Law of Peoples*. In both monographs, Rawls appears to obtain the building blocks for his theories of justice from the legal documents and public culture characterizing liberal democratic societies (particularly the United States), and liberal foreign policy, respectively. Moreover, as I already mentioned, the interpretive methodology itself was originally developed by Ronald Dworkin in the context of legal reasoning, and therefore lends itself quite easily to being applied to legal texts and normative discourses. But is this second account of the object of interpretation any better than the first? Unfortunately, it is not. In particular, the account is undermined by two serious objections.

First, relying on the normative commitments embedded in a society's positive law and public culture may, once again, lead us to morally repugnant conclusions. Certainly, the principles embedded in the constitution of an eighteenth-century slave society can hardly be interpreted in a way that is consistent with liberal principles. Such documents are clearly imbued with moral language and purport to establish moral values, but for a liberal, they are the wrong ones. More generally, positively held normative commitments need not reflect what is morally correct. Any plausible moral methodology must have guarantees against morally repugnant conclusions. Even when it focuses on legal documents and real-world normative discourses, the interpretive methodology, in its pure form, cannot categorically exclude such conclusions.[9] Whether such conclusions are going to follow from this methodology depends on what texts and discourses are being interpreted. If you pick the wrong legal system or public culture, you end up with the wrong principles.[10]

This observation should suffice to rebut this second account of the methodology. But let us now assume that liberals can (artificially) restrict the application of such a methodology to those legal and discursive

---

[9] I specify 'in its pure form', because Andrea Sangiovanni has recently put forward a particularly sophisticated version of the interpretive methodology, combining interpretive reasoning with a fundamental (non-interpretive) commitment to the moral equality of persons. See his 'Justice and the Priority of Politics to Morality', *Journal of Political Philosophy*, 16 (2) (2008), 137–64. I argue that, even though this version of the interpretive approach is less vulnerable to the charge of *status-quo* bias, it is still not fully satisfactory in Valentini, 'Global Justice and Practice-Dependence'.

[10] This kind of argument is a familiar one in critical discussions of Michael Walzer's interpretive approach to social justice. See his *Spheres of Justice. A Defense of Pluralism and Equality* (New York: Basic Books, 1983).

practices that are compatible with their fundamental commitments. That is, they interpret explicitly liberal rules of international conduct, and liberal-democratic constitutional documents. This is in fact, once again, what Rawls does in *Political Liberalism* and *The Law of Peoples*. Even with this restriction, the interpretive methodology turns out to be implausibly biased towards the *status quo*.

To explain why, let me briefly run through the three stages of interpretation in the case of international law and public culture. At the pre-interpretive stage, we consider liberal principles of foreign policy, currently embedded in international law and discourse. We then move on to the interpretive stage and ask: 'What values underpin them?' These, as statists rightly point out, are the values of peace, security, self-determination, respect for human rights, and cooperation between societies. Finally, at the post-interpretive stage, we consider what rules would best express these values. The obvious answer corresponds to the kinds of principles offered by statists. As we know from Chapter 4, these include rules of respect, non-interference, protection of human rights, and mutual aid between peoples.

These are without doubt morally sound rules, and they are far from being respected in the world as we know it. For instance, states often intervene (forcibly or not) into one another's affairs, they fail to respect their citizens' human rights, they refuse to come to one another's aid, they disregard restrictions on the conduct of war, and so forth. In this sense, there is clearly some critical potential in statist principles derived *via* the interpretive methodology. The question before us though is whether this critical potential is critical enough. It is not.

On this methodology, the design of normative principles is inherently constrained by the positive morality embedded in the relevant documents and public culture. It is no surprise that, following this methodology, the issue of egalitarian socio-economic justice is brought to the fore at the domestic level, but not at the international one. Indeed, while questions about citizens' welfare and socio-economic justice are central to the public culture of many existing liberal-democratic societies, they are largely marginal to international law or international discourse, which is instead dominated by a concern with human rights, fair trade, and international aid. If we let our philosophical imagination be constrained by our positive morality (even though this is a liberal one), we risk hampering moral progress.

This, notice, is not to say that principles of egalitarian socio-economic justice should apply to the world at large. This is a substantive conclusion that has not (yet) been established. All I am arguing is that the *reason why*, by following the interpretive approach in its classical forms, we conclude that they should not, is a bad one. The fact that the issue of global egalitarian socio-economic justice is not a particularly live one in international law should not prevent us from putting such an issue on the philosophical agenda. But this is precisely what the interpretive methodology does.

This methodology invites us to look at the world through the normative categories it generates. Because international law and discourse are essentially statist, the principles we will elaborate to express their underlying values will, in all likelihood, be statist as well.[11] Armed with these principles, we turn to the real world to determine whether actual international conduct conforms with them. As the principles presuppose a world of separate, largely independent states, we will tend to look at the international arena from this perspective. But by doing so, we are likely to miss those systemic power dynamics, and forms of global interdependence, which are arguably responsible for much of the suffering, poverty, and destitution existing in the world today. There is thus a clear link between this interpretive methodology, and the suboptimal capacity for guidance of statist principles discussed in Chapter 4.

To conclude, although initially appealing, the interpretive methodology is characterized by some serious flaws. In particular, its inherent bias in favour of the *status quo* makes it ultimately unviable.

5.4 THE AGENCY-BASED APPROACH

A second justificatory avenue leading to defend statist principles has recently been advocated by Saladin Meckled-Garcia, who takes seriously the fact that normative principles are designed to guide the conduct of particular agents or agencies. In his view, before we can say that a principle 'applies' to a particular domain, we must identify which agents (if any) should act on it. Principles without agents are normatively inert.[12] The central claim of this approach can therefore be summarized as follows.

> **Agency-based approach**: principles of distributive justice apply *only if* there are agents with both the *moral power* and the *capacity* to implement them.

Meckled-Garcia further claims that, to meet these requirements, agents of justice must satisfy the 'Authority Condition'. That is, they must possess 'the moral power to assign rights and duties and assure compliance (for example through a system of public law) equally over agents in [the relevant] domain'.[13] Given that no agency with this power exists at the international level,

---

[11] Saladin Meckled-Garcia, 'International Law and the Limits of Global Justice', *Review of International Studies*, 37 (5) (2011).
[12] Meckled-Garcia, 'On the Very Idea of Cosmopolitan Justice', p. 247.
[13] Meckled-Garcia, 'On the Very Idea of Cosmopolitan Justice', p. 258.

Meckled-Garcia concludes that principles of egalitarian justice are ill-suited to apply to the world at large.

Similar appeals to the state's capacity to implement principles of justice, and to its moral authority, figure prominently in contemporary statist writings. For example, in *Principles of Social Justice*, David Miller argues that, for justice to apply to a certain context, there must be

> a relatively homogenous political community whose directing agency, the state, has the capacity to shape its major social institutions – and thus the final distribution of social resources – in the way the principles embedded in the concept prescribe.[14]

Here, the applicability of principles of justice depends on the existence of an institutional agent (the state) *capable* of implementing them. While Miller places emphasis on the state's capacity to realize the demands of justice, Thomas Nagel's defence of statism also stresses its *authority* (or plausible claim to authority) to do so. Nagel contends that justice should be confined to domestic political communities because 'justice applies ... only to a form of organization that claims political legitimacy and the right to impose decisions by force'.[15] In short, on the agency-based approach, unless there is an agent with the capacity and the authority to implement principles of distributive justice at a global level, such principles do not apply. What can we make of this approach to the design and justification of normative principles?

5.5 THE AGENCY-BASED APPROACH: VIRTUES AND VICES

As in the case of the interpretive approach, the agency-based view has some obvious virtues. Most importantly, it takes seriously the fact that normative principles only make sense if they are intended to guide the actions of particular agents or agencies. Since 'ought implies can', agents cannot be under duties of justice if they lack the *capacity* to fulfil them. Therefore, making sure that there are agents around with the ability to act on whatever justice requires is a task any plausible approach to justice should undertake. Unfortunately, statements declaring the existence of rights, without specifying what agents should bear the correlative duties, are not infrequent in discussions about

---

[14] David Miller, *Principles of Social Justice* (Cambridge, MA: Harvard University Press, 1999), p. 246, see also pp. 18–19.
[15] Thomas Nagel, 'The Problem of Global Justice', *Philosophy and Public Affairs*, 33 (2) (2005), 113–47, p. 140.

global justice. This is an important shortcoming of these discussions, and one that the agency-based approach does well to reveal.

Equally important is the agency-based theorist's focus on authority. Not *every* agent is morally entitled to implement principles of justice, even if they have the capacity to do so. For instance, I may have the capacity to punish a criminal (by locking him into my house for years), but I certainly lack the moral power to do so. That power belongs to the state. The state is authoritative in this area.

Even though, as I have just pointed out, considerations of capacity as well as authority should place constraints on the design and justification of normative principles, the agency-based approach takes such constraints too far. By regarding the presence of authoritative agencies with the capacity fully to realize principles of liberal-egalitarian justice as necessary conditions for the applicability of such principles, the agency-based approach limits the normative reach of justice to those circumstances in which it is most likely to be already realized.[16] To appreciate this, we need to gain a better understanding of the relationships between (*a*) principles of justice, (*b*) duties of justice, and (*c*) authoritative institutions with the capacity to implement them.

This is clearly no small topic, but from the viewpoint of a broadly liberal-contractarian morality, state authority is typically justified by appeal to the human condition in a hypothetical state of nature. The fathers of contemporary Rawlsian liberal theory, including Locke, Rousseau, and Kant, all defend different versions of this general justificatory strategy. For present purposes, all we need to focus on is what these different versions broadly have in common.[17]

State-of-nature arguments typically begin with human beings in a pre-societal state of affairs, where everyone is seen as free and equal, and where each is supposed to respect the freedom and equality of others. To honour this requirement, men and women need to refrain from interfering in one another's life plans, leaving each other with a reasonably-sized 'sphere of agency' within which to pursue their ends and goals. However, in a bounded world

---

[16] Cf. Christian Barry and Laura Valentini, 'Egalitarian Challenges to Global Egalitarianism: A Critique', *Review of International Studies*, 35 (3) (2009), 485–512, sec. IV. Note that the argument against the agency-based approach advanced in this chapter differs from, and is in some sense complementary to, that advanced in the cited paper.

[17] See John Locke, *Second Treatise of Government* 1689 (Oxford: Basil Blackwell, 1966, 3rd ed.); Immanuel Kant, *The Metaphysics of Morals* (1797), translated by Mary Gregor (Cambridge: Cambridge University Press, 1991); Jean-Jacques Rousseau's second 'Discourse' in *Rousseau's Political Writings*, trans. by Julia Conaway Bondanella (New York and London: Norton, 1987); and Rawls, *Political Liberalism*, p. 267. My argument in what follows is broadly inspired by these texts. This is not to deny the fundamental conceptual differences between these thinkers, but as I said such differences are not of relevance to the present discussion. For an excellent overview of similarities and differences between Locke and Kant in particular, see Katrin Flikschuh, 'Reason, Right, and Revolution: Kant and Locke', *Philosophy and Public Affairs*, 36 (4) (2008), 375–404.

with scarce resources, where individuals interact with each other and thereby become more and more interdependent, respecting the requirement of non-interference becomes problematic. Since resources are scarce, interacting agents will lay mutually irreconcilable claims over them, claims that need to be adjudicated in accordance with the demands of freedom and equality. In a pre-societal state of nature, doing so proves extremely difficult, if not altogether infeasible, for at least two reasons.

First, different people have different reasonable interpretations of what respecting others as free and equal requires, and disagree about how these interpretations should translate into particular patterns of resource distribution. Unless fair decision mechanisms are in place allowing individuals to manage their disagreements in a way that reflects their freedom and equality, disagreements will have to be settled by brute force.

What is more, even assuming that individuals in the state of nature all agree on the demands of justice, without the panoramic perspective and enforcement capacities of the state, they would still be unable to meet them. How could they foresee and control the cumulative effects of their individual transactions? How could they make sure that those effects did not infringe on others' right to pursue their ends and goals?

For these reasons, under circumstances of sufficiently intense interdependence and interaction, agents simply *cannot* comply with the duty to respect one another's freedom and equality. The only way for them to do so is to set up a collective agent, with the authority and capacity to act and decide in the name of all: the state. Only an agent of this kind can make justice possible.

Meckled-Garcia is therefore right in arguing that justice can *only be realized* by an agent with 'the moral power to assign rights and duties and assure compliance (for example through a system of public law) equally over agents in that domain'. What is problematic about his argument is that it conflates the *instrumental* conditions for the realizability of justice – that is, an agent with the appropriate capacities and moral powers – with their *existence* conditions.[18]

As my brief sketch of a model liberal-contractualist strategy for grounding state authority shows, the establishment of an agent with the moral power and the capacity fully to realize justice does not pre-exist principles of justice. It is because principles of justice requiring respect for persons' freedom and equality cannot be otherwise realized that we have reason to establish a state in the first place. The state, on this account, represents a *solution* to the problem of justice in conditions of intense interaction, while on the agency-based account, the state needs to exist for the problem of justice itself to

---

[18] On this, see the discussion in Arash Abizadeh, from which I have learnt, 'Cooperation, Pervasive Impact, and Coercion: On the Scope (not Site) of Distributive Justice', *Philosophy and Public Affairs*, 35 (4) (2007), 318–58, esp. pp. 325–34.

become of any relevance.[19] For proponents of the agency-based approach, without the state (or a functionally equivalent agency), talk of liberal-egalitarian justice is simply out of place.

Of course, it is crucial to recognize that principles of justice will place different duties on different agents, depending on the particular position they occupy in the social context at hand. In the state of nature, each agent will be under a duty to do whatever is reasonably within her or his power to bring about circumstances under which justice can be fully realized. This, in turn, might take years if not centuries to achieve, because of coordination problems and simple natural limitations. We might therefore find ourselves in circumstances such that everyone is doing her/his duty – that is, doing what is reasonably within her/his power to realize justice – and yet justice itself is not fully realized. Proponents of the agency-based view might find this mismatch between judgements about individual compliance with duties of justice, and overall 'justness' of states of affairs, problematic. How can a social setting be unjust if everyone is doing what justice demands?

However conceptually odd this may seem, it is actually a familiar predicament in real-world circumstances. Realizing justice requires social change, and social change occurs slowly. What we cannot achieve now, we might be able to achieve in the future. What might look like a good measure or policy to further justice *ex ante* may turn out to be a failure *ex post*, because of unforeseeable circumstances, and so forth. The question before us is: 'What is the best way of capturing this familiar situation from a normative point of view?' Proponents of the agency-based approach would want us to deny the existence of injustice in the circumstances at hand. If everyone is doing her/his duty, if nobody is acting unjustly, where does the injustice possibly come from? This is an important concern, however, one that can be accommodated within a more nuanced and plausible moral framework than the one presupposed by the agency-based approach.

If we were to follow this approach, we would have to conclude that, so long as the demands of justice cannot be satisfied *here and now*, the fact that they remain unfulfilled is not morally problematic. As they cannot be satisfied, those demands do not apply in the first place. This way of thinking about our moral requirements places excessively heavy constraints on the applicability of principles of justice. Surely, we want to be able to say that the 'here and now' is suboptimal from the point of view of justice, and that there is room to strive to ameliorate it. But if we cannot assess the 'here and now' by reference to principles of justice, as proponents of the agency-based view argue, then we cannot come to this conclusion. If we follow the agency-based approach, justice once again ends up losing its critical potential.

---

[19] This point has also been forcefully made by Iris Marion Young in 'Responsibility and Global Justice: A Social Connection Model', *Social Philosophy and Policy*, 23 (1) (2006), 102–30.

More generally, we need to find a way of retaining the critical potential of justice, while at the same time recognizing the difference between (a) a situation in which justice is not fully realized because people are failing to act on their duties, and (b) a situation in which justice is not fully realized because its realization takes time, and requires long-term institution building and reform.

My suggestion is to distinguish between culpable and innocent underfulfilments of justice. Culpable underfulfilments of justice occur when agents who could act in the ways justice requires refuse to do so. Innocent underfulfilments occur when the demands of justice are not fully realized because the transition from the *status quo* to a just state of affairs inevitably takes time. While culpable underfulfilments of justice tell us that there are some blameworthy parties who are not doing their fair share in supporting or creating just arrangements, innocent underfulfilments tell us that everyone is doing her/his duty, but that her/his 'job' is not yet completed, so to speak. In cases of innocent underfulfilment, we are moving in the right direction, namely in the direction of justice, but we are not there yet.[20]

Let us now consider what conclusions would follow from this revised, more plausible, version of the agency-based approach. Recall that, for proponents of the 'orthodox' version of this view, egalitarian principles of justice can only apply to contexts characterized by the presence of state-like agents, with the capacity and the moral power to impose rights and duties, and secure the compliance of those subject to their authority. As there is no such agent at the international level, so the argument goes, principles of liberal-egalitarian justice cannot apply at that level. This is like saying: as we do not already have full capacity to solve the problem of justice, we cannot even start thinking about it.

By contrast, on the revised version of the agency-based view I am proposing, whether principles of justice should apply to a particular context or not depends on whether the problem of justice – that is, how to adjudicate the competing claims of interacting agents in a way that is respectful of their freedom and equality – arises in that context. In relation to the debate on global justice, this means that we need to consider whether the intense yet unregulated interaction that occurs in our imaginary state of nature and triggers the need to move to the state is somehow replicated at the international level. *If* it is true that worldwide transactions, interactions, and formal

---

[20] Cf. the distinction between violations and underfulfilments of human rights in Laura Valentini, 'Human Rights: A Freedom-Centered View' (manuscript). This distinction has been originally drawn (though with a slightly different meaning) by Thomas W. Pogge in *Word Poverty and Human Rights: Cosmopolitan Responsibilities and Reforms* (Cambridge: Polity Press, 2002), p. 47. For a helpful discussion of similar issues, see Pablo Gilabert, 'The Feasibility of Basic Socio-economic Human Rights: A Conceptual Exploration', *Philosophical Quarterly*, 59 (237) (2009), 659–81.

and informal social rules have become so intense that states no longer have the power to ensure justice at the domestic level, then perhaps they too should give up some of their authority to supranational institutions with the capacity to regulate at least some (if not all) aspects of international interaction, and solve conflicting claims among states.[21]

Notice that, for my argument against the agency-based view to succeed, I need not offer evidence in support of the antecedent of this conditional. What matters is not that we are actually in conditions that require building new authoritative institutions capable of realizing liberal-egalitarian justice worldwide. What matters is that the agency-based view is in principle unable to address this situation. It posits the existence of an authoritative agent as a condition for principles of justice to apply, without realizing that it is justice itself that prompts us to bring about authoritative agents and institutions in the first place.[22]

More generally, following the agency-based view, so long as institutions do not exist or are not fully capable of realizing liberal-egalitarian justice – say because they are badly designed – judgements of justice do not apply to them. Of course, 'ought implies can', but social institutions are human constructions and therefore capable of being ameliorated and perfected. Shouldn't justice contribute to determining when they are needed or badly designed and, if they are, prompt us to build or reform them? Paradoxically, by taking the agency-based view, we are bound to answer in the negative, concluding that principles of justice should apply only to those contexts in which they are most likely to be already realized.

At this point, supporters of this view might reply that their outlook does not have such a wildly implausible implication. In particular, they might argue that the 'authority condition' only concerns duties of justice that apply to institutional agents, and not duties to bring about institutions capable of realizing liberal-egalitarian justice. On this view, the absence of appropriate institutional agencies only limits the applicability of *duties of justice*, not that of duties to bring about institutions capable of realizing liberal-egalitarian justice.[23]

If this is what proponents of the agency-based approach have in mind, then our disagreement might amount to a mere question of formulation. Indeed, duties to bring about conditions under which justice can be realized are, no doubt, themselves grounded in justice. If the people of country A have a duty of justice towards the people of country B by virtue of their intense

---

[21] See Elisa Orrù and Miriam Ronzoni, 'Which Supranational Sovereignty: Criminal and Socio-Economic Justice Compared', *Review of International Studies*, 37 (5) (2011).

[22] On this, see Young, 'Responsibility and Global Justice'.

[23] I am grateful to Saladin Meckled-Garcia for pressing this reply. The argument mirrors the Rawlsian distinction between principles of justice that apply to institutions and the natural duty of justice to bring about just institutions when they are not in place. See Rawls, *A Theory of Justice* (Oxford: Oxford University Press, 1999 rev. ed.), pp. 98–101.

interactions, or participation in common practices, the fact that the duty can only be discharged through the construction of appropriate institutions makes no difference to its justice-based nature. It would indeed seem rather implausible to maintain that the *way* in which duties can be best discharged should make a difference to their *nature*.

To see this, consider, for instance, the case of a well-functioning Nozickian minimal state. Presumably, Rawlsian statists would want that state to be governed by egalitarian principles of socio-economic justice. In their views, its justice performance should be evaluated by reference to the principles of 'justice as fairness'. Yet, in order for that state to be able to fulfil Rawls's principles, a considerable effort in institution building would have to be undertaken. A minimal state simply does not possess the sorts of institutions that are needed to implement liberal-egalitarian justice.

If we follow the suggestion, seemingly advanced by proponents of the agency-based view, that there is a categorical difference between 'principles of justice' (e.g. Rawls's principles for the basic structure of society) and the duty to further just arrangements not yet established, we are bound to reach a contradictory conclusion in the case of the Nozickian society just described. We would judge that society to be unjust by Rawls's standards of justice, and yet deny that what that society (through its members) should do in order to comply with Rawls's principles – that is, further just arrangements not yet established – is also a matter of justice.

The most plausible way to look at the relation between the individual duty to support and further just institutions, and principles of justice applying to the basic structure of society, is to see them as grounded in the same type of moral concern (justice) and as jointly necessary for its realization. Unless citizens support just institutions, justice cannot be realized, and it is the joint agency of all members of society (citizens and officials) acting in their different institutional capacities, within and *via* the state, that makes a society just.

If proponents of the agency-based approach simply claim that, in the absence of appropriate institutional agencies, justice does not apply directly, but requires us to bring about or further just institutions not yet established, then I have little to object to their argument. If, however, they advance the more controversial claim that principles of justice only apply to the ways in which *already effective* sovereign authorities act towards their subjects, their approach cannot escape the charge of being biased in favour of the *status quo*.

5.6 THE RELATIONAL APPROACH

Recall that we have already encountered a version of this approach in our discussion of cosmopolitan views. Those who subscribe to it hold that liberal-egalitarian justice applies only among people who stand in particular kinds of relations *vis-à-vis* one another. While cosmopolitans argue that the relevant relations exist both domestically and internationally, statists believe they are confined to the domestic arena. But what relations are the relevant ones in their views? Two answers figure prominently in the literature. One refers to the particular kind of cooperation in which fellow citizens are involved, and the other to state coercion.

5.6.1 THE COOPERATION VIEW

On this view, principles of egalitarian justice determine the *fair returns* that those who are involved in social cooperation owe to one another. Social cooperation produces various goods, and a question arises as to how these goods ought to be distributed. On the view I am examining, liberal-egalitarian justice is the answer. Fair is the distribution of goods that all cooperating parties could accept, and only egalitarian distributions can pass this universal justifiability test. Schematically put, the view can be stated as follows:

> **Cooperation view**: egalitarian justice applies only among fellow citizens (and residents in the state) because of the particular type of cooperation in which they are involved.[24]

Since this particular type of cooperation, so the argument goes, does not exist across societies, egalitarian justice should be confined to the domestic realm. What can we make of this view? I will assume, for the sake of argument, that proponents of the cooperation view are right in thinking that egalitarian principles (as opposed to other kinds of principles) correctly determine fair returns of social cooperation. What I want to examine is the claim that cooperation of the relevant kind exists only at the domestic level.

It goes without saying that, in our evermore globalized world, cooperative processes extend across borders. Think about the many commercial products for which raw materials are extracted in one part of the world, the products themselves manufactured in a different one, and then sold worldwide. European chocolate is an excellent example of this dynamic. The cocoa beans used to produce it may come from the Caribbean or the Ivory Coast, the chocolate is manufactured in Europe, and then sold all over the world. This is the case

---

[24] See e.g. Brian Barry, 'Humanity and Justice in Global Perspective', in Brian Barry, *Liberty and Justice: Essays in Political Theory 2* (Oxford: Clarendon Press, 1991), 182–210, pp. 194ff.; Andrea Sangiovanni, 'Global Justice, Reciprocity, and the State', *Philosophy and Public Affairs*, 35 (1) (2007), 3–39; and Samuel Freeman, 'The Law of Peoples, Social Cooperation, Human Rights, and Distributive Justice', *Social Philosophy and Policy*, 23 (1) (2006), 29–68.

not only for chocolate, but for most of the goods we routinely consume. Moreover, international cooperation is becoming increasingly frequent in economic as well as environmental and political matters. There is thus a clear sense in which cooperation exists at the global level. If statists want to defend their views by appeal to a cooperation-based argument, they need to explain what makes international cooperation relevantly different from domestic cooperation.

Two *prima facie* plausible answers are available: one points to the different effects that international and domestic cooperation have on autonomy, and the other hinges on a distinction between domestic cooperation and international interdependence. I argue that the former fails to vindicate statist principles, while the latter is problematically biased towards the *status quo*.

Societal Cooperation and Autonomy

A particularly nuanced argument in support of cooperation-based statism has been recently offered by Andrea Sangiovanni. In his words: 'We owe obligations of egalitarian reciprocity to fellow citizens and residents in the state, who provide us with the basic conditions and guarantees necessary to develop and act on a plan of life, but not to noncitizens, who do not.'[25] On this view, what distinguishes between domestic and international cooperation is that the former, but not the latter, is needed in order to provide agents with the necessary conditions to lead autonomous lives.

From an empirical point of view this claim appears implausible. In a highly integrated and interdependent world, our ability to lead autonomous lives is to a good extent dependent on the agency of distant strangers. I doubt that the inhabitants of France or Italy would experience no deterioration in their ability to lead autonomous lives if suddenly all other countries were to disappear. Our agency is so deeply intertwined with that of foreigners (again, think about the global nature of financial markets and commerce) that they too make a meaningful contribution to the necessary conditions for our autonomy.

If there is a difference between domestic and global contexts to do with autonomy, this cannot be of a qualitative kind (i.e. the former is key to autonomy, the latter is not), but rather of a quantitative one. Perhaps, the point is that even though both domestic and international cooperation are jointly necessary for our ability to lead autonomous lives, our fellow citizens' contribution is greater than that of distant strangers.[26]

This claim is *prima facie* plausible. Even though globalization has brought about a considerable increase in international commerce and transactions,

---

[25] Sangiovanni, 'Global Justice, Reciprocity, and the State', p. 20.
[26] Sangiovanni, 'Global Justice, Reciprocity, and the State', p. 34.

there are several institutional barriers (including different legal regulations, banking systems, social protections, etc.) making international integration still much less intense than its domestic counterpart.[27] Notice, however, that, even if empirically correct, the claim would not suffice to support the statist conclusion that egalitarian socio-economic justice only applies domestically. The fact that fellow citizens affect one another in a more all-encompassing way than strangers need not entail that no justice-based *egalitarian* concerns arise at the international level.

Perhaps, egalitarian concerns apply across a wider range of goods domestically than internationally, depending on the types of cooperation involved. But nothing in this interpretation of the cooperation view excludes the possibility that *some* egalitarian concerns are appropriate, for example, in the organization of the global economy. Why should fair cooperation require equality at home, but no egalitarian concern abroad? Even though what makes cooperation fair might plausibly vary across different types of cooperative enterprises, there is no obvious reason why egalitarian concerns can only express fairness at the domestic level.

In short, an autonomy-based concern with social cooperation cannot sustain statist conclusions. At most, assuming that domestic and international cooperation impact on our autonomy in different ways, we may have different types of egalitarian justice applying domestically and internationally, along the lines of what weak cosmopolitans argue.[28]

Cooperation versus Interaction

A second sense in which domestic cooperation might differ from international cooperation is that, while domestically citizens act together to achieve common goals, globally this is not the case. For this reason, at the global level, we can plausibly talk about interaction and interdependence, but the idea of cooperation should be confined to the domestic arena. Fellow citizens are involved in a mutually beneficial project, underpinned by a complex set of formal and informal rules, coming together to constitute their state. Their cooperation is qualitatively different from international cooperation because it is so tightly organized that it gives rise to a group agent, a 'legal–political authority' speaking with one voice.[29] Since, internationally, no such group agent exists, we are dealing with interdependence, rather than full-blown cooperation.

---

[27] Dani Rodrik, 'Feasible Globalizations', in Michael M. Weinstein (ed.), *Globalization: What's New?* (New York: Columbia University Press, 2005), 196–213, p. 199. Cf. Barry and Valentini, 'Egalitarian Challenges to Global Egalitarianism', pp. 491–3.

[28] See Section 3.6 (III).

[29] Christian List and Philip Pettit, *Group Agency: The Possibility, Design, and Status of Corporate Agents* (Oxford: Oxford University Press, 2011).

For this argument to be successful, two conditions have to be met. First, it must be true that, globally, no cooperation intense enough to give rise to a group agent, speaking with one voice, exists. Second, and most importantly, the existence of such an agent, with a complex organizational structure, must constitute a plausible trigger of egalitarian justice. Neither of these conditions seems to me to be met.

To begin with, even though there exists no global state, there are international institutions that arguably qualify as group agents, acting with a common purpose. For instance, we often speak of the WTO as if it constituted a unitary agent, whose members all act together to achieve a common purpose: trade liberalization. Its 'guiding principles remain the pursuit of open borders, the guarantee of most-favoured-nation principle and non-discriminatory treatment by and among members, and a commitment to transparency in the conduct of its activities'.[30] In what sense, then, is the sort of cooperation occurring within the WTO unlike the cooperation occurring in the state?

Of course, this is not to say that the WTO should be governed by domestic principles of justice. However, if cooperation (as opposed to interdependence) is what triggers egalitarian justice, then egalitarian concerns will also apply to it. What fairness requires within the WTO may be similar to what it requires domestically in that in both cases we might be interested in agents' relative shares of goods: social primary goods in the domestic case; bargaining power or market gains in the case of the WTO.

One might attempt to reply to this argument by pointing out that the WTO is a much less cohesive institution than a state. While fellow citizens genuinely cooperate for mutual advantage, the members of the WTO do everything within their power to strike the best bargain, no matter how detrimental it might be for other countries. If they can get away with it, they will do it. This, one might further point out, is not cooperation in a genuine sense.

This reply rests on an implausibly moralized understanding of what counts as cooperation of the relevant kind. In the same way in which the WTO arguably involves exploitative or unfair interaction, so too real-world, non-ideal states do. As we already saw in Section 3.5, for the cooperation-based view to be plausible, the idea of cooperation it relies on must not be already moralized. Otherwise, it would lead to the absurd conclusion that justice only applies to those contexts in which it is already realized.[31] Justice applies to cooperative relations in order to make them fair, so fairness cannot be one of its conditions of applicability.

So far, I have disputed the claim that, globally, there are no instances of interaction and interdependence intensely regulated enough to be comparable to those we find within the state. Let me now turn to the even deeper question

---

[30] http://www.wto.org/english/thewto_e/whatis_e/wto_dg_stat_e.htm (last accessed 31 October 2011).

[31] See the discussion in Arash Abizadeh, 'Cooperation, Pervasive Impact and Coercion', p. 331.

of whether such intensely regulated cooperation is in fact necessary in order for concerns of egalitarian justice to apply. It would seem not. Explicitly regulated social interaction, giving rise to cooperative relations such as those we find domestically, is only *instrumentally* necessary for the realization of justice.[32] As we have already seen in our discussion of the agency-based approach, a complex group agent, with the capacity to manage social interaction so as to prevent it from eroding the background conditions for persons to lead autonomous lives, is not necessary for the applicability of egalitarian justice, but for its implementation. If, at the global level, interaction has become so intense as to erode states' capacity to secure domestic social justice, the only way to restore just conditions is to create tighter regulatory authorities with the explicit goal of making interaction, and its effects, fair.[33] To think otherwise is to conflate what makes justice empirically possible, with what makes it morally necessary.

In summary, I have looked at two versions of the cooperation view, and concluded that neither of them offers a plausible basis for defending statist conclusions. I now turn to another prominent relational approach to justice often defended by statists: the coercion view.

5.6.2 THE COERCION VIEW

This view can be succinctly stated as follows:

Coercion view: egalitarian justice applies only among fellow citizens because only they are subject to ongoing state coercion.

Although versions of this view have been recently advocated by a number of theorists including Richard Miller and Thomas Nagel, Michael Blake's defence of it is particularly insightful and well developed.[34] I will therefore rely on Blake's account in my discussion.

Blake's view is centred on the liberal principle of equal respect for persons' autonomy, that is, for their ability to lead their lives in pursuit of their ends

---

[32] Arash Abizadeh makes this argument in connection with the idea of the basic structure of society. In his view, the existence of a basic structure is only an instrumental condition for the realization of justice, and not one of its existence conditions. See his 'Cooperation, Pervasive Impact, and Coercion', to which I am indebted.

[33] For a similar perspective, see also Miriam Ronzoni, 'The Global Order: A Case of Background Injustice? A Practice-dependent Account', *Philosophy and Public Affairs*, 37 (3) (2009), 229–56.

[34] See Richard W. Miller, 'Cosmopolitan Respect and Patriotic Concern', *Philosophy and Public Affairs*, 27 (3) (1998), 202–24; Nagel, 'The Problem of Global Justice'; and Michael Blake, 'Distributive Justice, State Coercion, and Autonomy', *Philosophy and Public Affairs*, 30 (3) (2001), 257–96.

and goals. Clearly, coercive acts have a deep impact on persons' capacity to lead autonomous lives. Coercion represents a quintessential violation of autonomy. When I am coerced, I do not act out of my own will, I do not shape my own life, but I am a mere 'tool' of the will of another.

For instance, while choosing the medical profession because it looks like a good career option is perfectly admissible from the viewpoint of autonomy, it is not if 'someone else has made it the best option open to me by making other choices difficult or impossible to pursue'.[35] Similarly, consider the case of a robber pointing a gun to someone's head, threatening 'your money or your life'. The unlucky passer-by would have certainly chosen to continue to walk down the street with her/his money. But now the opportunity set containing those two options is no longer available to her/him. She/he can either keep the money (and die) or hand over the money and walk away.[36] There is little doubt that she/he would have preferred to keep her/his money and walk away; however, because of the mugger's threat, what would have otherwise been her/his 'chosen option' is replaced with a different one.

As Blake himself acknowledges, coercion is an inevitable fact of life, and while it may be autonomy undermining in the ways just described, it is not always to be condemned. In particular, coercion seems justified whenever the coercee has previously consented to it. Consider the following scenario. Before a big night out, I instruct my friend Elisa to drag me home in case I get drunk. If, once I have had too many drinks, she pushes me into a cab and sends me home, nothing wrong seems to have happened.[37] Similarly, if I breach a contract I have validly signed, it seems morally appropriate to force me to keep my commitment. After all, I knew that the terms of the contract were enforceable before signing it.

But what about circumstances in which agents have no chance to give their consent in the first place? What about the case of state coercion? No one can actually consent to the overall configuration of society's laws, and how these shape citizens' interactions. Despite this, unlike anarchists, liberals think of state coercion in general as justified. But why is that? Why should we not dispense with state coercion, given that it cannot be consented to and therefore appears to be inevitably autonomy undermining? Blake's answer is that, paradoxically, state coercion is *needed* for individuals to be able to lead autonomous lives. In his words:

> Only the state is coercive of individuals and required for individuals to live autonomous lives. Without some sort of state coercion, the very ability to pursue

---

[35] Blake, 'Distributive Justice, State Coercion, and Autonomy', p. 270.
[36] For a similar formulation, see Ian Carter, 'Positive and Negative Liberty', in Edward N. Zalta (ed.), *The Stanford Encyclopedia of Philosophy* (Fall 2008 edition), http://plato.stanford.edu/archives/fall2008/entries/liberty-positive-negative/
[37] Cf. Blake, 'Distributive Justice, State Coercion, and Autonomy', p. 273.

our projects and plans seems impossible. Settled rules of coercive adjudication seem necessary for the settled expectations without which autonomy is denied.[38]

For instance, in a completely anarchical scenario, it would be impossible for individuals to entertain expectations about one another's behaviour. Under those conditions, even if individuals in principle have the ability to develop and act on a plan of life, they cannot exercise it because they have no basis for forming minimally reliable expectations on others' conduct. Since legal coercion is an 'enabling condition' of autonomy, we cannot dispense with it. Instead, we have to make sure that the law shapes citizens' interactions in ways that are respectful of the autonomy of all.[39]

As we have seen, the standard way of justifying coercion appeals to individuals' genuine consent at a time (t') prior to the occurrence of coercion (at time t). In the case of state coercion, however, *actual consent* is unavailable. To overcome this difficulty, Blake suggests resorting to *hypothetical consent*. This provides a method for justifying the content of the law and ensuring that the state's coercive power is exercised with equal respect for the autonomy of all citizens understood as rational agents. The idea is that, when we cannot appeal to persons' actual will, we turn to the *reasons* they would have for agreeing to one configuration of domestic social institutions rather than another.[40]

Following Rawls's and T. M. Scanlon's contractualist thought experiments, the original position and the reasonable rejection test, Blake suggests that the only system of law that everyone would regard as justified – that is, which everyone would have reason to endorse – would engender roughly egalitarian distributive patterns. Since every individual has an interest in forming, revising, and acting on her/his conception of the good, the only social rules everyone has reason to accept are those under which everyone's interest in autonomy is equally protected through equal civil and political liberties, equal opportunities, and egalitarian distributions of wealth. On this reading, Rawls's difference principle justifies society's legal system (particularly property and tax law) to those who are subject to it, including the worse off, because they know that, under this principle, they fare better than they would under any alternative distributive arrangement.[41]

Can the coercion view so understood support statist conclusions? At first sight, it may seem not. After all, state coercion clearly exists also at the international level. Consider, for instance, wars of aggression, international economic sanctions, or simply border coercion against foreign migrants. Surely, these qualify as instances of state coercion, and thus stand in need of justification. Just as in the case of the cooperation view, proponents of the

---

[38] Blake, 'Distributive Justice, State Coercion, and Autonomy', p. 280.
[39] Blake, 'Distributive Justice, State Coercion, and Autonomy', p. 282.
[40] Cf. Section 1.2.
[41] Blake, 'Distributive Justice, State Coercion, and Autonomy', p. 283.

coercion view can only plausibly defend statist conclusions by explaining how international state coercion differs from its domestic counterpart.

I will argue that, even though proponents of this view can offer a plausible argument to this effect, their outlook is ultimately flawed because a narrow focus on state coercion fails to place under appropriate justice-based scrutiny a vast number of problematic constraints on autonomy that, from a liberal perspective, ought to stand in need of justification. If autonomy is what matters, then we have reason to worry about more than state coercion narrowly construed.[42]

Domestic and International State Coercion

Statists do not deny the obvious empirical fact that state coercion exists at the global level. What they do deny is that its justification requires egalitarian justice. In their views, at the global level, legitimate states should respect one another's sovereignty and self-determination, and refrain from interfering in one another's affairs. Coercive intervention might be justified against externally aggressive or internally oppressive states, but when societies are decent enough, no form of international coercion between them is justified. Indeed, by coercing one another, decent or reasonably just states would compromise their ability to secure social justice at home.

But what about border coercion?[43] For statists, to the extent that each state does what is in its power to assist others in need, this type of coercion is justified. The idea is that, by supporting the coercive institutional arrangements of their state, fellow citizens become responsible for one another's life conditions in a way that foreigners are not. Fellow citizens collectively determine how to shape their society's future, what policies to pursue, what risks to take, and what economic and cultural decisions to make.[44] In light of this, applying egalitarian principles of socio-economic justice – such as those liberals advocate domestically – would be to fail to honour some of liberalism's key values, such as that of self-determination. So long as each society has enough to be viable, so the argument goes, border coercion is justified on liberal grounds.

---

[42] What follows partly draws, and further elaborates, on Laura Valentini, 'Coercion and (Global) Justice', *American Political Science Review*, 105 (1) (2011), 205-20, pp. 207-9. For a different critique of the coercion view, see Eric Cavallero, 'Coercion, Inequality, and the International Property Regime', *Journal of Political Philosophy*, 18 (1) (2010), 16-31.

[43] David Miller has recently argued that border controls are not coercive in response to Arash Abizadeh, 'Democratic Theory and Border Coercion: No Right to Unilaterally Control Your Own Borders', *Political Theory*, 36 (1) (2008), 37-65. See David Miller, 'Why Immigration Controls Are not Coercive: A Reply to Arash Abizadeh', *Political Theory*, 38 (1) (2010), 111-20. I briefly explain why I find Miller's argument unsatisfactory in footnote 18, ch. 6.

[44] For similar arguments, see Rawls, *The Law of Peoples*, pp. 117-18; David Miller, 'Justice and Global Inequality', in Andrew Hurrell and Ngaire Woods (eds.), *Inequality, Globalization, and World Politics* (Oxford: Oxford University Press, 1999), 187-210, esp. pp. 193-5; and Blake, 'Distributive Justice, State Coercion, and Autonomy', pp. 289-94.

This argument has some plausibility. First, as we already saw in Chapter 4, denying the applicability of domestic egalitarian justice to the international arena does not *per se* entail a violation of the fundamental commitments of liberalism. Second, it seems plausible to claim that different types of justification are appropriate in the presence of different types of coercion. The ways in which domestic state coercion constrains foreigners' ability to act is different from the way in which it constrains fellow citizens. If state coercion is indeed the appropriate trigger of concerns of justice, it may very well be that different types of state coercion call for different types of justification.

The antecedent of this conditional is a very important one. Proponents of the coercion view believe that only state coercion triggers concerns of justice, but the content of this belief is by no means obviously correct. If it turns out to be unsustainable, then even if statists can successfully distinguish between domestic and international state coercion, this will not be enough to validate their views.

Why State Coercion?

Recall that statists' focus on state coercion rests on a deeper concern with equal respect for persons, and specifically with persons' entitlement to the necessary social conditions to lead autonomous lives. State coercion clearly places constraints on autonomy, but it is not the only way in which persons' ability to pursue their ends and goals can be limited. There are many practices with a potential for undermining autonomy, and it is such practices that, from a liberal viewpoint, should trigger concerns of justice. As state coercion is only one among them, state coercion is only a sufficient, but not a necessary and sufficient condition for the applicability of egalitarian justice.

A version of this argument has been put forward by Mathias Risse, who correctly detects a tension between statists' grounding of duties of justice in the equal autonomy principle (henceforth also 'autonomy principle'), and their focus on state coercion as the trigger of such duties. After all, there exists a multiplicity of ways in which institutions and actions may affect persons' autonomy, and not all of them involve commands backed by the threat of sanctions. Consider the following three examples, starting with IMF emergency loans. Decisions as to whether developing countries X and Y should be granted a loan, and on what conditions, are likely significantly to affect the autonomy of their inhabitants. Why then, asks Risse, does the autonomy principle require special justification for state coercion but not for conditional development aid?[45]

---

[45] Mathias Risse, 'What to Say About the State?', *Social Theory and Practice*, 32 (4) (2006), 671–98, p. 681.

Second, consider the case of a multinational corporation deciding to invest in society A, thus creating new employment opportunities for its inhabitants. This is a blessing, as many of them live in conditions of gruelling poverty. A few weeks before concluding the deal, the corporation's executive realizes that the company would have much better chances to make profit by investing in society B, where no one happens to be badly off.[46] As the company's decision has such severe consequences for the autonomy of A's inhabitants, one would think that an approach to justice based on the principle of equal respect for autonomy would condemn it. The coercion view, however, puts it beyond justice-based scrutiny.

Finally, think about agricultural subsidies helping farmers in Europe and the United States. These policies deeply affect the opportunities of farmers and producers in developing countries who often run the risk of losing their business because of international competition. Unable to sell their products at sustainable prices, they are likely to encounter severe hardship and to lack the necessary means for leading autonomous lives.[47] But since no coercion has caused their loss of autonomy – Europe and the United States are not threatening sanctions against these farmers – the coercion approach is in no position to condemn it.

In short, as Risse suggests, '*if it is because of the Autonomy Principle* that coercion requires justification, anything will require justification that constrains whether, or to what extent, people have a reasonable range of options to choose from'.[48] Risse's claim is perhaps too strong here. For instance, we would not want to argue that natural disasters, which often cause massive reductions in their victims' capacity for autonomy, require justification. A natural disaster may be bad, but is certainly neither just nor unjust. The important point is that, *if* liberals need to worry about potentially problematic restrictions of autonomy, then they need to worry about a lot more than *state coercion* alone.

The examples just offered all point to international and transnational dynamics placing significant constraints on the autonomy of both states and their citizens. In light of this, it appears inconsistent, for a liberal, to exclude them from justice-based assessment simply because they are not *coercive* in the way the state is. Why do restrictions of autonomy perpetrated by a group agent issuing commands backed by the threat of sanctions matter more than restrictions of autonomy occurring through some other avenues, including economic subsidies, conditional loans, trade barriers, and so forth? Without a

---

[46] I am grateful to Saladin Meckled-Garcia for suggesting this example.

[47] Ryan Pevnick, 'Political Coercion and the Scope of Distributive Justice', *Political Studies*, 56 (2) (2008), 339–413, p. 407.

[48] Risse, 'What to Say About the State?', p. 680, emphasis original.

plausible answer to this question, like the cooperation view, the coercion view only appears to offer a poorly justified defence of the *status quo*.

5.7 CONCLUSION

In this chapter, I have analysed three different methodological approaches leading to advocate statist principles of international justice, and found all of them problematic. The interpretive approach is either unable to deliver moral principles at all, or doomed to reproduce existing moral biases in the principles it advocates. The agency-based approach also suffers from a form of *status-quo* bias, because it takes the otherwise plausible idea that normative principles are meant to guide the conduct of specific agents and agencies too far. In particular, it suggests that the existence of a well functioning, nearly just state is necessary for liberal-egalitarian justice to apply. But surely, the existence of such a state is an instrumental, rather than an existence, condition of egalitarian justice.[49] Finally, I have looked at two versions of the relational approach: cooperation- and coercion-based views. I have argued that both fail to offer a plausible account of those disanalogies between the domestic and global realms that make liberal-egalitarian justice allegedly relevant to the former but not to the latter.

This chapter concludes the analytical and critical part of this book. From Chapter 6 onwards, building on the lessons learnt up to this point, I shall put forward a new normative framework for thinking about justice within and, most importantly, beyond borders. I first lay out a general account of the function and content of principles of justice. I then test its plausibility by reference to its capacity to account for familiar claims about domestic egalitarian justice. Finally, I consider the implications of my preferred framework when this is applied to the international arena. My task in doing so is to show that such a framework successfully overcomes the theoretical and practical shortcomings of cosmopolitanism and statism, steering a coherent middle course between the two.

---

[49] Abizadeh, 'Cooperation, Pervasive Impact, and Coercion'.

Part III

A Normative Framework

6

The Function of Justice: Assessing Coercion

6.1 INTRODUCTION[1]

In the course of our discussion, relational accounts of egalitarian justice have proven to be the most promising. On these accounts, egalitarian justice is a socio-political notion, which becomes relevant only in the presence of particular types of social relations. Agents belonging to altogether separate social systems may have humanitarian duties of assistance towards each other, but no duties of egalitarian justice.

We have also seen, however, that the relational approaches proposed by cosmopolitans and statists are unsatisfactory on a number of counts. Relational cosmopolitans, who by and large rely on the broad notion of the 'basic structure of society', are unable to differentiate between the social relations characterizing the domestic arena and those characterizing the international one. The notion of the basic structure, which indicates the fundamental legal, political, and economic arrangements of a particular social system, may encompass different types of institutions, calling for different standards of justification. There may very well be a global basic structure in this broad sense, but whether its justification requires the same egalitarian principles of justice as those liberals defend in the domestic context is dubious.[2]

Statists, by contrast, adopt too narrow an account of what triggers concerns of egalitarian justice – either in terms of social cooperation or in terms of state coercion – leading their theories to be implausibly biased towards the *status quo*. They might be right that the global arena differs from the domestic one in morally relevant ways but, as argued in Chapter 5, they have not succeeded in establishing that these differences warrant denying the applicability of egalitarian justice at the global level.

---

[1] A substantial portion of this chapter draws on Laura Valentini, 'Coercion and (Global) Justice', *American Political Science Review*, 105 (1) (2011), 205–20, by permission of Cambridge University Press.

[2] This was the conclusion reached in Chapter 3, with the provisional endorsement of what, following Beitz, I called 'weak cosmopolitanism'.

The aim of this chapter, and the next, is to remedy this shortcoming in the existing literature by offering a more nuanced account of the types of social relations that generate concerns of justice in general, and of egalitarian justice in particular. In doing so, I will rely on a notion closely associated with the idea of justice: coercion. I will, however, distance myself from recent statist treatments of this notion, such as those discussed in Chapter 5. Statists, I argue, implicitly assume what I call a *narrow* account of coercion – that is, coercion exercised by an agent through commands backed by the threat of sanctions. By contrast, I adopt a broader notion of coercion. In particular, I distinguish between *interactional* and *systemic* kinds of coercion, and show that these appropriately capture those constraints on freedom (i.e. on the social conditions to lead autonomous lives) that, from a liberal viewpoint, stand in need of justice-based assessment.[3]

Two key insights underpin the coercion-based normative framework I am about to defend. First, from a liberal perspective, certain restrictions of freedom – those I will define as coercive – demand special justification. The principles articulating the required justification are those we should designate as principles of justice. Second, the relevant restrictions of freedom need not be direct, perpetrated by an agent – collective or individual – against other agents. Instead, they can also be indirect, resulting from formal and informal social rules, supported by a large enough number of agents. Depending on the characteristics of the rules in question, different forms of justification apply.

The chapter is structured as follows. In Sections 6.2 and 6.3, I illustrate how the idea of coercion relates to that of justice, and explain where contemporary accounts of coercion, such as those defended by statists, go wrong. In Sections 6.4 and 6.5, I develop a new account of coercion, distinguishing between interactional and systemic versions of it. Interactional coercion is coercion exercised by one agent *vis-à-vis* other agents; systemic coercion is coercion exercised through a system of social rules enacted by a plurality of agents. I argue that both types of coercion are appropriate triggers of concerns of justice.

In Section 6.6, I consider the implications of my conceptual framework for our understanding of egalitarian justice at the domestic level. I show that coercion *by* the state is not necessary to generate requirements of egalitarian justice. Those requirements can in fact also be triggered by the systemically coercive practices existing *within* the state. Even when the state does not coerce its citizens, there may still be important restrictions of freedom standing in need of justification, and which can only be justified by appeal to familiar egalitarian principles of justice. In Section 6.7, I consider how we should conceptualize individual responsibility for interactional and systemic coercion, and then conclude with a few remarks anticipating the content of Chapter 7.

---

[3] The distinction between systemic and interactional coercion is partly inspired by Thomas Pogge's distinction between interactional and institutional accounts of human rights. See his *World Poverty and Human Rights: Cosmopolitan Responsibilities and Reforms* (Cambridge: Polity Press, 2002).

Let me make two important prefatory notes. First, in this chapter, I develop a particular account of the function of justice, focusing on coercion. The notion of coercion I adopt is admittedly unorthodox. Even though I explain why we have good reasons for understanding coercion the way I suggest, some readers are likely to remain unconvinced. This need not undermine the substantive claims at the heart of the chapter though. Those readers who find my definitions of interactional and systemic coercion inappropriate as definitions of *coercion* may still believe that these definitions correctly capture the object of assessment of principles of justice, and simply opt for a different label.

Second, in this chapter and the following one, I shall be concerned with developing a particular normative framework for thinking about justice. For the sake of clarity and simplicity, my discussion will focus on the relatively unproblematic realm of domestic political communities. I shall consider the implications of my framework for the question of global justice in Chapters 8 and 9.

6.2 LIBERALISM, JUSTICE, AND COERCION: AN OVERVIEW

Let me begin by recapitulating the normative links between egalitarian domestic justice and coercion, which we already encountered in Chapter 5. Central to contemporary liberalism is a commitment to equal respect for persons *qua* rational and autonomous agents. This commitment to autonomy leads liberals to (*a*) place great value on freedom, namely on the necessary *social* conditions for persons to lead autonomous lives,[4] and (*b*) be suspicious of all forms of coercion. The notion of coercion clearly evokes situations in which our ability to act autonomously is thwarted. Successful coercion entails a net loss of autonomy on the part of its victims.

Although liberals regard coercion as *prima facie* morally problematic, as discussed in Chapter 5, they do not consider all forms of coercion morally unacceptable. Most importantly, unlike anarchists, liberals are not opposed to *state* coercion as such. They realize that state coercion may threaten freedom, but they also acknowledge that it is *necessary* for it. In a completely anarchical scenario, without stable coordination mechanisms, a system of law securing access to resources, and effective enforcement

---

[4] I emphasize social conditions because non-social conditions, such as genetically determined mental and physical capacities, also affect one's ability to lead an autonomous life. Freedom, as I understand it, only focuses on those conditions on which society may plausibly have an impact.

procedures ensuring compliance, leading an autonomous life would be virtually impossible.[5] Coercion is thus Janus-faced: it is an obstacle to freedom and at the same time a means to it.

That said, liberals take state coercion to be indispensable for an autonomous life, and thereby just, only under strict conditions. Given their commitment to equal respect, they consider state coercion morally acceptable only when the distribution of freedom it engenders is in principle justifiable to those who are subject to it. For liberals, each citizen has *a right to a mutually justifiable degree of freedom* (a 'right to freedom' for brevity) and state coercion can only be just if it respects this right. But when is this requirement met? Plainly, whenever state coercion is exercised so as to give all citizens approximately equal freedom. Only a society granting its members roughly equal opportunities to lead autonomous lives, liberals argue, can be unanimously accepted by agents who wish to pursue their ends and goals. A social system falling short of this requirement could not be justified in the eyes of the people who are worse off, whose life prospects and opportunities would be significantly inferior to everyone else's.

Consider, for instance, despotic or hierarchical societies, in which the ability of some to act as they wish comes at the expense of the freedom of others. In a society marked by legally entrenched gender discrimination, for example, women have their opportunities severely restricted, while men enjoy full freedom to act as they see fit. This kind of society is obviously unacceptable from a liberal point of view. Indeed, it would hardly be capable of attracting the principled consent of all its members. Why should women accept to live in conditions of subordination and oppression?

On this liberal view, then, principles of justice tell us how the state should be organized for its coercive mechanisms to be justified in the eyes of all. *The function of justice, that is, is to evaluate the moral legitimacy of (state) coercion.* When liberties, opportunities, and wealth are roughly equally distributed among citizens – as prescribed by most contemporary liberal theories of justice – each is just as much in a position to pursue her/his ends and goals as everybody else,[6] and no morally problematic relationships of oppression or domination can be said to occur within society. By contrast, when these requirements are not met, as in the case of our sexist society, state coercion is unjust: it violates the fundamental liberal commitment to equal respect.

---

[5] As argued by Michael Blake, 'Without some sort of state coercion, the very ability to pursue our projects and plans seems impossible. Settled rules of coercive adjudication seem necessary for the settled expectations without which autonomy is denied.' See his 'Distributive Justice, State Coercion, and Autonomy', *Philosophy and Public Affairs*, 30 (3) (2001), 257–96, p. 280.

[6] Of course, there may be variations to do with character, temperament, and mental or physical ability, which cannot be socially influenced.

This account of the function of justice – referring to the justification of (state) coercion – not only is present in contemporary liberal theory but also has important predecessors in the history of liberal political thought, especially within the social contract tradition. There is, however, an important difference between the views advanced by contemporary proponents of the coercion view, and those of their predecessors. Contemporary accounts of this view suffer from what might be called a fetishism of state coercion. They mistakenly consider *state* coercion as the *sole* trigger of the problem of justice, and thereby conclude that, in the absence of a global state, liberal principles of egalitarian justice cannot apply at the international level. What they seem to be ignoring is that state coercion not only raises concerns of justice but also responds to them.[7]

As we saw in Section 5.5, this mistake was not made by earlier social contract theorists. In their views, a *group agent with the capacity to issue commands backed by the threat of sanctions* was necessary to put an end to the 'lawless' coercion occurring in the state of nature, and that threatened to undermine individual freedom. As Immanuel Kant said, '[i]f you are so situated as to be unavoidably side by side with others, you ought to abandon the state of nature and enter, with all others, a juridical state of affairs, that is, a state of distributive legal justice.'[8] The problem of justice, then, does not arise only in the presence of state coercion. The constraints on freedom that individuals place on one another in conditions of interaction and interdependence *prior* to the existence of the state also stand in need of justification. What is more, they can only be justified by creating justly governed, state-like, authorities.[9] This is precisely why liberals, unlike anarchists, believe that state coercion is in principle justifiable, that is, because it is necessary for freedom itself.

But how can those looser constraints on freedom, existing even prior to the establishment of the state, be appropriately characterized? In what follows, I develop a new conceptual framework for defining coercion that, I claim, gives us the necessary tools to capture them.

---

[7] As we have already seen, if state coercion was not necessary for freedom, liberals would side with anarchists and always regard it as unjustified.

[8] Immanuel Kant, *The Metaphysical Elements of Justice: Part I of the Metaphysics of Morals* (1797), translated by John Ladd (Indianapolis/Cambridge: Hackett, 1999, 2nd ed.), p. 114–15.

[9] See Kant, *The Metaphysical Elements of Justice*; Iris Marion Young, 'Responsibility and Global Justice: A Social Connection Model', *Social Philosophy and Policy*, 23 (1) (2006), 102–30; and Miriam Ronzoni, 'The Global Order: A Case of Background Injustice? A Practice-dependent Account', *Philosophy and Public Affairs*, 37 (3) (2009), 229–56.

6.3 COERCION: AN ESSENTIALLY CONTESTED CONCEPT

Careful readers will have noticed that, in the previous chapter and the present one, I have talked about coercion without ever explicitly defining it. This (less-than-optimal) practice is not unique to me. Contemporary proponents of the coercion view also assume that, whenever they talk about state coercion, their readers know what they are referring to. To some extent this assumption is warranted. In ordinary discourse, the state is said to coerce its citizens because it issues commands (laws) backed by the threat of sanctions. If we refuse to observe them, we will be either forced to comply, or punished for breaching the law.

Even though we all have a common-sense, intuitive idea of what state coercion consists of, philosophically, matters are considerably more complicated. Coercion is what W. B. Gallie called an 'essentially contested concept',[10] namely a concept for which we can identify a common core, but which can be given a number of competing definitions. From a philosophical point of view, then, claiming that concerns of egalitarian justice are triggered by state coercion leaves the conditions under which egalitarian justice applies significantly underspecified. To see this, it suffices to take a quick look at the competing definitions of coercion existing in the philosophical literature.[11]

Some think of coercion as synonymous with the use of physical force, yet most contemporary philosophers deny that simply forcing someone to act, or to refrain from acting, in particular ways counts as coercion. In their views, coercion is distinctive in virtue of its effects on the coercee's will.[12] The coercer issues commands backed by the threat of sanctions, and if the sanctions are serious enough, the coercee has *virtually no choice* but to execute the coercer's commands. Her/his will becomes an instrument to the will of the coercer.

Coercive threats clearly make their victims worse off, but philosophers disagree about the relevant baseline with respect to which to establish whether the victim's conditions are worsened. Some adopt a moralized baseline (i.e. 'what justice requires') and others a non-moralized one (the *expected* course of events, in the absence of the threat). A criminal who is told by the police 'surrender or otherwise we'll shoot' is coerced on the latter view, but not on the former. Had the police not intervened, the criminal would have been better off

---

[10] W. B. Gallie, 'Essentially Contested Concepts', *Proceedings of The Aristotelian Society*, 56 (1956), 176–98.

[11] In this discussion, I am heavily indebted to Scott Anderson, 'Coercion', in Edward N. Zalta (ed.), *The Stanford Encyclopedia of Philosophy* (Spring 2006 edition) http://plato.stanford.edu/archives/spr2006/entries/coercion/

[12] Robert Nozick, 'Coercion', in S. Morgenbesser, P. Suppes, and M. White (eds.), *Philosophy, Science, and Method: Essays in Honor of Ernest Nagel* (New York: St Martin's, 1969), 440–72. For a contemporary influential account of coercion, see also Alan Wertheimer, *Coercion* (Princeton, NJ: Princeton University Press, 1987).

(i.e. able to go about his business undisturbed), but the police's intervention is fully in line with what justice requires. By contrast, a Jew who is told by an SS officer 'give me all your belongings and I will spare your life', is coerced on the former view, but not on the latter. The SS officer's proposal makes the Jew better off compared to the expected course of events (i.e. being killed) but is clearly unjust.

To further complicate matters, some scholars reject the seemingly unproblematic claim that only threats can be coercive.[13] The nature of a proposal as an offer or a threat, they argue, depends on *how the proposal is perceived* in the particular context in which it is uttered, whereas its coerciveness depends on its effects on the coercee's will.[14] Consider, once again, the case of the SS officer and the Jew. In the context at hand, the SS officer might be interpreted as making an offer (albeit of a morally perverse kind), rather than issuing a threat, and we need not consider baselines to come to this conclusion. What is more, the offer appropriately qualifies as coercive.[15] What makes the SS officer's proposal coercive has nothing to do with its form (e.g. threat vs. offer) but is instead a matter of its effect. The agent who utters the proposal (the SS officer in this case) is getting others (the Jew) to act in certain ways, without their voluntary consent.

Considerations of this sort have led some theorists to develop the so-called non-baseline approaches to coercion. On these approaches, whether coercion occurs exclusively depends on the type of pressure the coercer applies to the coercee's will. The existence of coercion is not determined by reference to baselines, but simply by looking at the effects that a particular proposal has on the coercee's ability to exercise her/his volition. If the coercee feels so compelled by the proposal that she/he is no longer in a genuine position to choose freely which course of action to follow, coercion can be said to have occurred.[16] On this type of view, even bargaining under conditions of steep power inequalities might turn out to be coercive.[17] If the poor and destitute are faced with exploitative job offers they virtually cannot refuse, they can be said to be coerced, even if accepting the offers makes them better off in absolute terms.

Other, more nuanced positions on what counts as coercion have also been developed in the philosophical literature, but this is not the place to review them. My aim so far has only been to offer a brief illustration of some of the

---

[13] See Onora O'Neill, 'Which Are the Offers *You* Can't Refuse?' in her *Bounds of Justice* (Cambridge: Cambridge University Press, 2000); and Christine Swanton, *Freedom: A Coherence Theory* (Indianapolis: Hackett, 1992), pp. 104–9.
[14] This point is made by Swanton, *Freedom: A Coherence Theory*, pp. 104–9.
[15] Cf. the similar example in Nozick, 'Coercion', p. 450.
[16] See Joel Feinberg, *Harm to Self* (New York: Oxford University Press, 1986), ch. 23.
[17] Joan McGregor, 'Bargaining Advantages and Coercion in the Market', *Philosophy Research Archives*, 14 (1988–1989), 23–50.

controversies surrounding the notion of coercion. In the presence of such controversies, simply pointing to coercion as the trigger of concerns of justice, without specifying what coercion means, makes one's view overly vague. A plausible coercion-based account of the function of justice must rest on an equally plausible account of coercion. But what account should we opt for, given existing controversies?

To answer this question, we need to reflect on what makes coercion such a controversial notion in the first place. From a liberal perspective, coercion is so normatively laden because it evokes the idea of severe restrictions of persons' freedom (hence autonomy). From a rhetorical point of view, fixing the meaning of coercion helps us identify an array of actions that stand in need of special justification because of the particular effects they have on our ability to formulate and pursue our ends and goals. As David Miller puts it, 'coercion requires a particularly strong form of justification in order to be legitimate'[18] precisely because of its *prima facie* problematic impact on persons' ability to lead autonomous lives. Once we know what counts as coercion, we also know what needs to be assessed in light of particularly stringent moral principles: principles of justice.

If this is why coercion matters, a plausible account of coercion should be capable of capturing all those constraints on freedom that, from a liberal perspective, stand in need of special justification. Of course, commands backed by the threat of sanctions represent an instance of such constraints, but surely one's freedom can be significantly reduced in other ways too. The set of necessary social conditions for someone to lead an autonomous life, that is, one's freedom, can be compromised not only when one is forced to perform

---

[18] David Miller, 'Democracy's Domain', *Philosophy and Public Affairs*, 37 (3) (2009), 201–28, pp. 219–20. Notice that Miller's preferred account of coercion differs from the one I eventually defend. In particular, Miller distinguishes between coercion and prevention, and suggests that only the former needs special justification. Coercion occurs when an agent forces another to perform a *particular* action through commands backed by threats. Prevention occurs when commands backed by threats aim at preventing agents from acting in certain ways. Preventative threats, argues Miller, are much less autonomy-undermining than coercive ones. Is this claim, and the distinction it presupposes, plausible? I believe not. If I am poor and destitute, a law preventing theft undermines my autonomy just as much, if not more, than a law prescribing the payment of taxes. The former involves a preventative threat, the latter a performative one, but I see no morally relevant difference with respect to their impact on persons' autonomy. Perhaps, Miller's distinction is surreptitiously driven by our conviction that most of the state's prohibitions (e.g. on murder, theft, unfair competition, vandalism, injury, and so forth) are in fact morally justified. This, however, is compatible with saying that they stand in need of special justification. For further discussion, see David Miller, 'Why Immigration Controls Are not Coercive: A Reply to Arash Abizadeh', *Political Theory*, 38 (1) (2010), 111–20; and Arash Abizadeh, 'Democratic Legitimacy and State Coercion: A Reply to David Miller', *Political Theory*, 38 (1) (2010), 121–30.

certain actions on pain of sanctions but also when one is deprived of one's possessions[19] or is subject to physical compulsion.[20]

A burglar robbing my home while I am on holiday does not issue would-be coercive proposals, but still causes my freedom to shrink dramatically. There are many opportunities I no longer have, now that my valuables are gone. Why should this restriction of freedom be *prima facie* less problematic than the restriction perpetrated by the head of a hospital ward when he/she urges other doctors to work harder because otherwise they will lose their jobs? What is so special, from a moral point of view, about the latter type of freedom restriction as compared to the former? Even though the *way* the victims' freedom is restricted changes across these two cases, both may plausibly be regarded as instances of freedom restriction standing in need of stringent justification. In other words, both may be seen as belonging to the same set of morally significant social phenomena.

Taking the lead from these observations, in what follows I develop a new, very general account of coercion, according to which coercion encompasses a family of different actions and social relations standing in need of special justification because of their effects on persons' freedom. To develop this account, I start with our common-sense notion of coercion – which I call narrow coercion – and then generalize it.

> **Narrow coercion**: agent A coerces another agent B if A intentionally forces B to do, or to refrain from doing, X through a command backed by the threat of sanctions.

This understanding of coercion underpins our everyday judgements about the coerciveness of the state. On this account of coercion, the state plays the role of the coercer (A), its citizens (or foreigners) that of the coercees (B), and sanctions administered by public officials constitute the means through which the state intentionally restricts persons' freedom. The state thus coerces individuals just as a gunman coerces his victims. The structure of coercion remains the same across the two cases, only its content changes. While the gunman targets innocent bystanders threatening, 'Give me your money, or otherwise I'll kill you', the state targets potential lawbreakers threatening, 'Do not break the law, or otherwise I'll punish you.'[21]

This definition of coercion is 'narrow' in two respects: in its specification of *how* the coercer restricts the coercee's freedom (through intentional commands

---

[19] This is true on the generally plausible assumption that I need material resources to pursue my ends and goals.
[20] Cf. Arthur Ripstein, 'Authority and Coercion', *Philosophy and Public Affairs*, 32 (1) (2004), 2–35, pp. 8ff.
[21] Of course, there is a difference in that, unlike a gunman, the state is a complex *group* agent. See Christian List and Philip Pettit, *Group Agency: The Possibility, Design, and Status of Corporate Agents* (Oxford: Oxford University Press, 2011). I will expand on this later in the chapter.

backed by the threat of sanctions), and in its implicit understanding of *who* – that is, what sort of entity – can play the role of the coercer (i.e. an agent, be it collective or individual). I suggest that, by relaxing each of these conditions, we obtain a more general account of coercion, which captures all those constraints on freedom that ought to be recognized, from a liberal perspective, as needing justification. After developing this account, I shall test its plausibility by considering its implications for the question of domestic egalitarian justice.

6.4 GENERALIZING COERCION I: INTERACTIONAL COERCION

If coercive acts are those that call for special justification because of their freedom-restricting nature, the notion of coercion should be to a large extent insensitive to *how* A restricts B's freedom. All that coercion requires is (*a*) a responsible agent for (*b*) non-trivial constraints on someone else's freedom, (*c*) compared to a suitable baseline. Given these three conditions, we can define coercion between two agents – what I call 'interactional coercion' – as follows.

> **Interactional coercion**: agent A coerces another agent B if A foreseeably and avoidably places non-trivial constraints on B's freedom, compared to B's freedom in the absence of A's intervention (other things being equal).

This definition of coercion generalizes the narrow definition of coercion outlined above. While all occurrences of coercion under the earlier definition also count as occurrences of coercion under this newly developed one, the reverse is not the case. Unlike narrow coercion, interactional coercion does not focus only on those restrictions of freedom that are *intentionally* brought about *through the threat of sanctions*. In the interactional account of coercion, the intentionality condition is replaced with the weaker condition of foreseeability (and avoidability). While it is true that in order to intend something I must also foresee it, the opposite is not the case. Actions may have many foreseeable consequences I do not intend. Similarly, threats of sanctions are replaced with the broader category of constraints on freedom. To be sure, a gunman threatening to kill you unless you act as he commands restricts your freedom. But so does someone who physically forces you to act in particular ways, or who prevents you from accessing certain material resources.

To gain a clearer sense of what actions would count as coercive under the interactional account, we need to examine its component parts or parameters in detail. I will consider each of them in turn.

6.4.1 A Responsible Agent: Individuals and Groups

The first component of my definition – that is, a responsible agent – is necessary for acts of coercion to stand as possible objects of moral appraisal. By an agent, I implicitly mean a moral agent: an agent with the capacity to grasp, and act on, moral reasons and who can therefore bear responsibility for her/his actions. Human beings typically have these capacities while other species do not. For instance, while cats and horses may appropriately qualify as agents, they cannot grasp and act on moral reasons and are therefore not fit for attribution of responsibility. The sense of responsibility I am referring to here is often called 'responsibility as attributability' or 'outcome responsibility'.[22] To say that someone is responsible in this sense is to say that 'for a given action ... it is appropriate to take it as a basis of moral appraisal of that person'.[23] What counts as coercive thus depends on what we can plausibly hold agents responsible for.

In principle, someone is responsible for the consequences of her/his actions so long as they are both foreseeable and avoidable.[24] The existence conditions of responsibility posited here – that is, foreseeability and avoidability – are weaker than intentionality with respect to the consequences of those actions, but stronger than causal responsibility. What we require is for coercers to have a reasonable degree of control and foresight over the consequences in question but not necessarily to intend them.

Merely contributing to the causal chain of events that results in a restriction of a person's freedom does not count as coercion. If I leave my house and lock the door not knowing that my flatmate has forgotten her/his keys, I cannot be accused of coercing her/him. Although she/he is unfree to get in, this is a consequence of my action that I could not have reasonably foreseen.[25] By the same token, if I am an incurable sleepwalker and, while asleep, I go around threatening to beat people up unless they do as I wish, I cannot be said to coerce them. Since I have no control over my actions while sleepwalking, I cannot avoid performing them.

---

[22] I owe the term 'responsibility as attributability' to Thomas M. Scanlon, *What We Owe to Each Other* (Cambridge, MA: Harvard University Press, 1998), ch. 6. The notion of outcome responsibility was originally introduced by Tony Honoré, and further discussed by David Miller in *National Responsibility and Global Justice* (Oxford: Oxford University Press, 2007), ch. 4. See also David Miller's 'Constraints on Freedom', *Ethics*, 94 (1) (1983), 66–86, p. 72.
[23] Scanlon, *What We Owe to Each Other*, p. 248.
[24] I borrow these conditions from Thomas Pogge, who famously argues that the global order harms the poor because it foreseeably and avoidably perpetuates their plight. See Pogge, *World Poverty and Human Rights*.
[25] I am here indebted to David Miller's examples in 'Constraints on Freedom', pp. 70–1. Notice, however, that Miller's account of coercion is different from mine. See footnote 18, ch. 6 above for discussion.

Now consider another scenario. The CEO of a big company fires half of his/her employees. As this will lead to a foreseeable and avoidable curtailment of their freedom, the action of the CEO does count as coercive, and his/her conduct stands in need of stringent justification. While I owe my flatmate no explanation for why I left the house, the CEO owes the employees an explanation for why he/she has fired them.[26] Of course, the CEO might have had good reasons for doing so, in which case his/her action would turn out to be justified. For instance, the employees may have breached the terms of their employment contract, and secretly tried to sabotage the firm they worked for. Or the economy might have taken a bad turn, forcing the CEO to cut costs and dismiss many employees. Assuming no other cost-cutting measures were available, the CEO's actions seem justified. If he/she had done nothing, the company would have gone bankrupt, leaving twice as many people unemployed. The important point is that, whether or not the CEO's actions are justified, given their coercive nature, they stand in need of justice-based assessment.

All the examples offered so far involved individual agents. It is, however, crucial to recognize that certain groups can also bear agential status and thus engage in interactional coercion.[27] The notion of a group agent is a familiar one in ordinary discourse. Firms, associations, and other institutional entities are routinely treated as unitary agents. For instance, when we claim that British Petroleum (BP) is responsible for the recent oil spill in the Gulf of Mexico, we treat the complex organizational apparatus constituting this company as a unitary agent. Similarly, when the IMF is accused of imposing unreasonable conditions on its loans, or when statists claim that the state coerces its citizens, these complex social institutions (the state, and the IMF) are treated as unitary agents.[28]

But when does a collective possess group-agential status? To begin with, the collective must be a group, rather than what Christian List and Philip Pettit call a 'mere collection'.[29] A group differs from collections insofar as its identity does not change with changes in membership. For instance, those in line at a post office counter constitute a mere collection, while the members of a state constitute a group, because states typically maintain their identities relatively independently of the specific people who inhabit them. Italy is Italy no matter who precisely its inhabitants are. Similarly, charities, NGOs, universities, and hospitals exist as groups with a stable identity independently of their specific membership.

---

[26] Of course, libertarians might find this claim implausible. But here, I am only appealing to the moral sensitivities of liberal egalitarians, to whom this book is primarily addressed.

[27] See List and Pettit, *Group Agency*.

[28] See the discussion in Anna Moltchanova, 'Collective Agents and Group Moral Rights', *Journal of Political Philosophy*, 17 (1) (2009), 23–46.

[29] List and Pettit, *Group Agency*, ch. 1.

But when do groups so conceived count as *agents*? Plainly, it is when they are so organized as to meet the general conditions for ascription of agency, namely grasping reasons for action, and acting on their basis.[30] For this to be the case, a group needs to possess sufficiently complex deliberative and decision-making capacities. As I have already mentioned, the complexity of such decision-making capacities varies across agents. While non-human animals can only grasp very basic reasons (e.g. a lion's hunger is a reason for it to attack a gazelle) human beings can engage in highly complex reasoning processes involving prudential, moral, and other kinds of reasons. Unless an agent has these more complex reasoning capacities, it cannot be held responsible for the consequences of its actions. Indeed, even if the lion's attacking the gazelle has foreseeable and avoidable effects on the latter's well-being, we do not take the lion's action to be an appropriate object of moral appraisal.

Groups such as states, universities, churches, and hospitals clearly have a capacity for 'collective will formation' sophisticated enough to warrant attribution of *moral* agency. This, in turn, allows us to hold them responsible for their conduct. The British State, for example, may plausibly be held responsible for the foreseeable and avoidable consequences of the substantial public-sector funding cuts announced in October 2010.[31] Similarly, a particular hospital might be held responsible for the harm caused by its faulty medical procedures, and so forth. All of the aforementioned collectives typically possess complex enough organizational structures, and sufficiently sophisticated decision-making procedures, to qualify as agents, and specifically as moral agents.

To conclude, any instance of interactional coercion requires a moral agent in a position to foresee and avoid the consequences of his/her/its actions. In turn, the agent can be either an individual, or a collective. Not only individuals, but also corporate persons such as firms, multinationals, and states can therefore engage in interactional coercion.

---

[30] See List and Pettit, *Group Agency*, ch. 1. For other accounts of group agency, see Toni Erskine, 'Assigning Responsibilities to Institutional Moral Agents: The Case of States and Quasi-States', *Ethics and International Affairs*, 15 (2) (2001), 67–85, p. 72. Erskine's account in turn draws on Peter French's seminal book *Collective and Corporate Responsibility* (New York: Columbia University Press, 1984). See also Anna Stilz, 'Collective Responsibility and the State', *Journal of Political Philosophy*, 19 (2) (2011), 190–208.

[31] Polly Curtis, 'Budget 2010: Public-sector cuts a "declaration of war", says union', *The Guardian*, 22 June 2010, http://www.guardian.co.uk/uk/2010/jun/22/budget-public-sector-cuts-unions (last accessed 30 October 2011).

6.4.2 Non-trivial Constraints on Freedom

Just like coercion, freedom is a widely debated concept in political philosophy. Some scholars, for instance, define it in terms of non-interference on the part of human agents, others in terms of non-domination. According to freedom as non-interference, an agent is free to the extent that she/he is not interfered with by other agents. One's freedom is thus a function of the opportunities one has available.[32] According to freedom as non-domination or republican freedom, an agent is free to the extent that she/he is not subject to arbitrary power or alien control.[33] So, while for the freedom-as-non-interference theorist a slave whose benevolent master leaves many opportunities open to him/her is relevantly free, for a freedom-as-non-domination theorist he/she is not, because his/her choices are in principle subject to the master's arbitrary power.[34]

Although scholars disagree about the appropriate definition of the concept of freedom, one task that any plausible account of freedom must fulfil is capturing the social conditions for a person to lead an autonomous life. Liberals care so much about freedom because it is a necessary condition for autonomy, and this is reflected in all the above-mentioned accounts of freedom. Lack of opportunities, continued interference in one's affairs, and domination clearly undermine autonomy.

As my aim in this chapter is only to offer a general framework, for the time being, I take no stand on which account of freedom we should endorse.[35] Instead, I limit myself to observing that, in many (but not all) real-world cases, our judgements about freedom and unfreedom – hence about coercion – will converge independently of the particular conception of freedom we employ.

What about the non-triviality condition? Not every restriction of freedom counts as coercive. When evaluating whether an action is coercive, we should set aside *trivial* restrictions of freedom.[36] What counts as trivial is bound to be, to some extent, a matter of debate, but we can again be confident that people's judgements will often converge. For instance, if A and B are both having their tea break and A eats the last remaining biscuit on the table, she/he thereby foreseeably and avoidably deprives B of the opportunity to eat it herself/ himself. Although there is a sense in which A restricts B's freedom, this restriction is so trivial that it should not count as coercive: it can hardly be said to undermine B's autonomy. This is not to say that A's action is beyond

---

[32] See e.g. Isaiah Berlin, *Four Essays on Liberty* (London: Oxford University Press, 1969); and Ian Carter, *A Measure of Freedom* (Oxford: Oxford University Press, 1999).
[33] See Philip Pettit, *Republicanism: A Theory of Freedom and Government* (Oxford: Clarendon Press, 1997).
[34] For an overview of different accounts of freedom, see the contributions in David Miller (ed.), *Liberty* (Oxford: Oxford University Press, 1991).
[35] I shall consider the question of freedom in greater detail in the next chapter.
[36] Cf. Miller, 'Constraints on Freedom', p. 76.

moral assessment. It may be unfair of her/him to take the biscuit (assuming she/he already had her/his fair share). However, by saying that her/his appropriation of the last biscuit is not coercive, the implication is that it is not an appropriate object of justice-based evaluation, where justice is understood politically, as concerning matters apt to fall under the purview of political institutions.[37]

Things would be different if A acted so as to restrict B's access to food, shelter, education, or health care. In that case, A would certainly restrict B's freedom non-trivially, thereby perpetrating an act of coercion. But acts that, by any reasonable standard, only trivially restrict someone's freedom should not count as coercive in the sense we are interested in here.

6.4.3 A Suitable Baseline

Finally, we need to specify the baseline against which to evaluate whether someone's freedom has been restricted. As we already know, such a baseline can be of two kinds: either moralized or non-moralized.[38] On a non-moralized account, the benchmark with respect to which we establish whether there is a restriction of freedom is the expected course of events in the absence of A's (the putative coercer's) intervention. On a moralized account, such a benchmark is the 'morally expected' course of events: the course of events that would occur in a just state of affairs. Which baseline should we opt for? If coercion is to serve as a plausible criterion for the applicability of justice, we should opt for a non-moralized baseline – that is, 'the absence of A's intervention'. Otherwise, we could no longer say that coercion stands in need of justification. Instead, we would have to say that coercion is *always* unjust, and conclude that many acts of what normally qualifies as justified coercion are not coercive at all. So, for instance, on a moralized account of the baseline, a criminal who is sent to jail for a good reason would not be subject to coercion. If putting the criminal in prison is what justice requires, then the restriction of her/his freedom following from her/his imprisonment cannot be regarded as coercive. This will strike many as implausible, and suggests that, in establishing whether coercion has occurred, we should adopt a non-moralized baseline.

To recapitulate, (*a*) a responsible agent, (*b*) non-trivial constraints on freedom, and (*c*) a suitable baseline are the key components of the notion of interactional coercion. As I have shown, this definition substantially generalizes the narrow definition. But it still does not do so enough. Up to now, our account of coercion implicitly assumes that the coercer (A) can only be a

---

[37] Cf. my remarks in Chapter 1, n. 6.   [38] See Anderson, 'Coercion'.

morally responsible agent, individual, or collective. But this condition is too restrictive, because it fails to capture some of those constraints on freedom that are most relevant to the question of justice as this is typically conceived of in the domestic context.

To see this, let us return to the CEO example and focus on the employees' situation after being made redundant following an economic downturn. Assume, for the sake of argument, that they do not benefit from unemployment insurance or public assistance of some other kind. As a result, they have hardly enough to feed their families and are virtually forced to accept any job offer that comes their way, no matter how inequitable it is. This situation is certainly bad, but we have established that the CEO did not behave unjustly. As previously noted, the survival of the firm depended on adopting drastic cost-cutting measures, and letting off a large portion of the employees was the only available option.

From a liberal point of view, however, there is still something *prima facie* problematic if citizens' freedom is, to a large extent, at the mercy of free market processes. Although unconstrained capitalism appears systematically freedom threatening, the perspective of interactional coercion does not allow us to detect such restrictions of freedom as standing in need of justification, because they are not perpetrated by a *single* agent. Indeed, judged by the criteria for group agency I have outlined, 'the market' hardly qualifies as one.

One might object that, in the case under discussion, we can blame the group agent state for citizens' being at the mercy of free market processes.[39] After all, if the state intervened to constrain these processes, the employees' ability to lead autonomous lives would not be so severely undermined. Although this objection appears *prima facie* plausible, there are reasons for doubting its actual bite. If what we are looking at is interactional state coercion, it is unclear how abstention from constraining market processes might be described as an instance of it. The state's *inaction* on a particular matter cannot plausibly qualify as coercive on the interactional account. If while Bob assaults Mary, I stand by doing nothing, there is *no* sense in which I am coercing her. I may be failing to help her, and problematically so, but surely the only coercer here is Bob.

Faced with this reply, one might nevertheless insist that, by enforcing property rights, the state helps to sustain the market. Its agency is therefore implicated in the overall coercive effects of market transactions. This is certainly true, but from this it does not follow that the state bears *full* responsibility for the consequences of market dynamics. Especially in our contemporary world, we are familiar with situations such that, even if the

---

[39] This seems to be the view implicitly defended in Saladin Meckled-Garcia, 'On the Very Idea of Cosmopolitan Justice: Constructivism and International Agency', *Journal of Political Philosophy*, 16 (3) (2008), 245–71.

state were to act, it would not be able to remedy the harmful effects of market processes. There is no sense in which global financial crises like the one erupted in 2007 are a product of state agency alone, and fully under the state's control. The overall freedom-restricting effects of market processes may be partly traced to the actions of the state, but cannot be entirely reduced to them.

If there are coercive phenomena, seemingly standing in need of justification, but which cannot be captured by the notion of interactional coercion, we need to broaden our notion of coercion further. This time, instead of focusing on *how* coercion is performed, we focus on *who*, or rather, *what* can be coercive.

6.5 GENERALIZING COERCION II: SYSTEMIC COERCION

Depending on the nature of the coercer, coercion can be either interactional or systemic. So far, we have discussed interactional coercion, assuming A to be an individual or a group agent. I now turn to the case of systemic coercion, that is, the sort of coercion exercised through a system of formal and/or informal rules, enacted by a sufficient number of agents. On this account, coercion is defined as follows.

> **Systemic coercion**: a system of rules S is coercive if it foreseeably and avoidably places non-trivial constraints on some agents' freedom, compared to their freedom in the absence of that system.

Once again, let me analyse the components of this definition in turn.

6.5.1 A System of Rules

By a system of rules (S) I mean a broad set of phenomena, including formal institutions, informal social practices, stable patterns of interaction, or a combination of these. For instance, complex organizations such as universities and hospitals can be described as systems of rules, but so can more informal social structures, such as families, or markets, that typically combine formal legal regulations, informal social conventions, and regular patterns of interaction. In short, rules may be either formal or informal, they may be officially established, or they may spontaneously emerge from repeated practice, but so long as agents' behaviour follows a recognizably rule-governed pattern, a system of rules can be said to exist.

Even though, as we have seen in the previous section, some systems of rules are complex enough to give rise to group agents, it is crucial to bear in mind that, when discussing systemic coercion, it is on systems of rules *qua* systems that we focus. When a coercive act can be clearly attributed to a unitary agent (whether individual or collective), by contrast, it is an instance of what I have called interactional coercion.

As in the case of individual actions, a system of rules can stand as a possible object of justification only so long as the consequences of its operation are foreseeable and avoidable. But given that a system of rules *qua system* is not an agent – that is, it is not the sort of entity to which responsibility can be attributed – who should be held responsible for the foreseeable and avoidable consequences of its operation? When we come to assess a system of rules, responsibility for its effects is *indirect*: it falls on all those who support the system in question through their actions and behaviour.[40]

Consider, for example, a society with gender-neutral laws, but in which discrimination based on sex is a widespread phenomenon, especially at the workplace. There is a tacit rule, followed by the vast majority of employers in that society, according to which men should always take precedence over women, even when the latter are clearly better qualified than the former. Women's employment opportunities, and life prospects, are therefore much worse than men's.

Even though we can plausibly assume that the practice of discrimination on the basis of sex is appropriately coercive (it restricts women's freedom compared to a plausible baseline – more on which later) and unjustifiably so, we cannot so easily identify who is responsible for it. To be sure, some employers may coerce women interactionally. But notice that, even so, none of them could be individually responsible for the restrictions of freedom systematically suffered by women in general. Moreover, by refusing to offer female candidates a job, most employers will not actually coerce them. As 'unemployment' is the normally expected course of events for women in this sexist society, refusal to employ them does not amount to coercion. Whose fault is it, then?

Responsibility for the sort of indirect systemic coercion occurring within sexist societies falls on *all* those who support the practice of discrimination on the basis of sex.[41] This includes not only employers and professionals who explicitly act in sexually discriminatory ways, but also those who avail themselves of the services of businesses that engage in the relevant practice, thereby contributing to its continued existence. For example, if a particular company does not itself engage in sexual discrimination but its suppliers do, it can

---

[40] This account of responsibility is defended in Pogge, *World Poverty and Human Rights*; and Young, 'Responsibility and Global Justice'. See also Christopher Kutz's notion of 'relational and positional accountability' in *Complicity: Ethics and Law for a Collective Age* (New York: Cambridge University Press, 2000).

[41] Cf. Aaron James, 'Power in Social Organization as the Subject of Justice', *Pacific Philosophical Quarterly*, 86 (1) (2005), 25–49, pp. 43–4.

still be held partly responsible for the effects of this morally unacceptable practice.[42]

The important conclusion to draw from this discussion is that, from a systemic perspective, while coercion occurs through the (more-or-less formal) system of rules governing a particular practice (e.g. sexual discrimination), responsibility for it falls on those who support the system by complying with its rules as well as on those who benefit from the consequences of its operation.[43]

6.5.2 Non-trivial Constraints on Freedom

As participation in a practice requires following its rules, practices inevitably place some constraints on participants' actions. Parallel to the case of interactional coercion, systemic coercion will only exist when practices avoidably and *non-trivially* constrain their members' or other agents' freedom. Judgements about non-triviality have to be made on a case-by-case basis, and there are likely to be reasonable disagreements about what counts as non-trivial. However, we can once again expect these judgements to converge at least in some cases. For instance, if we think of a small tennis club or an amateur cooks' association, we can assume that, no matter what rules apply to them, they do not place significant constraints on anyone's freedom – unless the tennis club and cooks' association are very peculiar ones indeed.[44] By contrast, if we think of the rules governing family structures or market systems, we have every reason to believe that they have a 'deep and pervasive impact' on their members' and (possibly) some third parties' capacities to set and pursue ends for themselves. As such, they appropriately qualify as coercive on the present definition.

6.5.3 A Suitable Baseline

So far, I have spoken about systems of rules placing constraints on freedom, without discussing the relevant baseline with respect to which such constraints should be evaluated. In the case of interactional coercion, the appropriate baseline corresponded to B's freedom in the absence of A's intervention, other

---

[42] Cf. the discussion in Miller, *National Responsibility and Global Justice*, p. 120.

[43] See the discussion of how the global wealthy are appropriately regarded as responsible for the plight of the global poor because they contribute to sustaining, and benefit from, a global institutional system that foreseeably and avoidably harms them. Pogge, *World Poverty and Human Rights*.

[44] Cf. Andrea Sangiovanni, 'Global Justice, Reciprocity, and the State', *Philosophy and Public Affairs*, 35 (1) (2007), 3–39, p. 18.

things being equal. Can a similar baseline be employed in the case of systemic coercion? In principle it can, but at the cost of considerably complicating matters. Envisaging what the world would be like in the absence of a particular system of rules or practice can be an extremely complex task, especially if the system is itself complex and extensive. When this is the case – that is, when the system has a subtle and far-reaching impact on many lives – things are unlikely to remain equal in its absence. This is why there may be more than one plausible account of the relevant baseline.

If S are the rules governing a society, a world without S could be either one containing S' – that is, a different system of rules – or one containing S'', S''', and so forth.[45] Because the relevant counterfactual baseline is likely to be controversial – is it S', S'', or S'''? – some might object that my proposal is very hard, if not impossible, to operationalize. Two points can be made in response. First, the difficulties with my proposal are in principle no different from the difficulties routinely encountered in the evaluation of causal claims in complex social systems. The higher the system's complexity, the harder is the evaluation of the relevant counterfactuals. This, however, does not seem to be a good enough reason to abandon the aspiration of making causal claims in the social sciences, and it is therefore also not a good enough reason to reject my proposal either.

Second, even though counterfactuals are hard to adjudicate, in the last analysis less hinges on them than one might initially think. Independently of what we take to be the relevant baseline, in almost all conceivable cases, some agents' freedom will be greater than under system S; hence, S will turn out to be coercive on the present definition.[46] It is indeed safe to assume that the baseline will *rarely* be one where *everyone* is less free than under the current system. A plausible account of the baseline will be one where some are worse off and others better off. Even if more agents are better off (in terms of freedom) under the current system S than under its relevant counterfactual counterpart S', so long as some of them are better off under S', S counts as coercive. If some agents' freedom is restricted, they are owed a justification as to why the system is designed in the way it is.

This account of coercion is admittedly inclusive, but its inclusiveness simply reflects the plausible idea that, by creating social practices, we *ipso facto* place constraints on one another's freedom. The existence of such practice-mediated constraints on freedom is a by-product of our living in a social world with moderate scarcity. Our lives and actions inevitably place constraints on those

---

[45] Notice that a *completely* anarchical scenario – one without any rules, formal or informal (and not just without S) – would not constitute an appropriate term of comparison. Without any rules enabling agents to form minimally reliable expectations about one another's behaviour, freedom and autonomy are simply impossible.

[46] I am grateful to Christian List and Henry Shue for helping me sharpen this point.

of others. The question we need to ask, then, is whether the way these constraints are crystallized within existing social rules is morally defensible.[47]

Having generalized the narrow definition of coercion, I now test the resulting view, to establish whether it provides a plausible account of the function and conditions of applicability of justice. To do so, I look at two possible interpretations of the type of coercion occurring in the context of domestic societies. The first understands it in terms of interactional coercion on the part of the state, and the second understands it in terms of systemic coercion. If a focus on systemic coercion, independent of its occurring within a group agent, is sufficient to generate concerns of justice at the domestic level, my view will be vindicated.

6.6 SYSTEMIC COERCION AND DOMESTIC JUSTICE

Recall that most contemporary proponents of the coercion view interpret the phenomenon of state coercion as a special instance of interactional coercion, whereby the state plays the role of the coercer (A), its citizens that of the coercees (B), and sanctions administered by public officials constitute the means through which the state foreseeably and avoidably (in fact, intentionally) restricts its citizens' freedom.

On this understanding of state coercion, the state is treated as a full-blown agent, who 'wants' citizens to behave in certain ways and 'pushes them around' to make sure that they do. Of course, the agency of the state is not altogether separate from that of its citizens in that the state is what we have called *a group agent*. As we shall see in the next section, this clearly has implications for the allocation of responsibility for state conduct.[48] Statist proponents of the coercion view, such as Nagel, show some awareness of this.[49] They recognize that responsibility for state coercion, especially in democratic societies, ultimately falls upon citizens and officials, because they are 'joint authors of the coercively imposed system', and not merely subject to its rules. Yet it seems crucial that the rules in question give rise to an agent in its own right, a coercer, acting 'in our name'.[50] Without a coercing agent, putatively acting in

---

[47] Cf. James, 'Power in Social Organization as the Subject of Justice'.
[48] See e.g. Anna Stilz, 'Collective Responsibility and the State'.
[49] Thomas Nagel, 'The Problem of Global Justice', *Philosophy and Public Affairs*, 33 (2) (2005), 113–47, p. 128.
[50] Nagel, 'The Problem of Global Justice', p. 129 says 'The society makes us responsible for its acts, which are taken in our name and on which, in a democracy, we may even have some influence.' Clearly, for the society to be able to 'act', it must constitute an agent in its own right, a group agent. Similarly, Blake, 'Distributive Justice, State Coercion, and Autonomy', p. 287, says 'the state has to offer different guarantees to different persons [i.e. citizens and foreigners], not

our name, and issuing commands backed by the threat of sanctions, there can be no coercion; hence, the question of justice cannot arise in the first place. This, I argue, is a mistake.

The establishment of an institutional apparatus such as the state, whose internal organization warrants the ascription of group agency, is to be seen primarily as a *response* to the systemic, yet lawless, coercion that already exists prior to it.[51] Iterated social interaction gives rise to informal social rules, and foreseeable externalities. In all likelihood, these rules and externalities place constraints on freedom (against a plausible account of the baseline), and thus qualify for justice-based assessment. In turn, their justification requires that they be regulated so as not to infringe on persons' right to freedom, and this can only be achieved by building complex institutional apparatuses such as the state. As we saw in Section 5.5, without strong regulatory capacities, the preservation of persons' freedom over time cannot be guaranteed. Without a system of institutions managing the cumulative effects of market transactions, for example, resource inequalities and power differentials between individuals might become so steep as to compromise the ability of some to lead autonomous lives.[52] The state, or some branches of it, is thus necessary to discharge the duties of justice generated by the existence of more diffuse, informal, unregulated, coercive systems.[53]

This is not to say that the existence of group agents such as states does not *also* trigger duties of justice. Any instance of coercion does, be it channelled through a group agent or not. The important point to emphasize, though, is that principles of egalitarian justice, such as those liberals defend at the domestic level, are triggered by systemic coercion as such, independently of whether this goes along with a complex organizational apparatus constituting a group agent. What matters, from the perspective of systemic coercion, is not that the state is a group agent, but rather that it is the *locus* of relevantly freedom-restricting systems of rules.

To see this, consider a society marked by racial discrimination. Discrimination may not be formally authorized by the law, but simply result from widespread prejudices and informal social rules. These rules are therefore not 'imposed' by the state upon its citizens (just as they were not 'imposed'

---

because it cares more about one set or the other, but because it is doing different things to some [i.e. coercing] – things that stand in need of justification.' This also presupposes an account of the state as an agent in its own right.

[51] Iris Marion Young, 'Responsibility and Global Labor Justice', *Journal of Political Philosophy*, 12 (4) (2004), 365–88, p. 376.

[52] John Rawls, *Political Liberalism* (New York: Columbia University Press, 1996), p. 267, and Ronzoni, 'The Global Order: A Case of Background Injustice?'

[53] Of course, not every state is a just one. That is, not every state succeeds in shaping social interaction in a way that is consistent with persons' right to freedom. However, *state capacities* are necessary to do so. Whether any particular state in fact exercises such capacities in a way consistent with justice is a different question.

by the state in the earlier case involving discrimination on the basis of sex). Against any plausible account of the relevant baseline, these informal social rules would be freedom restricting, hence coercive. Specifically, in the society under consideration, the members of one racial group – for example, African-Americans – are *de facto* second-class citizens. They have much worse educational and employment opportunities than the dominant group – say, whites – and their capacity for autonomy is significantly restricted compared to that of other members. Since our society clearly fails to respect the right to freedom of some of its citizens, from a liberal perspective, it must be condemned as unjust. But who bears responsibility for it?

In our society, there is no specific agent we can point to who can be accused of restricting African-Americans' opportunities. We cannot even point to the state itself as being the *author* of such discrimination, as nothing in its coercive pronouncements (i.e. its laws) mandates these forms of social disadvantage. It is instead a set of informal social rules that causes African-Americans' freedom to shrink (unduly). There is no individual agent who can be said to act in a way that causes such a dramatic restriction in African-American citizens' freedom. If we want to blame someone, we need to look at society as a whole. Since a system of rules is not freestanding, and its existence depends on the compliance or regularly repeated behaviour of a large enough number of individuals, it is ultimately they who bear responsibility for the joint consequences of their actions. In turn, rectifying this sort of injustice will probably require the adoption of a set of state policies and regulations, aimed at compensating for African-Americans' disadvantage. These may include affirmative action programmes, quota systems, additional educational opportunities for those who are discriminated against, and so forth. As this example shows, the availability of a formally coercive group agent can help us *solve* a problem of justice *already* generated by informal, coercive, social rules. The existence of such an agent is not itself *a necessary* trigger of the demands of (egalitarian) justice.

At this point, those endorsing a broadly Rawlsian, basic-structural approach to justice, might be generally sympathetic to my conclusions, namely that the racist society under discussion is unjust, but disagree with the way I propose to attribute responsibility for this injustice. The basic structure, they might argue, *ought* to maintain the social conditions that allow justice to be realized. If justice demands fair equality of opportunity, in a racist society, colour-blind laws will not suffice to put an end to unfair discrimination. This means that, in the case under discussion, primary responsibility for the injustice of society as a whole still falls on 'the basic structure', that is, on its institutions, rather than on its citizens.

There are two things to say in response to this worry. First, even though the notion of the basic structure is hard to define with precision, my sense is that its scope is broader than that of the state, understood as a group agent. For example, it seems perfectly plausible to claim that the basic structure of society has racist elements even if state laws are gender-neutral. Systemically coercive patterns of interaction originating in individual behaviour may belong to the basic structure of society, without thereby also belonging to the state. If I am right about this, then there is no fundamental disagreement between basic-structural views and the account I am proposing. The only difference lies in how the boundaries between different concepts are drawn. While I distinguish between the state as a group agent and systemically coercive dynamics generated by informal patterns of interaction, more orthodox Rawlsian theorists capture both of these phenomena with the broader notion of the basic structure of society.[54]

Second, and more substantively, while I agree that if the state has the capacity to tackle privately generated racial discrimination, it has a duty to do so, I think it is more accurate to conceive of its responsibility in remedial terms.[55] In the example examined, citizens themselves, through their privately unjust behaviour, are *primarily* (or 'outcome') responsible for systemic racial injustice. If they did not behave the way they do, no macro-level injustice would occur.[56] This does not make the state immune from responsibility, of course. If the state *could* remedy such private injustices, and yet failed to do so, it would certainly be acting wrongly. What my perspective allows us to say, though, is that even when the state does not have the capacity to address these injustices, there is still someone responsible for them: those who engage in discriminatory practices. On the view I defend, justice is triggered not only when the state coerces its citizens, or when it has the capacity to compensate for the effects of unjust systemic coercion. Systemic coercion activates demands of justice independently of the presence of a capable state.

To further clarify the implications of the view I am proposing, it might be useful to offer another example. A free capitalist market may be regarded as coercive (against any plausible baseline) and, from a liberal perspective, unjustly so, even if its coercion is not exercised by a single agent. As argued by G. A. Cohen, in a capitalist society, the proletariat is appropriately said to be *forced* (coerced) to sell its labour because the structure of capitalism 'is sustained by a great deal of deliberate human action'.[57] This is not the human action of *individual* capitalists, but of the capitalist 'class' as a whole.

---

[54] I am grateful to Miriam Ronzoni for raising this point. For an insightful discussion of Rawls's basic-structural approach, see her 'What Makes a Basic Structure Just?', *Res Publica*, 14 (3) (2008), 203–18.

[55] For the notion of remedial responsibility, see David Miller, 'Distributing Responsibilities', *Journal of Political Philosophy*, 9 (4) (2001), 453–71.

[56] Cf. also the discussion in G. A. Cohen, 'Where the Action Is: On the Site of Distributive Justice', *Philosophy and Public Affairs*, 26 (1) (1997), 3–30.

[57] G. A. Cohen, 'The Structure of Proletarian Unfreedom', *Philosophy and Public Affairs*, 12 (1) (1983), 3–33, p. 7. See also David Zimmerman, 'Coercive Wage Offers', *Philosophy and Public Affairs*, 10 (2) (1981), 121–45.

Consider, for example, the relation between a particular capitalist employer C and a proletarian worker P. Even though C offers P an underpaid job, *ex hypothesi* P cannot refuse it. Analysed in relation to the relevant counterfactual, that is, a world in which C makes no offer, P cannot be said to be coerced. C's offer enhances, rather than curtails, P's freedom; otherwise, why would P take it in the first place? This interactional perspective is blind to the existence of coercion in the relations *between C and P*.

But if we now take a systemic perspective, we are bound to conclude that capitalists are coercing proletarians through supporting a system of rules that, on any plausible account of the baseline, imposes (unjustifiable) constraints on their freedom. What is (most) troubling in the relations between C and P is that (*a*) P lives under a system that places him in a position such that he has no choice but to accept C's exploitative offer, and (*b*) C shares responsibility for the existence of such a system, to the extent that he contributes to supporting it.

From the perspective of systemic coercion, capitalists can be said to coerce proletarians unjustly even if the rules governing the market system do not form a unified group agent. What is more, regulation on the part of the state represents a *possible solution* to a logically independent problem of justice generated by free market processes. Redistributive schemes, anti-trust laws, and social security measures can all tame the effects of unconstrained market transactions, thus making them compatible with the freedom of all.

This is not to deny that capitalist markets emerged in the context of the modern state, where the capitalist class represented the ruling elite.[58] However, what goes hand in hand historically (capitalism and the state) need not go hand in hand conceptually. That is, the fact that free market capitalism existed *within* the context of modern states is not *conceptually* relevant to the question of whether the market system itself should be placed under justice-based assessment.[59] Market processes that are not encapsulated in, and sustained by, a unitary group agent like the state (think of international market processes, for example) are just as much in need of justification, insofar as they constitute systems of rules placing non-trivial constraints on agents' freedom.[60] To be sure, the agency of different states might be implicated in these processes, but it will certainly not account for all of them. The international economy goes well beyond the actions of specific agents, encompassing states, corporations, individuals, and international organizations.

---

[58] In fact, Cohen himself points this out.

[59] To be sure, this historical truth will probably have an impact on our assessment of how responsibility for this kind of injustice should be distributed, as explained in the following section.

[60] See Aaron James, 'Distributive Justice without Sovereign Rule: The Case of Trade', *Social Theory and Practice*, 31 (4) (2005), 533–59, pp. 555ff.

In short, whenever systemic coercion exists, principles of socio-economic justice much like those we encounter at the domestic level apply, independently of whether they are encapsulated in a group agent. In many cases, the justification of systemic coercion, and the rectification of the problems of justice it gives rise to, will require formal regulation through complex institutional apparatuses, often giving rise to collective agents, of which the state is one prominent example.

6.7 RESPONSIBILITY FOR COERCION

Before concluding, we need to take a closer look at how responsibility for coercion might be attributed when coercion is perpetrated by collectives, be they group agents, or more loosely connected sets of individuals. Even though I have already suggested that collectives are suitable bearers of responsibility, holding their members responsible for things they did not individually bring about, and over which they had no 'individual' control, might seem dubious and unfair. Is it plausible to hold citizens responsible for what their states do, given that they have no choice but to belong to them? Does it make sense to hold an individual responsible for systemic coercion even if opting out of the relevant system of rules is not an option, and even if her/his contribution is not strictly necessary for the relevant freedom restrictions to occur? To answer these questions, I first briefly consider the principles governing the attribution of responsibility to individuals, and then investigate whether similar principles can plausibly apply, *mutatis mutandis*, to collectives.

6.7.1 Individual Responsibility

Earlier in our discussion, we saw that a person is 'outcome-responsible' for something (also 'responsible' for short) when we can think of her/him as the 'author' of certain foreseeable and avoidable outcomes. One may be causally responsible for producing particular outcomes, but to the extent that the outcomes are not under one's control, one's agency is not involved in a way that matters for attribution of responsibility. When the conditions for responsibility so understood are satisfied by a particular agent, it is usually appropriate to let him reap the benefits, or bear the costs, associated with the outcomes generated.[61] For example, if thanks to his hard work Richard obtains good grades in his final exams, he is responsible for this outcome, and entitled to

---

[61] See the discussion of 'outcome responsibility' in Miller, *National Responsibility and Global Justice*, ch. 4. In developing these thoughts, I have also benefitted from the discussions in Young,

harvest the benefits following from it (e.g. better employment opportunities). If, on the other hand, Daniel is lazy and refuses to study, it seems appropriate to let him bear the costs of his shamefully bad grades.

When the outcomes produced are relevant to the performance of a duty to others, responsibility typically goes hand in hand with moral blameworthiness (or praiseworthiness). The greater the involvement of one's agency is in bringing about morally salient outcomes, the greater one's responsibility and blameworthiness (or praiseworthiness) are. For instance, while we all have a stringent moral duty not to injure others, our responsibility and level of blameworthiness for breaching it depend on the extent to which our agency is involved in causing injuries to others. If, say, Connie shoots Carl in the leg, she violates her duty not to harm and is responsible as well as blameworthy for wounding him. However, her blameworthiness is greater if she deliberately shoots him than if she merely accidentally does so. Her agency is clearly more deeply involved in the production of the relevant outcome in the former case than in the latter. Similarly, if Sarah neglects to look after her children, and they hurt themselves as a result, she is clearly responsible, and blameworthy. But her responsibility and blameworthiness for this outcome would be even greater if she had actively contributed to bringing it about, for instance, by deliberately injuring her kids.

In the present context, the duties of interest to us are duties of justice. On my account, these duties forbid individuals from placing, or contributing to placing, unjustifiable constraints on others' freedom. *One's outcome responsibility for justice, then, depends on the extent to which one's agency is involved in placing morally objectionable constraints on the freedom of others.*[62] The greater the involvement is of one's agency, the greater one's responsibility (and blameworthiness) is. For example, if in breach of a contract we both signed, I refuse to give you a thousand pounds in exchange for your services, I thereby foreseeably and avoidably place non-trivial constraints on your freedom, compared to a counterfactual scenario in which I honour my duties. If, however, it turns out that my refusal to pay you is the result of duress – say I have encountered sudden financial difficulties – my responsibility and blameworthiness are instantly reduced. I have excuses, and the involvement of my agency in failing to meet my duties is not as significant as it would have been had I refused to pay you out of self-interest. While in the former case my intensions are 'pure' but my circumstances harsh, in the latter I am acting out of the wrong intentions.

'Responsibility and Global Justice', pp. 116–18; and Robert E. Goodin, 'Apportioning Responsibilities', *Law and Philosophy*, 6 (2) (1987), 167–85.

[62] Of course, there may be agents, such as the state, that also have special, remedial, responsibilities for justice. But it is on primary, outcome, responsibilities that I focus here.

Even though ascertaining individual responsibility in specific cases may be extremely difficult, the practice of attributing responsibility to individuals is generally regarded as sound. By contrast, the practice of ascribing responsibility to collectives is rather controversial. Because, as we have seen, collectives play a key role in our thinking about the function and conditions of applicability of justice, we cannot sidestep the question of whether and, if so, how responsibility should be attributed to them. In the present context, two types of collectives are of significance: group agents (such as the state) and sets of individuals participating in systemic coercion.

6.7.2 Responsibility for Interactional Coercion by Group Agents

Let us begin by considering a real-world example of unjustifiable interactional coercion on the part of a group agent. The example I have in mind is the Deepwater Horizon incident, allegedly caused by the company British Petroleum (BP) in the Spring of 2010. Deepwater Horizon was an offshore drilling platform, located in the Gulf of Mexico, owned by the company Transocean and operated by BP. On 20 April 2010, gases released from an exploratory well provoked an explosion leading to the death of eleven platform workers, and to a massive oil spill causing severe environmental and economic damage to the Gulf coast.

In the beginning of September 2010, BP eventually admitted to being (partially) responsible for the incident. According to the company's and other investigations, the catastrophe was the result of a sequence of 'mistakes': engineers misread pressure indicators; managers took risky decisions concerning the design of the well; the company invested too little in safety measures; and so forth.[63] Had these and other mistakes not been made, the disaster could have been avoided.

As is easy to imagine, the different companies involved in the incident have tried to shift responsibility and blame onto one another.[64] For the sake of simplicity, however, let us assume that the incident was caused by BP alone. Even though BP did not intend to cause the oil spill (thereby massively shrinking the freedom of those living in the affected areas), *its* agency was heavily involved in it. As BP qualifies as a group agent, on the view defended here, it is appropriate to hold *it* and, indirectly, its members, responsible for the resulting harm.

---

[63] Graeme Wearden, 'BP to admit partial blame for Deepwater oil spill', *The Guardian*, 8 September 2010, http://www.guardian.co.uk/business/2010/sep/08/bp-deepwater-report (last accessed 31 October 2011).

[64] Damian Carrington, 'BP oil spill report lists series of failures – mostly by others – that led to disaster', *The Guardian*, 8 September 2010, http://www.guardian.co.uk/environment/2010/sep/08/bp-oil-spill-failures (last accessed 31 October 2011).

But 'why is this so?' an objector might ask. After all, only a subset of individuals were involved in the causal chain of events that culminated in the disaster, including those engineers who misread pressure indicators, and those managers who took risky decisions concerning the design of the well. Should we not blame and place responsibility only on them? Wouldn't we otherwise let other, 'innocent', members of the group (e.g. shareholders) bear the costs of outcomes for which they are not personally responsible?

Even though attributing responsibility to the group and, derivatively, to its members might seem *prima facie* unfair, on reflection, it is not. Despite not being personally responsible for the disaster, by voluntarily joining a particular company, shareholders both benefit from its gains and make themselves liable to paying a price for the company's mistakes.[65] Their responsibility rests on their membership in, and support for, the group agent that has culpably caused a harmful outcome.[66] Their agency is partly constitutive of the agency of the group. Although they are not responsible or culpable *as individuals*, they are liable to paying the costs associated with their participation in the group agent, and share in the blame that is appropriately cast on it.

Not only is the attribution of responsibility to the group as a whole morally legitimate, but the opposite strategy of blaming only those who were personally involved in the incident would lead to great unfairness. Those who misread the pressure indicators, or took risky decisions, are undoubtedly to blame and should pay for their mistakes. But can we hold them responsible for the billions of dollars of damages caused by the oil spill? Surely, we cannot think that someone who has merely misread a pressure indicator is as responsible and blameworthy as a terrorist who has killed eleven people and caused severe environmental and economic damage. Moreover, holding only a few people responsible would be insulting towards the victims of the incident, who could never obtain adequate compensation for the harms suffered. No matter how harsh the sanctions on those personally involved are, it would simply be impossible to extract adequate compensation from them. In short, by refusing to place responsibility on the group agent as a whole, we would make a few individuals pay too much, and yet let victims receive too little.[67]

That said, it seems crucial for the attribution of responsibility to members of group agents that membership can be regarded as voluntary. Only then, one might argue, can we think of their agency as being genuinely implicated in that

---

[65] On this, I have learnt from Stilz, 'Collective Responsibility and the State', pp. 194–5; and Miller, *National Responsibility and Global Justice*, ch. 4.

[66] List and Pettit helpfully distinguish between: (*a*) enactor responsibility; and (*b*) member responsibility in relation to group agents. In the case at hand, shareholders may not be regarded as having enactor responsibility, but certainly have member responsibility. See *Group Agency*, ch. 7.

[67] See the discussion of what List and Pettit call 'responsibility gaps' in *Group Agency*, ch. 7.

of the collective. This is indeed the case for most corporations, associations, and organizations. Shareholders voluntarily join them and know that, in so doing, they accept certain benefits as well as the risk of incurring certain costs. But voluntary membership is hardly ever a feature of the group agents that are of most interest to us: states. How can we plausibly hold citizens responsible for the acts of their states if their membership is not voluntary? It might make moral sense to hold shareholders of a multinational partly responsible for its deeds, but if the shareholders had no choice but to support the multinational, if they were forced to buy shares, would the same conclusion follow? It would seem not.

How, then, can we hold citizens responsible for the actions performed by their states? To answer this question we need to go back to the liberal hypothetical consent approach canvassed earlier in the book. As we saw in Chapter 1, and subsequent chapters, even though individuals cannot actually consent to all aspects of the social arrangements they are subject to (e.g. they cannot consent to state membership), these aspects are morally justified to the extent that they satisfy a hypothetical consent test. If a state is one that could be in principle acceptable to all citizens living under it – by virtue of its particular distribution of freedom – then we may regard *all* citizens, just like members of a corporation, as collectively responsible for its acts. Even though they do not actually consent to living in a state, they have *reason* to do so; hence, their agency is appropriately seen as implicated in the actions performed by the group agent. They obtain certain benefits from the state, they support its structure, and are therefore partly liable for its mistakes.[68]

Of course, this is not true of citizens of oppressive states, who have no reason to consent to state laws and policies. In those circumstances, instead of members of the relevant group agent, citizens are best seen as victims of its unjustified coercion. Consider, for example, the position of Jews in Nazi Germany. It would clearly be absurd to hold them responsible, *qua* members of the Nazi state, for the atrocities perpetrated by the Third Reich.[69] But when states are reasonably just, when the distribution of freedom they engender is in principle acceptable to all citizens, citizens are rightly regarded as partly responsible for the state's acts. Their specific degree of responsibility will depend on the particular position they occupy within the state. The more powerful they are, the more they benefit from participating in the state, the more responsibility they bear for the state's acts.

---

[68] Anna Stilz puts forward a similar argument, inspired by Kant's political writings and to which my discussion is indebted, in her 'Collective Responsibility and the State', p. 199. See also David Miller, who suggests that participants in a group engaged in a cooperative enterprise are responsible for what the group does, provided cooperation is fair. *National Responsibility and Global Justice*, pp. 119ff.

[69] Miller, *National Responsibility and Global Justice*, p. 132.

The Function of Justice: Assessing Coercion 151

In sum, group agents can be held responsible for the consequences of the actions they perform. In turn, this collective responsibility indirectly falls on their members, provided they have *voluntarily* joined the group, or that even though their membership is not *de facto* voluntary, they have *reason* to consent to it. But how are we to conceive of responsibility for outcomes produced by a multiplicity of agents who *do not* give rise to a higher-level group agent?

6.7.3 Shared Responsibility for Systemic Coercion

The logic that allows us to attribute responsibility for unjust interactional coercion to a group agent is, as we have seen, a familiar one. We focus on a particular action, or set of actions, performed by the agent itself, that can be easily linked to particular freedom-restricting effects. Depending on the magnitude of the effects, and the nature of the involvement of the group's agency in bringing them about (e.g. Were they merely foreseeable? Were they intended?), we assign responsibility (and blame) to it. At a second stage, we then consider how responsibility should be apportioned among the group's members.

This way of assigning responsibility works for group agents, but is ill-suited to conceptualize responsibility for systemic coercion. When coercion is systemic, there is no single agent to whom we can assign responsibility for a specific outcome. Instead, we have a multiplicity of actions that, together, contribute to foreseeable and avoidable ongoing restrictions of freedom. Connecting each action to the relevant effects is virtually impossible.[70]

Consider, once again, the case of an unconstrained capitalist market system, under which some are left poor and destitute. We can safely complain that, in this scenario, the poor and destitute are suffering injustice: the distribution of freedom within society is certainly one they could not possibly consent to. As we already saw, however, blaming the state as uniquely responsible for this injustice would not be appropriate. While the state might be partly implicated in this form of coercion, for example by enforcing property rights, it cannot plausibly be seen as solely (outcome) responsible for it. To a large extent, the main coercer is the market system itself.

If not (only) the state, who should we regard as being responsible for perpetrating these injustices, given that the market does not exhibit agential features? Plainly, those who participate in the market system and thereby help sustain it. Producers and consumers, employees and CEOs. In the words of Iris Young, in cases like this, individuals bear responsibility 'because they

---

[70] See Young, 'Responsibility and Global Justice'.

contribute by their actions to the processes that produce unjust outcomes. [Their] responsibility derives from belonging... in a system of interdependent processes of cooperation and competition through which [they] seek benefits and aim to realize projects'.[71] By virtue of sustaining a system of rules leading to foreseeable and avoidable unjust outcomes, individuals share responsibility for its effects. None of them is uniquely responsible for the harm caused, but neither is there a group agent we can hold responsible and blame for it. Responsibility is therefore most straightforwardly traceable to the multiplicity of individuals who fuel the processes in question.

An objector might again wonder whether holding individuals responsible in this way is ultimately unfair. After all, it is virtually impossible for anyone not to participate in the market system. Not sustaining the market in some way or other is simply not an option. Moreover, no individual could avert the entire harm caused by that system. Under these circumstances, how can we possibly hold individuals, who do not have a choice, responsible for the effects of market dynamics?

Just as in the case of coercion on the part of the group-agent state, to respond to this worry we need to invoke the idea of hypothetical consent. The poor and destitute within the market system would have no reason to accept the way it is currently structured. Holding *them* responsible, therefore, would indeed make little sense.[72] They are the victims, rather than the agents, of market-based coercion. But there are many others, capitalists, CEOs, bankers, middle-class professionals, and so forth who clearly unfairly benefit from the system and have self-interested reasons to support it. This being the case, it seems appropriate to hold *them* responsible for the harmful consequences of market transactions. So long as they do whatever is reasonably within their power to compensate for such harmful consequences, they are responsible but not blameworthy (as they do not have a choice but to participate in the said processes); if they fail to compensate for them, they are also liable to being blamed.[73]

This, of course, does not mean that all those who support (rather than being the 'victims' of) a certain system of rules have exactly the same responsibilities as everyone else with regard to its effects. One's degree of responsibility will depend on the particular position one occupies within the system, and on the contribution of one's agency to it. Plausibly, the owner of a large and successful firm has greater responsibility for the morally problematic effects brought

---

[71] Young, 'Responsibility and Global Justice', p. 119. Young makes these remarks in relation to what she calls the 'social connection model of responsibility'. Her idea of social connection and her understanding of the social structures that give rise to concerns of justice have elements in common with the idea of systemic coercion.

[72] Notice that Young disagrees on this point. For her, even the victims of structural injustice may be regarded as responsible for it. See 'Responsibility and Global Justice', p. 123.

[73] Miller, *National Responsibility and Global Justice*, p. 122.

about by the market system than the owner of a small family business. The point, however, is that as no one's actions, taken in isolation, could bring about the relevant outcomes, responsibility for them is *shared* among those who support the system, and have reason for doing so.[74]

Quantifying the degree of responsibility of each individual and, more importantly, identifying what each ought to do in order to rectify the injustices she/he has contributed to are extremely complex issues, indeed issues that cannot be resolved in the abstract. To address them properly, we need to look at each person's position within the relevant system of rules, consider what actions are available to her/him, and what she/he could possibly do in order to improve the unjust situation that she/he contributes to create. This renders duties of redress for participation in unjust systemic coercion necessarily *imperfect in kind*: their content and mode of performance are, to some extent, up to the agent's own evaluations.

While, in a social system characterized by free market processes such as the one we are considering, it is fair to say that the rights to freedom of the destitute are being underfulfilled (given that the system is unjust), there is no specific individual whose actions can be causally connected to the rights underfulfilments suffered by any specific person – which is why I talk about underfulfilments rather than violations.[75] Similarly, it is equally difficult to determine with precision what one ought to do in order to rectify them. For example, rectification might involve campaigning for greater market regulation on the part of the state, raising awareness among colleagues, trying to improve the conditions of some of the worse-off people by donating to charities.[76] Indeed, holding on to the resources accumulated through unjust market transactions is equivalent to perpetuating injustice.

Even though the responsibilities falling on individuals by virtue of their participation in systemic coercion are fluid and difficult to define in detail, this does not detract from the fact that they are stringent, justice-based, ones. If they are not respected, one can be appropriately accused of failing to honour stringent duties of justice, and hence other people's rights, even if the link between right-holders and duty-bearers is a loose one.[77]

---

[74] For the notion of shared responsibility, see Larry May, *Sharing Responsibility* (Chicago: University of Chicago Press, 1992), ch. 2.

[75] For the notion of underfulfilment, see Chapter 5, pp. 110ff.

[76] Crucially, without thereby however fooling oneself into thinking that the grounds for so donating are charitable ones, rather than justice-based.

[77] This is contrary to the Kantian dogma that duties of justice are necessarily perfect in kind, that is, their content and mode of performance are fully specified. Those who are attached to this dogma (not everyone is) will find my conclusion too brisk. Why should we not stick to the Kantian dogma? The reason is simple: doing so would lead us to conclusions that clash with our most deeply held convictions about justice. Most duties of justice can only be perfect when institutions precisely allocate them. But what if institutions are defective and *fail* properly to allocate them? In this case, insisting that duties of justice can only be perfect implies denying the

6.8 CONCLUSION

In this chapter, I have argued that a coercion-based outlook on justice cannot plausibly be grounded in the narrow account of coercion implicitly defended by statists, but is much better developed on the basis of the multifaceted conceptual framework I have presented. This framework meets the desideratum of capturing the multiplicity of constraints on freedom which, from a liberal perspective, need justification. As the normative significance of coercion stems from its association with potentially problematic restrictions of freedom, confining coercion to restrictions occurring through threats is unduly limiting. The range of potentially problematic restrictions of freedom is much wider than that.

For instance, a person's ability to pursue her/his ends and goals is severely limited not only when she/he is forced to act in a particular way at pains of sanctions but also when she/he is robbed of all her/his possessions, or is subject to physical compulsion. This wide variety of potentially problematic constraints on freedom is fully captured by my proposal to consider coercion as indicating a family of phenomena, including narrow, interactional and systemic coercion. While in so doing we can still distinguish between different *types of coercion*, depending on *how* they restrict freedom, we no longer run the risk of confining weighty justificatory demands only to some, but not all, potentially problematic constraints on freedom.

Moreover, my coercion-based conceptual framework enables us to see that principles of justice such as those typically defended by liberal-egalitarians in the domestic context are normatively relevant even prior to the existence of the state. An all-encompassing group agent issuing commands backed by the threat of sanctions is not a necessary condition for the applicability (as opposed to the realizability) of justice. For justice to apply, we only need a system of rules placing non-trivial constraints on freedom. This will obviously have important implications for the question of global justice since, at the global level, there are complex systems of rules, but there is no overarching global Leviathan. Before moving on to the question of global justice, however, we need to gain a better sense of what, exactly, counts as a constraint on freedom, and of what type of social order could be seen as respecting persons' right to freedom.

---

existence of any such duties. But this conclusion is surely implausible. When institutions fail to allocate justice-based responsibilities, justice is still very much operative, and presumably demands institutional reform. For further discussion, see Henry Shue, 'Mediating Duties', *Ethics*, 98 (4) (1988), 687–704; and Laura Valentini, 'Justice, Charity, and Misery: What, if Anything, Is Owed to Haiti?' (manuscript).

disagreement about which economic inequalities are compatible with the right to freedom. I therefore conclude that, on the approach I defend, we cannot develop a conclusive theory of what economic justice positively requires, but should limit ourselves to identifying what it must exclude. Whether, beyond a relevant threshold, economic inequality is justified, and to what extent, is a contextual and controversial matter, which is best settled by each society's free and fair decision-making processes.

The chapter is structured as follows. In Section 7.2, I defend the notion of freedom as independence, and show that it better captures the necessary social conditions for autonomy than rival views. In Section 7.3, I examine the difficulties involved in constructing an appropriate metric of freedom so understood, and explain why these difficulties should not excessively worry us in the present context. In Section 7.4, I consider the implications of this particular account of freedom for the coercion-based conceptual framework developed in Chapter 6. In Section 7.5, I turn to its implications for justice. I offer a sketch of what a reasonably just society, one whose distribution of freedom is universally justifiable to its members, would look like, and suggest that whether a just distribution requires full-blown economic equality is a largely context-dependent matter. On the view I defend, economic inequality is justified so long as it is in principle compatible with a mutually acceptable distribution of freedom. Once again, my discussion is set against the familiar background of domestic politics. I shall consider the implications of my view for the question of global justice in the next chapter.

7.2 FREEDOM AS INDEPENDENCE

Let me start by recalling that the reason why liberals care about freedom lies in the role freedom plays in enabling people to lead autonomous lives. In order for a person to be able to exercise her/his capacity for autonomy, both natural and social conditions have to be met.[1] From a natural point of view, a person must possess the necessary mental and physical abilities. From a social point of view, she/he must be reasonably free from others' interference. By focusing on the *social* determinants of autonomy only, freedom is a necessary (but not a sufficient) condition for persons to live autonomously.

However, it is important to note that the social determinants of autonomy may have greater impact on persons' ability to lead autonomous lives than normally appreciated, for they include not only resource holdings but also the

---

[1] Cf. the discussion in Joseph Raz, *The Morality of Freedom* (Oxford: Oxford University Press, 1986), pp. 372ff.

7

The Content of Justice: Freedom and Equality

7.1 INTRODUCTION

In Chapter 6, I have developed a novel account of the function and conditions of applicability of justice in general, and egalitarian justice in particular. I have suggested that concerns of justice arise in the presence of coercion, be it interactional (exercised by an agent) or systemic (occurring through a system of rules). Central to my definitions of coercion and justice is the idea of freedom. Coercion, I have argued, always involves a non-trivial restriction of one or more agents' freedom, while justice demands that the distribution of freedom within a particular social system be in principle acceptable to all of its members. Only when the distribution of freedom meets this mutual acceptability requirement, members' right to freedom is respected.

But what is freedom? My aim in the present chapter is to answer this question, thereby further developing my accounts of both coercion and, crucially, justice. Combining insights from both the liberal and the republican tradition, I argue that a person's freedom is a function not only of the number and quality of the options she/he can take advantage of but also of their 'robustness'. On this account of freedom, which I call *freedom as independence*, someone who enjoys access to many valuable opportunities, but only thanks to the generosity of the most powerful, is not fully free to take advantage of them. Her/his ability to pursue her/his ends and goals is ultimately dependent on others' will.

This account of freedom has important implications for how we understand the value of economic equality. Whereas, as we have seen so far, for many liberal-egalitarians economic equality is a *fundamental* demand of justice, on my view, it is not. Economic inequalities, I argue, are unjust only to the extent that they violate persons' right to freedom, by leading to social oppression. Some such inequalities clearly have this effect, for instance, when the worse off are poor and destitute, but it is not obvious that others also have. Once a relevant sufficiency threshold has been met, there is bound to be reasonable

effects that resource holdings have on our mental and physical abilities.[2] Poverty, for instance, may easily lead to physical and psychological damage. Similarly, oppression undermines persons' ability to lead autonomous lives not only by making many 'external' options unavailable but also by affecting victims' psychology: the oppressed are prone to developing adaptive preferences, thereby losing the disposition genuinely to choose for themselves. In short, even though genetics and nature play a part in determining our fate, our ability to lead autonomous lives is to a great extent dependent on our social environment, and hence on our freedom.

The idea of freedom so understood can be variously interpreted. As anticipated in Chapter 6, freedom is an 'essentially contested concept', object of intense debate among philosophers. For the sake of simplicity, I focus on two possible, and popular, interpretations of this notion: what we might call freedom as option-availability and freedom as independence. In the main text, I do not delve into the complexities of the by-now extremely rich debate on freedom. Details that are not essential for my purposes, but probably of interest to those familiar with the literature on freedom, are discussed in notes.

Freedom as *option-availability*, as the name suggests, holds that a person's overall freedom is a function of the options she/he can choose from without being subject to others' interference. Put metaphorically, this view says that the extent of a person's freedom is determined by the set of 'open doors' she/he can walk through unhindered by others.[3]

This approach can take different forms, depending on what aspects of persons' options are deemed relevant to the evaluation of how free they are. For instance, some might think that persons' freedom is a function of the sheer *number* of options open to them: the more options they have, the more free they are.[4] In terms of our metaphor, on this purely *quantitative* account of freedom, the extent of one's freedom is entirely determined by *how many*

---

[2] Thomas W. Pogge, 'A Critique of the Capability Approach', in H. Brighouse and I. Robeyns (eds.), *Measuring Justice. Primary Goods and Capabilities* (Cambridge: Cambridge University Press, 2010), 17–60, p. 28.

[3] This is a broad characterization of the so-called 'negative', as opposed to positive, conceptions of freedom. While negative freedom focuses on non-interference, positive freedom focuses on self-realization or self-mastery. The latter account of freedom is typically considered inimical to an overall liberal moral outlook, which is why I shall not discuss it here. For the distinction between positive and negative freedom, see Isaiah Berlin, 'Two Concepts of Liberty', in his *Four Essays on Liberty* (Oxford: Oxford University Press, 1969); and Ian Carter, 'Positive and Negative Liberty', in Edward N. Zalta (ed.), *The Stanford Encyclopedia of Philosophy* (Fall 2008 edition), http://plato.stanford.edu/archives/fall2008/entries/liberty-positive-negative/. Berlin famously uses the 'open doors' metaphor. For a discussion of what I call freedom as option-availability, see also S. I. Benn and W. L. Weinstein, 'Being Free to Act, Being a Free Man', *Mind*, 80 (318) (1971), 194–211; and W. A. Parent, 'Freedom as the Non-Restriction of Options', *Mind*, 83 (331) (1974), 432–4.

[4] A particularly sophisticated version of this view is defended by Ian Carter in *A Measure of Freedom* (Oxford: Oxford University Press, 1999).

doors one can walk through, independently of the particular opportunities they give access to.

Alternatively, one might believe that only the *quality* of one's options matters: there is a difference between the freedom to dine at expensive restaurants and the freedom to practice one's religion.[5] On this second understanding of freedom as option-availability, the latter type of option would be considered more relevant to one's overall freedom than the former. Dining at expensive restaurants might be a pleasant experience, but it is arguably not as crucial to the pursuit of one's ends and goals as practicing one's religion. We would probably judge a society in which everyone can dine at expensive restaurants, but nobody can practice their religion, as less free than one in which expensive restaurants are unavailable, but freedom of religion is protected. The motivation behind this type of judgement is well captured by Charles Taylor, who locates the importance of freedom in our being purposive, autonomous agents. The more a particular opportunity is key to the fulfilment of our purposes, the more it contributes to our overall freedom, and the more free we are.[6]

Finally, we might take the – I believe more plausible – view that one's freedom is determined by a combination of both the quantity and the quality of available options.[7] That is, we might think that freedom is two-dimensional, and that a person's overall freedom is given by the weighted number of the options open to her. Every option will contribute to determining that person's freedom, but some (the most valuable ones) will count more than others. This is because even options that have very little value *per se* matter to some degree, as the presence of options is itself a necessary social condition for autonomy. To be an autonomous agent, I must be in a position to choose, and learning to

---

[5] On this, see Matthew H. Kramer, *The Quality of Freedom* (Oxford: Oxford University Press, 2003).

[6] Cf. Charles Taylor, 'What's Wrong with Negative Liberty?', in his *Philosophy and the Human Sciences* (Cambridge: Cambridge University Press, 1985), pp. 211–29. See also Amartya Sen, 'Welfare, Preference, and Freedom', *Journal of Econometrics*, 50 (1/2) (1991), 15–29, on the need to take individual preferences seriously when measuring freedom. Theorists like Ian Carter claim that our judgements can be explained solely by appeal to quantitative considerations because 'important' freedoms also give us access to more actions. Since freedom of religion (allegedly) gives us access to more actions than the freedom to dine at expensive restaurants, we can explain why the former freedom contributes more to one's overall freedom than the latter simply by reference to quantitative considerations. See Carter, *A Measure of Freedom*, p. 140. While I concede that judgements such as the one about freedom of religion versus the freedom to dine at expensive restaurants are also consistent with a purely quantitative approach to freedom, I am not persuaded that such an approach correctly *explains* them. Intuitively, freedom of religion matters more than the freedom to dine at expensive restaurants not because of how many actions it allows one to perform, but because of *how important those actions are* to one's plan of life. For a thorough critique of the purely quantitative view see Kramer, *The Quality of Freedom*, ch. 5.

[7] This is what Ian Carter calls the 'hybrid' approach to freedom. See his *A Measure of Freedom*, pp. 135ff. See also David Miller, 'Constraints on Freedom', *Ethics*, 94 (1) (1983), 66–86, p. 67. For a defence of this approach, see Kramer, *The Quality of Freedom*.

discriminate between good and bad options is therefore something I have reason to value.[8]

Even though these three approaches (quantitative, qualitative, and 'mixed') clearly differ from one another, what unites them all is the belief that a person's freedom is a function of the options open to her/him because of others' non-interference *in the actual world*. For proponents of freedom as option-availability, for example, I am free to go to the cinema so long as I am not prevented from performing this action by some other agent. The reason *why* I am not prevented from performing this action has no bearing on the question of whether I am free to perform it.

This interpretation of the notion of freedom can be contrasted with the view that freedom consists in being *independent* of other persons' choices. On this view – which owes much, but is not identical, to the republican idea of freedom as non-domination (more on this later)[9] – the more my life prospects and decisions are vulnerable to the choices of other people, the more I qualify as unfree. My freedom is not just a function of my 'sphere of agency', of the options actually available to me, but it depends also on the reasons *why* my sphere of agency is shaped in the way that it is. A world where you enjoy (a reasonable degree of) freedom as independence 'must be a non-interference world...not by accident, but by virtue of your being secured against the powerful'.[10]

Consider again the 'cinema' example. On the option-availability view of freedom, I am free to go to the cinema so long as no one actually interferes with my performing the relevant action.[11] There may be very many reasons why I am not interfered with. For instance, I may be free to go to the cinema because I have enough money to pay for a ticket, or I may be 'free' because, although I cannot afford a ticket, the manager of the cinema is kind enough to let me in. On the option-availability account of freedom, I am just as free to go to the cinema in the second scenario as I am in the first. On the freedom as independence view, I am not. For proponents of this view, my freedom is

---

[8] See Carter, *A Measure of Freedom*, p. 64.

[9] Philip Pettit, *Republicanism: A Theory of Freedom and Government* (Oxford: Clarendon Press, 1997). Another prominent contemporary proponent of republicanism is Quentin Skinner. See e.g. his *Liberty before Liberalism* (Cambridge: Cambridge University Press, 1998). In this chapter, my characterization of republicanism will exclusively draw on Pettit's work. As I have mentioned in the main text, the notion of freedom as independence, which is partly inspired by Kant's political writings, has much in common with the idea of freedom as non-domination central to the republican tradition. Despite obvious similarities between the two, as I shall explain later in the chapter, the two differ in that freedom as non-domination is arguably moralized in a way that freedom as independence, *as I understand it*, is not.

[10] Philip Pettit, 'Freedom as Antipower', *Ethics*, 106 (3) (1996), 576–604, p. 24.

[11] How much this specific freedom will contribute to my overall freedom is of course a matter of debate and depends on which particular approach one adopts among the three previously outlined.

greater in the first scenario because in the second my ability to go to the cinema entirely depends on the kindness of the manager. The manager could interfere with my actions at any time, requiring that I pay my ticket, and thereby preventing me from going to the cinema. In this case, my 'freedom' to go to the cinema is somewhat illusory: it is under someone else's control.[12]

In line with this, Arthur Ripstein, an advocate of the 'freedom as independence' view, explains that:

> The sense in which freedom is a central issue for political philosophy is relational: to be free is to be independent, that is, to not be subject to the choice of another person... So a slave is always [in a sense] unfree, because his or her decision about what ends to pursue is always subject to the will, or grace, of his or her master.[13]

An illuminating way of capturing the specificity of freedom as independence, as opposed to freedom as option-availability, is to focus on what Christian List calls its distinctive 'robustness'.[14] The master's ability to act in pursuit of his goals is robust across different possible worlds, by virtue of the particular social structure of which he is a member. If, for instance, one of his slaves refuses to cooperate, the master's autonomy is not thereby undermined. There are virtually no nearby possible worlds in which his ability to do what he wishes lies in the hands of a few others. His capacity to realize his ends and goals could only be seriously compromised by a societywide rebellion. To be

---

[12] Some advocates of negative freedom (what I here call freedom as option-availability), particularly Ian Carter in *A Measure of Freedom* and Matthew Kramer in *The Quality of Freedom*, have argued that the concerns of freedom as independence can also be captured by factoring the *probability of interference* into the evaluation of how free a person is. On this view, you may be more or less free to go to the cinema depending on how likely it is that you will be interfered with. Even though this represents a useful modification of the standard negative-freedom/option-availability view, it does not fully capture the concerns behind the notion of freedom as independence. One might be unlikely to be interfered with because of the benign dispositions of the more powerful, or one might be unlikely to be interfered with because of the existence of effective legal constraints on the more powerful. From the perspective of the probabilistic version of the negative conception of freedom, one's freedom is exactly the same across these two scenarios. From the perspective of freedom as independence, it is not. In particular, those who owe their freedom simply to the benign attitude of the powerful are less free than those who are secured against the powerful's intervention. The former's choices are still ultimately dependent on the will of their superiors, but the latter's choices are not. Put in more technical terms, while there may be many nearby possible worlds in which the former are actually interfered with (all that is needed is a change in attitude on the part of a few people), the latter's freedom is robust across many nearby possible worlds (to challenge it, the structure of the entire legal system of a particular society would have to change). For discussion, see Pettit, *Republicanism*; and Christian List, 'Republican Freedom and the Rule of Law', *Politics, Philosophy & Economics*, 5 (2) (2006), 201–20. The issue of robustness will also be discussed in the main text.

[13] Arthur Ripstein, 'Authority and Coercion', *Philosophy and Public Affairs*, 32 (1) (2004), 2–35, p. 8. For an excellent discussion of the notion of freedom as independence, as understood by Kant, see Anna Stilz, *Liberal Loyalty: Freedom, Obligation, and the State* (Princeton: Princeton University Press, 2009), ch. 2.

[14] List, 'Republican Freedom and the Rule of Law'.

sure, there may be a possible world, accessible from the master's world, in which slaves rebel and put an end to their condition of subjugation. However, that possible world is far away from the existing one. Therefore, the master's access to a number of valuable options is 'robust' across a wide range of possible worlds.

The slave's situation is obviously very different. His ability to make certain choices, to act on his life plans, is entirely dependent on the master's will. Even if, in the *actual world*, the master benevolently lets the slave take his own decisions, in many nearby possible worlds this would not be the case. For proponents of freedom as option-availability, the master's benevolent attitude in the actual world is sufficient to warrant the claim that the slave is *fully* free to make certain choices. For proponents of freedom as independence, it is not.[15]

On the latter account of freedom, what matters are not merely the quality and quantity of the options a person has at her/his disposal, but the relations in which she/he stands with respect to other agents and which determine the shape of her/his option set. Deeply asymmetrical relations will often generate dependence, and hence unfreedom. For instance, a social system where property is concentrated in the hands of a few wealthy individuals is likely to be marked by profound dependence relations. In the words of F. A. von Hayek, unless property is sufficiently dispersed, an individual becomes 'dependent on particular persons who alone can provide him with what he needs or who alone can employ him'.[16] The fact that, in the actual world, people may be generous or kind enough to provide him with what he needs does not make him as free as someone who can pursue his ends and goals robustly shielded from others' interference.

On the account of freedom as independence, then, *actual* interference is not the only type of 'hindrance' to freedom we need worry about. As the examples mentioned so far show, the absence of mechanisms – usually a social structure – that effectively and stably prevent interference also counts as a hindrance to freedom. Indeed, if I am constantly liable to being interfered with by other, more powerful, agents – even if they do not always *actually* interfere with my actions or are at any rate unlikely to do so – my capacity to form, set, and pursue ends for myself is severely compromised. As Hayek, once again, says '[w]e are rarely in a position to carry out a coherent plan of action unless we are certain of our exclusive control of some material objects', and the certainty that matters can only be given by an effective legal system

---

[15] List, 'Republican Freedom and the Rule of Law', p. 210.
[16] F. A. Hayek, *The Constitution of Liberty*, in Ian Carter, Matthew Kramer, and Hillel Steiner (eds.), *Freedom: A Philosophical Anthology* (Oxford: Blackwell, 2007), p. 259.

recognizing and enforcing our entitlements.[17] This is precisely the reason why, in Chapter 6, coercive law was said to be necessary for freedom, and hence for autonomy: without a coercively enforced system of rules enabling us to form reliable expectations on each other's conduct, and securing us against the powerful, autonomy becomes chimerical. The kind of security necessary for autonomy can only be obtained when people enjoy non-interference robustly, and not merely by virtue of the contingent dispositions of a few powerful agents.

This shows how the notion of freedom as independence better reflects liberals' concern with persons' autonomy than the alternative account of freedom as option-availability. If what ultimately matters is my capacity to set and pursue *my own* ends, then no matter what, or how many, options are in principle open to me, my freedom is only illusory if my decisions do not express my own will. To be (more or less) free is to enjoy (to a greater or lesser extent) the necessary social conditions to be the author of one's own life, and the idea of freedom as independence, more than that of freedom as option-availability, captures this core liberal insight.

At this point, a sympathetic reader might be convinced of the substantive advantages of the notion of freedom as independence, and yet wonder in what sense this notion differs from the republican idea of freedom as non-domination. After all, the idea of *robust* non-interference also appears to be the distinctive element of the neo-Roman republican account of freedom.

Even though freedom as independence and freedom as non-domination have much in common, there is one important respect in which they come apart. As Philip Pettit has argued, the idea of freedom as non-domination differs from freedom as option-availability (or non-interference) along two dimensions. First, for advocates of freedom as non-domination, only *arbitrary* interference counts as freedom-undermining. Second, non-domination considers not merely actual interference but also the very *possibility* of interference, problematic from the perspective of freedom.[18]

Freedom as independence shares with republican freedom a focus on the possibility of interference, but is *not* committed to the view that only arbitrary interference is freedom-undermining. This means that freedom as non-domination is arguably moralized in a way that freedom as independence is not.[19] If the concept of non-domination is meant to capture the master value

---

[17] Hayek, *The Constitution of Liberty*, p. 258. See also Arthur Ripstein, 'Private Order and Public Justice: Kant and Rawls', *Virginia Law Review*, 92 (7) (2006), 1391–438, p. 1402.

[18] See Philip Pettit, *A Theory of Freedom: From the Psychology to the Politics of Agency* (Cambridge: Polity Press, 2001), pp. 138ff. In particular, Philip Pettit says that non-arbitrary interference is not an 'assault on people's possession of freedom; at most it conditions, but does not compromise, freedom.

[19] I say 'arguably' because Pettit has explicitly denied that the republican notion of freedom as non-domination is moralized in 'The Determinacy of Republican Policy: A Reply to McMahon',

that an ideal republican society should promote, its specification of what counts as arbitrary interference must presuppose an account of justice. To see this, let me briefly discuss Pettit's seminal definition of this notion.

On Pettit's view, 'someone dominates or subjugates another, to the extent that (*a*) they have the capacity to interfere (*b*) on an arbitrary basis (*c*) in certain choices that the other person is in a position to make'.[20] This account of domination is moralized to the extent that clause (*b*) refers to the idea of a person's significant interests. From this perspective, interference is arbitrary when it does not take into account the 'relevant interests' of those affected. Pettit specifies that, in the political context, the 'relevant' interests are those we share with our fellow citizens.[21] From this, it follows that the sort of interference exercised by a just legal system, one that, by definition, equally protects the shared interests of all citizens, is *not* freedom-undermining in the relevant sense. On this account, a just legal system does not hinder freedom, and is thus optimal from a republican point of view.[22]

By contrast, on my account of freedom as independence, a just legal system places constraints on freedom, but such constraints are *fully justified* insofar as they are *in principle* acceptable in the eyes of all. Coercion – that is, the placing of non-trivial restrictions on persons' freedom – is not the same as domination. Domination is always morally problematic, because of its arbitrariness, while coercion is not.[23] Instances of coercion that restrict freedom in a justified manner are beyond moral criticism. In sum, even though freedom as non-domination and freedom as independence have much in common, the former contains a (moralized) non-arbitrariness clause that the latter rejects.

Philosophy and Public Affairs, 34 (3) (2006), 275–83. I explain why I find this claim unconvincing and in tension with other aspects of Pettit's view in footnote 22, ch. 7.

[20] Pettit, *Republicanism*, p. 52.

[21] Pettit, *Republicanism*, p. 55.

[22] Pettit has claimed that his arbitrariness criterion is non-moralized, because whether interference is arbitrary or not depends on 'the factual question of whether the interference is subject to suitable controls' ('The Determinacy of Republican Policy', p. 279), namely whether it is forced to track the interests of the interferee *as the interferee herself/himself would define them*. But this non-moralized account of non-domination cannot possibly deliver the ideal of a just society Pettit wishes to defend. For instance, many believe that redistributive taxation is not in their interest, and convicted offenders typically deny that penalties are in their interest, yet Pettit defines state interventions of this kind as non-arbitrary (Pettit, *Republicanism*, pp. 55–6, and *A Theory of Freedom*, pp. 135–6). It seems that only a moralized account of non-arbitrariness, referring to 'morally relevant interests', can explain this judgement. For discussion of this point, see Ian Carter, 'A Critique of Freedom as Non-domination', *The Good Society*, 9 (3) (2000), 43–6; and more generally Christopher McMahon, 'The Indeterminacy of Republican Policy', *Philosophy and Public Affairs*, 33 (1) (2005), 67–93.

[23] For further discussion of the moralized nature of the idea of non-domination, and a sketch of a republican account of global justice, see Cécile Laborde, 'Republicanism and Global Justice: A Sketch', *European Journal of Political Theory*, 9 (1) (2010), 48–69. I am indebted to Cécile for discussions on these issues.

To sum up, on the freedom-as-independence view, freedom is three-dimensional. A person's overall freedom is a function of three variables: (*a*) the number of options open to her/him; (*b*) the quality of those options; and crucially (*c*) the reason why they are open to her/him, which in turn determines whether they are robustly or only weakly open to her/him.

The notion of freedom as independence presented in this section is meant to help us formulate judgements about both coercion and justice. While coercion, be it interactional or systemic, always indicates non-trivial restrictions of freedom as independence, justice requires that freedom as independence be distributed in a way that is in principle acceptable to all. But in order to decide when freedom so understood has been restricted, or when it is appropriately distributed, we need a metric allowing us to assign particular 'quantities' of freedom to individuals and make comparisons across them.

7.3 MEASURING FREEDOM: INCOMPLETENESS AND PARTIAL COMPARABILITY

Developing an appropriate metric of freedom as independence (from now on also 'freedom' for brevity) is a complex technical task, requiring not only philosophical but also mathematical and social-scientific knowledge. In light of this, instead of defending a particular metric, I will limit myself to describing the properties that any such metric should have, and outlining what considerations we should take into account when developing it. As I shall argue, the absence of a complete metric of freedom is not a serious limitation for present purposes. We can in fact still make many judgements about both coercion (freedom restriction) and justice (justified distributions of freedom), without committing to any specification of the metric.

To design a metric of freedom, we need to evaluate the quantity, quality, and robustness of the options available to each.[24] Counting options, and evaluating their robustness and quality are all non-trivial theoretical exercises. The first presupposes an account of action-individuation enabling us to distinguish between different options, the second a way of identifying nearby and more distant possible worlds, and the third a criterion on the basis of which to assign a specific value to different options.[25] Of these three

---

[24] The problem of constructing a metric of freedom has been analysed in great detail by Ian Carter in *A Measure of Freedom*. Although my discussion is indebted to Carter's work, my preferred account of freedom significantly differs from his purely quantitative approach. For an alternative account of how to measure overall freedom, which, unlike Carter's, emphasizes the importance of the quality of the options available to an agent, see Kramer, *The Quality of Freedom*, ch. 5.

[25] The first of these questions is explored in Carter, *A Measure of Freedom*, ch. 7.

theoretical exercises, I take the third to be of particular relevance for present purposes. While we can reasonably assume that accounts of action-individuation, and methods for identifying close and distant possible worlds, can be unproblematically applied cross-contextually, the value of options lacks such a straightforward cross-contextual character.

The quality of one's options may in fact depend on objective, subjective, or intersubjective evaluations.[26] Objective evaluations would have the advantage of making comparisons across persons easy and manageable, as each option would always have the same objective, subject-independent value. Unfortunately, despite their attractiveness, objective evaluations of this kind are incompatible with the reasons that make freedom valuable in the first place. Freedom matters because it enables us to lead autonomous lives, pursuing our chosen ends. Its importance is premised on the existence of a plurality of choice worthy ends, and of disagreement about which ones we should pursue and why.[27] An objective assessment of the quality of options is a non-starter, because it presupposes what we do not have: namely an objective, uncontroversial, and all-encompassing theory of the good.

What about a subjective account of the value of options? This would also be problematic, as it would render freedom comparisons across persons almost impossible, and inject excessive arbitrariness in our evaluations. Adopting a fully subjective understanding of the value of options may lead us to claim that, say, an incarcerated psychopath is more free than an ordinary prisoner in the event he greatly values the freedom to walk up and down his cell. But surely, the psychopath and ordinary prisoner are roughly equally unfree, and it would be absurd to claim that the former is considerably more free than the latter. Similarly, subjective evaluations might be problematically based on adaptive preferences. An oppressed housewife in a sexist society might deeply value the option of being able to serve her husband, yet we would not want this sort of option to have a genuine positive impact on the evaluation of her overall degree of freedom. If anything, the disproportionate value she places on this option is revelatory of her unfreedom.

Given the difficulties with subjective and objective approaches, we are probably on firmer ground establishing the quality of options intersubjectively. On this approach, we can reasonably assume that human beings have standard needs and interests, and that being able to attend to those needs and interests is of great value to all of them. One can take it for granted that opportunities for nutrition, health, shelter, leisure, meaningful occupation, and so forth are of significance to all humans. They are key components of virtually any plan of life.

---

[26] Cf. Carter, *A Measure of Freedom*, pp. 119–20.
[27] See Berlin, 'Two Concepts of Liberty'.

Beyond this set of universally important types of freedom, though, we should still expect considerable cross-cultural, societal, or interindividual variation. The freedom to buy stylish clothes, for instance, may be valuable in a fashion-obsessed society, but much less valuable in one whose predominant social ethos is insensitive to fashion norms. Apart from a core set of freedoms, what people value, and what they need to realize their ends, varies across time and space.

As Onora O'Neill puts it, '[i]f we view autonomy [what I here call freedom] historically then we are confronted with very wide variations in the amount and types of autonomy which persons of different sorts and epochs typically have' and value. Such cross-cultural variation leaves liberal theorists with a considerable difficulty, for 'it seems that a serious and determinate liberalism must take a historical view of autonomy [freedom] but that in taking a historical view of autonomy [freedom] liberalism becomes... indeterminate'.[28]

Perhaps O'Neill's claim is too strong here, but its thrust is correct. Given variations in how different people and cultures value certain options, people's overall degrees of freedom might not be fully comparable. In the best case scenario, our freedom comparisons across persons will have to be partial, rather than complete. On the view I defend, then, the aspiration fully to compare each aspect of persons' freedom status is somewhat chimerical.[29]

The complexity, and limits, of freedom measurements become all the more transparent when, in addition to considering how to evaluate the quality of persons' options, we also think about how to balance the different variables contributing to one's overall freedom: the quality, quantity, and robustness of the options. To see this, consider the following two scenarios.

In the first, Master Adrian tells slave Bobby: 'From now on, you can use my possessions as you please. You can lead a life of luxury and pleasure, without following my orders or being subject to my interference. I promise that, though you are legally my slave, I will treat you as an equal.' Bobby now has very many valuable options at his disposal, but his access to them is far from being secure. Adrian can take his word back at any point, and even if, *de facto*, he does not, this possibility renders Bobby's freedom somewhat illusory. Perhaps, worried about his Master's possible reaction, Bobby still feels compelled to lead a life of subordination and restraint. His access to options is fragile, as there are many nearby possible worlds in which he might be deprived of it. Under these conditions, we can hardly say that our slave fully

---

[28] Onora O'Neill, 'The Most Extensive Liberty', *Proceedings of The Aristotelian Society*, 80 (1980), 45–59, pp. 54–5 and 58, emphasis added.
[29] As Amartya Sen has emphasized, we have to reckon with the fact that, on most plausible metrics, rankings and comparisons will often be incomplete. See his *The Idea of Justice* (Cambridge, MA: Harvard University Press, 2009).

enjoys whatever conditions are necessary to lead an autonomous
certainly free to at least some degree, but not as much as simply looking
option set in the actual world would suggest.

Now consider the case of Johnny. He is a cleaner in a big chocolate factory, his finances are modest, and there is very little he can afford, beyond subsistence. Even though he is not privileged, he can be reasonably certain that his access to subsistence is secure. He cannot buy luxury goods, but he knows that if he does his job as instructed, at the beginning of each month he will receive a small sum of money he will be able to spend as he likes. He does not have much, but he has certainties in life, and can plan his present and future around them.

What can we say about the relative freedom status of Bobby and Johnny? We can safely claim that Bobby scores more highly than Johnny with respect to the quality and quantity of his options, while Johnny scores more highly with respect to their robustness. Who is more free, overall? It is hard to say. Perhaps, knowing all the relevant facts – both scenarios are underdescribed – we would be able to formulate an intuitive judgement about the relative freedom status of our two characters. If so, then we should try to construct our metric of freedom so as to make it compatible with this, and other, common-sense judgements. The more our metric will reflect, and illuminate, the considered judgements we advance with most confidence, the more it will appear correct and compelling.[30] When developing a metric of freedom, and balancing its three dimensions, we proceed by testing it against our judgements. Whenever our metric fails the test, we have a more or less strong reason to revise it, depending on the gravity of the failure. A metric of freedom that led us to conclude that, say, a convicted man in prison is more free, or as free, as a middle-class professional with no criminal record, would clearly have to be rejected.

That said, no matter how well designed our metric is, it still remains true that we cannot assume comparisons to be possible across all cases. As I have already mentioned, when measuring freedom, we must not expect too much from our theories. Comparisons will be possible, but only to a certain extent. This should not be taken as a shortcoming specific to this approach, or as an 'embarrassment'.[31] As Richard Arneson points out '[t]he idea that a *complete* measure of human good can be rationally warranted is wildly absurd'.[32]

---

[30] This in accordance with Rawls's method of reflective equilibrium. See John Rawls, *A Theory of Justice* (Oxford: Oxford University Press, 1999 rev. ed.), pp. 18–19 and 42–5. For discussion of reflective equilibrium in the context of designing a metric of freedom, see Carter, *A Measure of Freedom*, ch. 4.

[31] Amartya Sen, 'Well-Being, Agency and Freedom', *Journal of Philosophy*, 82 (4) (1985), 169–221, p. 200.

[32] Richard J. Arneson, 'Two Cheers for Capabilities', in H. Brighouse and I. Robeyns (eds.), *Measuring Justice. Primary Goods and Capabilities* (Cambridge: Cambridge University Press,

Justice in a Globalized World

tric is – be it freedom, welfare, advantage, and so forth – rtial comparability will be virtually unavoidable. More- e avoidable, this would not make theories that cannot y less plausible or incorrect. Consider an account of which, instead of focusing on the quality, number, and tions, we need only look at their quantity and quality. In ssion, we would have to conclude that Bobby the slave is more free than ... ny the cleaner. This, however, is far from obvious. If we focused only on the quality and quantity of persons' options, our notion of freedom would fail to capture all of those social factors that are relevant to our ability to lead autonomous lives.[33] As such, it would be incomplete.

So far, I have advanced a few considerations highlighting what kinds of difficulties we would have to face in order to construct a plausible metric of freedom. As I have already mentioned, the elaboration of such a metric is a largely technical task beyond the scope of this book, requiring not only philosophical expertise, but also mathematical and social-scientific knowledge. What matters, for our purposes, is that such a metric can in principle be devised, and that many of our most important judgements about both coercion (freedom restriction) and justice (justifiable distributions of freedom) can be made even *without* committing to any particular specification of such a metric. I shall substantiate these claims in the following two sections.

7.4 COERCION AND FREEDOM AS INDEPENDENCE

In Chapter 6, I distinguished between two forms of coercion: interactional and systemic. We can now reformulate our definitions of these two types of coercion replacing the 'general' notion of freedom with its more specific interpretation in terms of freedom as independence, and consider its implications for specific cases. I first look at interactional coercion, and then turn to its systemic counterpart.

> **Interactional coercion**: agent A coerces another agent B if A foreseeably and avoidably places non-trivial constraints on B's freedom-as-independence, compared to B's freedom-as-independence in the absence of A's intervention (other things being equal).

2010), 101–28, p. 116, emphasis added. Notice that, on the view I am proposing, freedom may be appropriately regarded as a good, or rather, as a meta-good, allowing us to pursue our ends and goals.

[33] Of course, for fine-grained comparisons we would also have to consider possible intersubjective differences.

Consider, first, a thief (A) and her/his victim (B). If A steals B's possessions, she/he thereby foreseeably and avoidably deprives B of resources with which B could pursue her/his ends and goals. This causes B's option set to shrink in a way that makes B less free than she/he would otherwise be. This conclusion can be reached by proponents of freedom as option-availability and freedom as independence alike.

However, on the account of freedom as independence I have defended, B's freedom would have to count as diminished not only by A's actual interference, but also by her/his counterfactual interference: in case she/he did not rob B in the actual world, but there were some nearby possible worlds in which she/he would. How could this be possible? B, for example, might live in a very unsafe neighbourhood, plagued by the presence of a skilled thief the police has so far been unable to catch: A. B might be lucky, and never become one of A's targets, but the fragility of her/his access to certain opportunities makes her/him certainly less free than she/he would be, absent A's activities. A's repeated incursions into B's neighbourhood place constraints not only on the freedom of A's direct victims, but on B herself/himself, putting her/him on the edge, making her/him reluctant to leave her/his apartment unsupervised, and so forth. From the perspective of freedom as independence, there is a sense in which B is indeed coerced in the present scenario – her/his freedom is diminished by A's repeated interventions – and, on any plausible account of justice, unjustly so.

Alternatively, think of the case of a criminal who is rightly imprisoned. There is no doubt that this person's freedom is thereby curtailed. If I am put into jail, I can hardly be said to be significantly free from others' interference to pursue my ends and goals. Not only is my option set dramatically reduced compared to my option set prior to my arrest, but what is going to happen to me, whether I will ever be able to lead a normal life outside the narrow confines of my cell, depends on a judge's decision. The prisoner's freedom is reduced not only because she/he can no longer access certain options but also because her/his access to some such options is extremely fragile, and ultimately outside her/his control. For instance, even though, in the actual world, a prisoner manages to obtain abundant meals, this may only be due to the generosity of one of the prison's cooks, who gives her/him particularly generous portions. Were this prison's cook to be replaced, or to change her/his attitude, the prisoner would have to come to terms with a constant, low-level hunger. Her/his access to 'sufficient nutrition' is not under her/his control, but ultimately dependent on others.

Consider, finally, the following scenario.[34] Mary aspires to be a lecturer in London. At one point, her partner, James, obtains a very well-paid job in the

---

[34] I am grateful to David Miller for suggesting it to me.

Philippines. James has no intention to give up this job. Mary wants to follow him, and has to abandon her aspiration to become a lecturer in London. Does this mean that James has coerced her by depriving her of the opportunity to be *both* a lecturer in London *and* James's partner? It would be disingenuous to deny that there is a sense in which Mary's freedom is restricted by James. Her ability to pursue her aspiration to be both a lecturer in London and James's partner is frustrated by his decision. The realization of her plans of life clearly depends, at least in part, on what James does.

But endorsing the plausible claim that, by deciding to move to the Philippines, James places constraints on Mary's freedom does not entail the implausible claim that, in so doing, James acts unjustly. As explained in Chapter 6, coercion is not a moralized notion: it indicates the conditions under which concerns of justice are appropriate, and not instances of injustice. Indeed, coercion is virtually unavoidable: complete and absolute freedom as independence is a mirage. Human beings are not self-sufficient, god-like creatures. By their very nature, they are vulnerable and interdependent.[35] This means that a just society cannot be one where no dependence relations, no unfreedom, exists. Rather, it is one where dependence relations exist, and yet are not excessively asymmetrical. In such a society, there is mutual dependence (interdependence), but no one is so powerful as to force others to act in pursuit of her/his own ends and goals. In the case just described, there would be clearly something morally problematic if Mary were entirely economically dependent on James, and therefore had no choice but to follow him to the Philippines.

However, assuming Mary does not find herself in a situation of economic dependence, her predicament does not involve any form of injustice. Indeed, it would seem obviously unjust to place James under a publically enforceable obligation to act in such a way as to promote Mary's goals, regardless of his own preferences. Even if it just so happened that his goals and Mary's were perfectly aligned, this would nevertheless constitute an unacceptable restriction of his own freedom.

Let me now turn to the case of systemic coercion, understood as the imposition of non-trivial constraints on freedom as independence.

> **Systemic coercion**: a system of social rules S is coercive if it foreseeably and avoidably places non-trivial constraints on some agents' freedom-as-independence, compared to their freedom-as-independence in the absence of that system.

To see what is special about systemic coercion so understood, consider an imaginary society: Samaritania. Samaritania is organized on the basis of

---

[35] This aspect of human nature is emphasized by Onora O'Neill in *Towards Justice and Virtue: A Constructive Account of Practical Reasoning* (Cambridge: Cambridge University Press, 1996).

libertarian norms of justice (Samaritania-L).[36] Taxation is kept to a minimum, and used only to finance the state's police, military forces, and basic infrastructure. Samaritanian markets are almost entirely unregulated, allowing for considerable wealth accumulation on the part of some, and considerable deprivation plaguing others. Let us now zoom in on one of Samaritania's citizens: Martin Lucky.

Despite being 'legally' poor and propertyless, Martin leads a good life. He occasionally dines at nice restaurants, owns a little but functional car, and has a modest but welcoming home. This all thanks to the generosity of an old lady, Mary Kind-Hearted, whom he met when he was a young man. Feeling sorry for Martin's predicament, Mary took him under her protection, and started giving him financial support on an amicable, unofficial, basis. Martin is leading a relatively problem-free life, but the conditions of his happiness are fragile. Were Mary to decide that she has had enough of him, or were more pressing matters brought to her attention (e.g. her grandson in financial difficulty), she could easily abandon Martin, who would quickly slide back into poverty. As it happens, Mary continues to like Martin and, shortly before her death, decides to make him one of her heirs. But Martin knows that things could have easily gone very differently.

Now consider a counterfactual counterpart of our scenario. Samaritania is no longer organized in accordance with libertarian principles, but with egalitarian ones (Samaritania-E). Markets are regulated, tax rates are relatively high, and the collected revenue is then employed for redistributive purposes as well as to finance a vast range of public services. Once again, let us zoom in on Martin. He still leads a good life: he occasionally eats at fancy restaurants, drives a small but functional car, and has a welcoming home. As it happens, the number and quality of the opportunities available to him is identical to the number and quality of those accessible to his counterpart in Samaritania-L. Against this background, we need to ask: 'Is the system of rules underpinning Samaritania-L's social organization coercive of Martin, given his situation under the alternative set of rules governing Samaritania-E?'

While proponents of freedom as option-availability would have to deny that it is, advocates of freedom as independence would not. For even though Martin has the same quality and quantity of options in both Samaritania-L and Samaritania-E, the robustness of those options varies across the two. In particular, it is much greater in Samaritania-E than in Samaritania-L. While in Samaritania-L he is *de facto* entirely dependent on Mary, in Samaritania-E he is not. His life prospects and prosperity are not ultimately under someone else's control and, to that extent, he enjoys a greater degree of freedom under Samaritania-E than under Samaritania-L.

---

[36] For a libertarian account of a just society, see Robert Nozick, *Anarchy, State, and Utopia* (Oxford: Blackwell, 1974).

Now consider a more realistic scenario. This involves Aanjay, a young Indonesian woman whose poverty and destitution make working in a sweatshop her only chance of survival. When the manager of a sweatshop offers her a job, he, personally, does *not* place constraints on her freedom. If anything, he increases her sphere of agency by giving her the opportunity to earn some (however little) money. Yet it would be disingenuous to claim that she is fully *free* to work in that sweatshop. Because of her poverty and destitution, she cannot but accept the manager's job offer, no matter how exploitative it is. It is only thanks to the manager's business interests that she now has the possibility to feed herself. She depends on him for her survival. Whatever opportunities she can now enjoy are ultimately under someone else's control. From the perspective of freedom as independence, this very fact is of great relevance to the assessment of her overall freedom status.

Aanjay's situation would strike most people as morally problematic, as being at least *prima facie* unjust. Indeed, how could we think of the distribution of freedom existing in her society as justified in her eyes? But whose fault is it? From the perspective of my coercion-based approach to justice, Aanjay's employer cannot be said to coerce her. As already mentioned, his offer increases, rather than diminishes, her freedom – even though it does so in a fragile way. But if his actions are not coercive, and hence not subject to justice-based assessment, how can we plausibly make sense of the thought that Aanjay is the victim of injustice?

To do so, we need to turn to the perspective of systemic coercion. Her poverty and destitution can arguably be imputed to the systems of social rules structuring her life circumstances: from national laws and policies to the international economy. From a systemic viewpoint, Aanjay and other women like her can be said to be coerced because it is not hard to imagine a counterfactual counterpart social system in which they would enjoy much greater freedom. A better regulation of the international economy, in conjunction with stricter domestic legislation and labour standards, would probably allow women like Aanjay to lift themselves out of poverty, and to have robust access to more and better opportunities, without relying on the generosity, or business interest, of others. In light of this, we can plausibly conclude that women like Aanjay are systemically coerced (under plausible specifications of the baseline) and, I would add, unjustly so (under any plausible account of justice).

To summarize, I have argued that the notion of freedom as independence is particularly promising from the perspective of a liberal political morality in general, and from the perspective of the coercion view in particular. On this account of freedom, one's overall freedom is a function of three variables: the number and quality of the options at one's disposal, and their robustness. In illustrating how this notion of freedom can be employed to evaluate the coerciveness of particular actions or social systems, I have also occasionally

appealed to our intuitive judgements about justic[e]
instances of coercion (whether interactional or sy[stemic])
reasonably just or unjust (recall, the case of
terrorizing B's neighbourhood). Intuitive judg[ements help]
somewhat, but cannot take us very far. If we w[ant to assess]
the justice or injustice of particular social sy[stems, we need an]
account of what justice requires. That is, [we need to know how justice]
conditions the distribution of freedom within [society and what it owes]
to all its inhabitants.

7.5 JUSTICE AND FREEDOM AS INDEPENDENCE

How are we to determine when a particular social system meets the universal justifiability condition? Two crucial difficulties arise in this context. First, as we saw in Section 7.3, we cannot defend a complete metric of freedom that can claim validity across all persons, cultures, and societies. Interpersonal and cross-cultural variations in what people value make the design of such a metric chimerical. Call this the '*substance-of-freedom*' problem. Second, different people might disagree about what counts as an acceptable distribution of freedom. Some, for example, might opt for equality of freedom, others for maximin freedom (i.e. for maximizing the freedom of the least free), and still others for a minimum of freedom for all. As we saw in Chapter 4, universal justifiability tests aimed at expressing the ideal of equal respect are underdetermined. Consequently, different possible distributive principles seem to be compatible with the demands of justice. Call this the '*distribution-of-freedom*' problem.

How can such problems be resolved? The substance-of-freedom problem can be addressed by focusing on those opportunities access to which is crucial for an autonomous life, no matter what society one belongs to – within reasonable temporal limits.[37] As I mentioned earlier, the quality of certain options is, plausibly, fully intersubjectively recognizable not only within each society but also across societies. When considering persons' relative freedom positions, then, we do well to focus on these universally valuable options.

This idea is a familiar one in political philosophy and underpins, *mutatis mutandis*, Rawls's primary goods approach.[38] For Rawls, primary social goods

---

[37] I am not saying that my claims about the value of certain options with respect to one's overall freedom would also be valid, for instance, if applied to ancient Greece or the Incas civilization.

[38] Or indeed in Sen's and Nussbaum's capability approach. See H. Brighouse and I. Robeyns (eds.), *Measuring Justice*.

...ose means to achieve whatever ends', and include civil and ...erties, opportunities, income and wealth, and the social bases of ...ct.[39] In any contemporary society, Rawls plausibly assumes, secure ... to these goods is key to people's ability to lead autonomous lives and ...efore significantly contributes to determining their overall freedom status. ...ven though Rawls's list of primary goods is open to improvement and refinement, overcoming the substance-of-freedom problem will require the adoption of a strategy similar to his.[40] To evaluate the distribution of freedom across members of society, we focus on those options that anyone has reason to value, no matter what their particular ends and goals are.

What about the distribution-of-freedom problem? Rawls himself, for instance, can be interpreted as defending a principle of maximin freedom, whereby inequalities in freedom are justified only so long as they increase the absolute level of freedom of the least advantaged. This characterization of Rawls, as an advocate of maximin freedom, may not seem obvious at first. His principles require persons to have equal basic liberties and fair equality of opportunity, and maximin only explicitly applies to the distribution of economic goods such as income and wealth. In what sense, then, does Rawls's theory apply maximin to the distribution of freedom?

To see this, we need to bear in mind that access to economic goods enables citizens to take full advantage of their formal freedoms in the first place (what Rawls calls basic liberties and opportunities). For example, I may be entitled to formal freedom of movement, but if I lack the necessary means to buy a car, or a train ticket, my freedom of movement is limited. The extent of my freedom of movement is thus importantly determined by the economic means I have at my disposal. If this is correct, then we can plausibly claim that, on a full or substantive understanding of freedom, Rawls's theory prescribes 'maximin-governed' distributions of freedom.[41] From the perspective of the parties in his original-position thought experiment (discussed in Chapter 2), departures from equality are only justified so long as they benefit the worse off people in absolute terms.

Maximin, however, is not the only distributive rule that could in principle attract the consent of all (prospective) citizens. It would not seem irrational for persons concerned to lead autonomous lives to prefer a principle guaranteeing, say, an *equal* distribution of income and wealth, or a *minimum level of income and wealth* for all, without considering socio-economic inequalities above that level morally problematic. That is, principles that are either more or

---

[39] Rawls, *A Theory of Justice*, p. 54.
[40] For challenges to the primary goods metric, see Brighouse and Robeyns (eds.), *Measuring Justice*.
[41] On this, see Carter, *A Measure of Freedom*, pp. 81–2. As Carter rightly points out, for Rawls, the distribution of economic goods has an impact on the 'worth' of liberty. However, many would regard the worth of liberty as being itself part of freedom.

less egalitarian than Rawls's own could also plausibly pass a universal justifiability test, depending on what reasonable assumptions we make when devising the test itself.

Rawls's own test – the original position – assumes that individuals are risk-averse, and that excessively steep socio-economic inequalities are morally problematic, *inter alia*, because they lead to social stigma and relationships of domination within society. These assumptions can reasonably be challenged. Rational persons need not be as risk-averse as Rawls takes them to be, and socio-economic inequalities may be more or less undermining of persons' self-respect, and more or less conducive to domination, than Rawls thinks.[42]

For instance, we can easily imagine a society whose citizens would prefer sufficientarian principles to Rawls's maximin. On their views, so long as each citizen has *enough* socio-economic goods to lead her/his life without being constantly dependent on others, economic inequalities are justified. As a result, some will be considerably better off than others, but so long as this does not translate into excessively debilitating forms of domination or stigmatization, such intrasocietal differences could be unanimously accepted.

Alternatively, we can think of a society whose citizens single out an equal distribution of socio-economic goods as the only universally acceptable one, say due to the fear that alternative distributions might undermine the self-respect of the worse off to such a point as to globally compromise their agency. Inequalities incentivize productivity, but they can also lead to high rates of crime and poor health, and disrupt social relations generally. Faced with this risk, some might conclude that socio-economic inequalities are simply unacceptable.[43]

In fact, the later Rawls himself 'abandoned the aspiration that the contractual argument reduces eligible conceptions of justice to a singleton'.[44] Even though he explicitly defends a principle of maximin freedom in *A Theory of Justice*, in his later work, he emphasizes how the fundamental liberal commitment to equal respect for persons *qua* free, autonomous, agents need not lead to a single distributive criterion. There may be a number of possible

---

[42] For discussion, see Martin O'Neill, 'What Should Egalitarians Believe?', *Philosophy and Public Affairs*, 36 (2) (2008), 119–56; and Thomas M. Scanlon, 'The Diversity of Objections to Inequality', Lindley Lecture, University of Kansas (Lawrence, Kansas: 1996).

[43] See Robert H. Wade, 'Should We Worry about Income Inequality?', in David Held and Ayse Kaya (eds.), *Global Inequality* (Cambridge: Polity Press, 2007), 104–31. See also Norman Daniel's criticisms of Rawls's potentially too inegalitarian conclusions in 'Equal Liberty and Unequal Worth of Liberty', in Norman Daniels (ed.), *Reading Rawls: Critical Studies on Rawls' 'A Theory of Justice'* (Stanford, CA: Stanford University Press, 1975), 253–81.

[44] Gerald F. Gaus, 'The Demands of Impartiality and the Evolution of Morality', in Brian Feltham and John Cottingham (eds.), *Partiality and Impartiality* (Oxford: Oxford University Press, 2010), p. 15. See also the arguments in Sen, *The Idea of Justice*, p. 46, to the effect that social contract-style thought experiments do not lead to select a unique set of principles.

distributive arrangements that agents concerned with furthering their life plans might consider acceptable.[45]

In light of the underdeterminacy of universal justifiability tests, what can we say about what would count as a just distribution of freedom in general, and in relation to socio-economic goods in particular? Although we cannot identify with precision what distributive criterion counts as universally acceptable, because in principle more than one does, we can still plausibly establish which distributions of freedom a just society must *exclude*, since rational agents concerned with furthering their life plans could never consent to them. Hypothetical consent does not enable us to determine what is perfectly just, but is of great help in establishing what is *reasonably just or legitimate*. (Unless otherwise stated, from now on I shall use the term 'justice' and the adjective 'just', meaning reasonably just or legitimate.)

For example, a system of laws failing to give some of its citizens access to Rawls's primary goods, or a functional equivalent thereof, would never pass a universal justifiability test.[46] Why would citizens accept to live under circumstances in which their freedom of movement, or access to basic subsistence, is almost non-existent compared to that of others? How could they possibly want to run the risk of finding themselves in the situation of Aanjay, or Martin Lucky in Samaritania-L?

In line with these reflections, and in a Rawlsian spirit, I suggest that a society certainly *cannot be just* unless it provides the following guarantees for its citizens: (*a*) *equal* civil and political rights – including freedom of religion, movement, thought, association, occupation, as well as the right to vote and to hold political office; (*b*) *equal* opportunities; and (*c*) *adequate* economic rights – allowing each to take reasonable advantage of one's liberties and opportunities.[47]

Falling short of such minimal criteria of justice, a society clearly becomes unacceptable to at least some of its members. We can safely exclude that persons concerned with pursuing their life plans would have any reason to accept to be governed by institutions where their agency, and physical integrity, is constantly at risk: either because their civil and socio-economic rights are not respected, or because, lacking mechanisms of accountability, their protection rests on the partisan preferences of the powerful. Without equal political rights, a person's life prospects may be dependent on the will of a few privileged who exercise exclusive control over 'would-be collective'

---

[45] John Rawls, *The Law of Peoples* (Cambridge, MA: Harvard University Press, 1999), pp. 14ff. and 143ff.

[46] Cf. the discussion of how Kant's equal right to freedom might be operationalized in Stilz, *Liberal Loyalty*, ch. 2.

[47] Rawls, *The Law of Peoples*, p. 14. Cf. also Henry Shue, *Basic Rights: Subsistence, Affluence and U.S. Foreign Policy* (Princeton, NJ: Princeton University Press, 1980, 2nd ed. 1996).

decision-making processes. Democratic control and accountability therefore contribute to securing the robustness of one's access to certain fundamental goods.

For the reasons offered earlier, I also suggest that we should limit ourselves to focusing on those economic guarantees that *must* certainly be respected by any society to pass a hypothetical consent test: these include access to subsistence, health, shelter, education, and sanitation, but not equality of income or wealth. Whether the latter form of equality is in line with the demands of justice is, as we have seen, a controversial matter. Different rational persons will reasonably disagree on this, and hypothetical consent itself cannot settle such disagreements. From the liberal perspective adopted in this book, these disagreements cannot be theoretically resolved, but have to be practically managed through free and fair decision-making.

This gives us further reasons for valuing equal political rights, over and above the instrumental considerations I mentioned earlier. If the outcome of hypothetical consent is underdetermined, to identify what might count as a mutually justifiable distribution of freedom, we should resort to democratic deliberation and decision. This is not to say that democratic processes succeed in concretely realizing the ideal of universal justifiability. As we all know, such processes are imperfect, and most commonly operate on the basis of majority rule, rather than unanimity. The point I am making is rather that such processes offer us the best approximation of universal justifiability in real-world circumstances. When hypothetical consent runs out because of reasonable disagreement about its outcomes, democracy begins.[48]

To conclude, *beyond a certain threshold,* there can be reasonable disagreement about how a political community should be internally organized to be in principle acceptable to all of its citizens. A crucial role for international political philosophy, then, is to set such a threshold, establishing what civil and political rights have to be enshrined is a society's constitution, and *what forms of socio-economic inequality* cannot be tolerated, no matter what society we are looking at. While we can confidently assert that extreme forms of inequality (e.g. such that the worse off people lack access to basic goods) are certainly unjust, the unjust nature of other forms of inequality, especially wealth inequalities, is a matter of debate, and will partly depend on the specific nature of the society at hand. When it comes to economic goods, our accounts of justice can be reasonably ecumenical. Insisting on one specific interpretation of what justice requires might lead us to impose what is in fact a parochial interpretation of universal justifiability on others, without adequate reason.

---

[48] I offer a more detailed defence of this claim in Laura Valentini, 'Justice and Democracy', (manuscript). Cf. the distinction between minimal and maximal justice in Rainer Forst, 'Towards a Critical Theory of Transnational Justice', *Metaphilosophy*, (32) (1/2) 2001, 160–79.

7.6 CONCLUSION

In this chapter, I have further developed my coercion-based normative framework, specifying that coercion always involves non-trivial restrictions of freedom as independence – as opposed to freedom as option-availability – and that justice requires freedom as independence to be distributed in a way that is in principle mutually acceptable to society's inhabitants. Interestingly, since hypothetical consent tests are, by their very nature, underdetermined, this has led us to conclude that economic equality is not as central a value in a liberal account of domestic justice as participants in the global-justice debate from both sides, cosmopolitan and statist, seem to assume. The only limits on economic inequality *required* by justice are those that are necessary for a society to be in principle acceptable to all its members. But beyond a certain threshold, there is reasonable disagreement about what the relevant limits are, a disagreement which is best settled by the democratic processes of each community.

Having examined the function, and content, of principles of justice at the domestic level, we now have all the necessary conceptual tools to extend our normative framework from the domestic context to the international arena.

8

The Scope of Justice: Global

8.1 INTRODUCTION

In Chapters 6 and 7, I have developed a normative framework delineating the function and content of principles of justice. I have argued that their function is to assess the moral legitimacy of coercion, and that their content depends on what respecting persons' right to freedom requires. In developing this normative framework, I have for the most part focused on the domestic arena. In this chapter, I take a step further, and analyse the implications of my framework for the question of justice beyond borders.

I show that, when applied to the contemporary global order, this framework delivers an account of global justice that steers a middle course between cosmopolitanism and statism. Global justice, I argue, requires more than statist assistance, yet less than cosmopolitan equality. My framework grounds duties of mutual non-interference and assistance between political communities, as well as justice-based responsibilities to bring about international institutions with the capacity to regulate global systemic coercion. For these institutions to be just, they must be so organized as to be in principle compatible with everyone's right to freedom.[1]

The chapter is structured as follows. In Section 8.2, I bring together the reflections advanced in Parts I, II, and III, and offer a concise overview of the normative framework defended in this book, specifically focusing on the relationship between equal respect, duties of justice, and duties of humanitarian assistance. In Section 8.3, I consider the implications of this framework for two hypothetical scenarios: a world of mutually independent political communities and a global state. The framework delivers statist principles in the first scenario, and cosmopolitan ones in the second. Which of these two solutions is ultimately correct depends on which scenario provides the most accurate description of the current state of the world. In Section 8.4, I suggest – as readers might by now expect – that both are equally incorrect: we live neither in a world of fully independent peoples, nor in a global state, but somewhere in between these two

---

[1] I have briefly sketched this conclusion in Laura Valentini, 'Coercion and (Global) Justice', *American Political Science Review*, 105 (1) (2011), 205–20.

extremes. In Sections 8.5, 8.6, and 8.7, I show that, thanks to its dual focus on interactional and systemic coercion, the view I defend coherently combines statists' concern with the justification of intersocietal relations with cosmopolitans' focus on the moral legitimacy of global practices, especially of economic ones. I argue that, in our deeply interconnected world, the values of sovereignty and self-determination dear to statists cannot be effectively secured unless the systemic coercion characterizing the global economy is regulated and constrained. After advancing a number of tentative suggestions concerning how to make the world more just, I conclude by briefly recapitulating the main elements of my approach to global justice.

Before getting started, I should warn the reader that what follows is by no means a blueprint for the construction of a just world. This is in part due to space and time constraints, but also to the interdisciplinary character such a blueprint ought to have. The elaboration of plausible proposals for international reform requires not only the ability to develop an abstract normative framework (my task in this book) but also expertise that goes far beyond that of the political philosopher, encompassing disciplines such as law, sociology, political science, and economics. I shall be happy if this book offers a plausible account of the moral grounds on which such proposals for reform should be designed and defended.

8.2 EQUAL RESPECT, JUSTICE, AND HUMANITY

Liberals, we already know, are committed to the principle of equal respect for persons *qua* rational and autonomous agents. From the discussions throughout this book (especially in Chapters 1, 3, and 4), it has emerged that this principle generates two fundamental classes of duties: duties of justice and duties of humanity. The function of duties of justice is to place limits on how we may legitimately constrain one another's freedom. Since duties of justice concern the way we affect others' life conditions, they become relevant to the moral assessment of persons' conduct when particular kinds of social relations are present or could be brought about through that conduct: those social relations I have defined as coercive. Whenever we are involved in coercive exercises, be they interactional or systemic, we owe others a special justification for the ways we limit their freedom. Some of these constraints will be compatible with the demands of justice while others will not be.

Since we live in an imperfect world, justice is insufficient as a guarantee that all will be in a position to exercise their agency to a reasonable degree. Human beings are vulnerable to natural catastrophes, other people's violence, and their own recklessness. Misfortune, injustice, and imprudence also seriously undermine people's ability to lead autonomous lives. This is why, in addition to duties of justice, equal respect grounds duties of humanitarian assistance to help those in need when this is not too costly to oneself.² For instance, if my property has been stolen and I find myself without any means of subsistence, others who are not (outcome) responsible for my condition still have a duty to help me, so long as this does not unreasonably burden them.³

Unlike duties of justice, *duties of humanity are not correlative to rights*.⁴ Those who act in fulfilment of these duties use *their own* entitlements to promote the good of others. For instance, Carl the beggar is not entitled to the five pounds Lisa the passer-by drops in his hands. By contrast, John is entitled to the five pounds his friend Mark hands him in return for a bus ticket. While Carl could not protest if Lisa left nothing, John could complain if Mark failed to pay him. Of course, Lisa would be acting wrongly if her refusal to leave a donation was a manifestation of general indifference towards human need. Such indifference is clearly at odds with the demands of humanity. But failures of humanity differ from failures of justice. While Lisa's indifference wrongs 'humanity' as such – contingently represented by Carl – Mark's refusal to honour his duty of justice wrongs John, who has a right against him.⁵

Moreover, as we saw in Chapter 3, *ceteris paribus, duties of humanity are less stringent than duties of justice*: if I have duties to help others to lead autonomous lives, *a fortiori*, I have duties not to undermine the social conditions for their autonomy, namely their right to freedom. For instance, if I have a duty to help the starving, I must have an even stronger duty not to place others in conditions where they are condemned to starvation.⁶ The more my agency is involved in bringing about others' plight, the more stringent are my duties to address it.

In sum, on the view I defend, equal respect grounds two types of duties: duties of justice and duties of humanitarian assistance. The former place limits on the constraints we may legitimately impose on one another's freedom, thereby determining our rights and entitlements. The latter tell us how we ought to use our own entitlements, whenever others fall below a minimal

---

² For discussion, see Onora O'Neill, *Towards Justice and Virtue: A Constructive Account of Practical Reasoning* (Cambridge: Cambridge University Press, 1996), ch. 7.

³ The notion of outcome responsibility was discussed in Chapter 6. This notion was originally introduced by Tony Honoré, and further discussed by David Miller in *National Responsibility and Global Justice* (Oxford: Oxford University Press, 2007), ch. 4.

⁴ Notice, however, that as I have made explicit in footnote 77, ch. 6, correlativity to rights does not entail that duties of justice are perfect, namely that their content and mode of performance are fully specified. Thinking otherwise would lead us to hold an implausibly conservative account of justice. On this, see e.g. Christian Barry and Laura Valentini, 'Egalitarian Challenges to Global Egalitarianism: A Critique', *Review of International Studies*, 35 (3) (2009), 485–512, Section IV.

⁵ For discussion, see David Miller, '"Are They *My* Poor?" The Problem of Altruism in a World of Strangers', *Critical Review of Social and Political Philosophy*, 5 (4) (2002), 106–27.

⁶ For the *ceteris paribus* qualification, see Thomas Pogge, 'Severe Poverty as a Violation of Negative Duties', *Ethics and International Affairs*, 19 (1) (2005), 55–83, p. 76.

threshold of agency through no fault of our own. What are the implications of this view for our duties at the global level?

8.3 TWO PICTURES OF THE INTERNATIONAL REALM

Duties of humanity have, by their very nature, global reach. No particular social relations need to be in place for individuals to bear humanitarian duties towards one another. Their common humanity is all that matters. Duties of justice are more complex. On the view I have developed, our answer to the question of whether and, if so, how we should extend principles of justice beyond state borders depends on what forms of international coercion there are (or can be). To help our thinking on this matter, I consider two hypothetical configurations of the international arena. The first, which I call the 'separate-islands model', describes an international order characterized by complete independence between different political communities; the second, which I call the 'global-polity model', describes a world dominated by a global state.[7]

8.3.1 Separate Islands

Imagine an international order comprised of a multiplicity of independent, self-contained, and self-sufficient peoples. Each of them meets reasonable, though not identical, standards of domestic justice (as defined in Section 7.5), and although they are aware of one another's existence, there are no cultural, commercial, or political links between them. Each of them can therefore be aptly described as an 'island of justice'. What would liberal equal respect demand for these imaginary political communities?

In this case, the implications of equal respect are relatively straightforward, consisting of justice-based duties of non-interference, and duties of humanitarian assistance, respectively. I consider each of them in turn.

(I) Justice-based Non-interference

Since respect for persons entails respect for the conditions that enable them to lead autonomous lives – and, as argued in Chapters 5 and 6, membership in a just society is one of them – in the envisaged scenario, peoples ought to refrain

---

[7] These scenarios are inspired by A. J. Julius's description of different configurations of the network structure of the international realm. See A. J. Julius, 'Nagel's Atlas', *Philosophy and Public Affairs*, 34 (2) (2006), 176–92, pp. 189–90. Predictably, my conclusions on the inadequacies of these two scenarios parallel Julius's.

from interfering in one another's internal affairs. Any action that foreseeably and avoidably places constraints on other peoples' freedom is, *ipso facto*, unjust. No form of international interactional coercion is justified between different 'islands of justice'. What is more, on my view, no principles of socio-economic justice apply between mutually independent societies, even if some are economically better off than others, and even if this simply results from differential luck.[8]

As discussed in Chapter 3, some will find this conclusion counterintuitive. Suppose we have two internally just societies, Brightland – which is rich and prosperous – and Gloomyland – which is reasonably well of, but not as well off as Brightland, because of bad brute luck. Under these conditions, wouldn't justice require us to redistribute resources from Brightland to Gloomyland? Isn't it unfair that Gloomylanders are worse off through no fault of their own?

There may be something 'cosmically unfair' about Gloomylanders' predicament, but nothing socially unjust. Denying the existence of egalitarian distributive duties between our two societies is in fact perfectly consistent with a commitment to respect for persons *qua* rational and autonomous agents. First, a stringent duty to place limits on resource inequalities can in principle apply only among those who stand in relations of mutual dependence. As we saw in Sections 3.3 and 7.5, when this is the case, steep inequalities (beyond a sufficiency threshold) may indeed undermine persons' ability to lead autonomous lives by generating social hierarchies or skewed power relations.[9] But between societies that, *ex hypothesi*, are independent of one another, considerations about domination and social stigma have no reason to arise in the first place. Second, Brightland's refusal to forgo some of its resources does not express disrespect towards Gloomylanders. Brightlanders can say to Gloomylanders: 'Thanks to your industriousness and hard work, you have built a just and well-organized society. You should be proud of your achievements, and do not need our help or compassion.'

My moral analysis of the relationship between Brightland and Gloomyland is not only consistent with equal respect but also psychologically plausible. As argued in Section 4.4, if we take seriously the claim that justice is premised upon limited altruism, we cannot establish duties of justice presupposing that people are entirely selfless. It is too much to expect of human beings that they concern themselves with making sure that everyone is as well off as they are, even if all meet a relevant threshold of sufficiency. This behaviour would of course be a mark of great generosity but, I argued, it is not required by justice.

---

[8] Presumably, if the worse off people were to blame for their situation, the claim that no international distributive duties apply would be all the more plausible.

[9] Cf. the helpful arguments in Martin O'Neill, 'What Should Egalitarians Believe?', *Philosophy and Public Affairs*, 36 (2) (2008), 119–56.

In sum, if we assume fully independent, and internally just, political communities, differences in socio-economic prosperity across them, even when due to purely differential luck (and hence, *a fortiori*, when the worse off are responsible for their predicament), do not raise concerns of justice. The only duties of justice applying between internally just and independent societies amount to non-interference.

(II) Humanity

This does not mean that, from the perspective of my normative framework, no distributive duties apply between mutually independent societies. Some such duties do fall upon them, but rather than being duties of justice, they are humanitarian duties activated by absolute deprivation. To illustrate this point, let us go back to the case of Brightland and Gloomyland, but assume that the latter is in conditions of absolute, rather than relative, deprivation, once again through no fault of its own. (If duties of justice do not apply in this case then, *a fortiori*, they would not apply were Gloomyland responsible for its plight.)

In these circumstances, the inhabitants of Brightland ought to respond to the suffering of Gloomylanders on humanitarian grounds, provided this would not be too costly to them. If Brightlanders eventually come to Gloomylanders' help, they may be regarded as morally praiseworthy for sacrificing some of *their own* resources for the sake of others. Of course, if Brightlanders had caused Gloomylanders' destitution, for instance through past aggressive behaviour, their assistance would hardly qualify as a matter of humanity, but would rest on a stringent demand of rectificatory justice.

Responding to the suffering of distant strangers – even when one is not outcome responsible for it – reveals a morally good character, whereas a failure to respond reveals a morally flawed character, even though it does not result in rights violations. Gloomylanders have no justice-based rights against Brightlanders, but Brightlanders have humanitarian duties towards Gloomylanders. If Brightlanders fail to honour such duties, they act wrongly, even though they do not thereby violate Gloomylanders' rights.

At this point, an objector might protest that Brightland's duties cannot be duties of humanity because they are obviously enforceable. Unless one subscribes to the implausible view that Gloomylanders cannot permissibly *enforce* Brightlanders' duties by appropriating some of their resources, one must accept that these are duties of justice.

This objection presupposes the view that duties of humanity, unlike duties of justice, may never be permissibly enforced. But, as I argued in Section 3.3, this view is implausible. While it is true that duties of justice, unlike duties of humanity, may in principle be enforced *without wrongdoing*, it is not true that duties of humanity may *never* be permissibly enforced. They may be enforced, but their enforcement always involves a moral loss. This is precisely the case in the present example. It would certainly be unreasonable to ask Gloomylanders to let themselves die for the sake of respecting Brightland's rights. But this does not mean that, by removing resources from Brightland, Gloomylanders would not violate Brightlanders' rights. All it means is that they would be all-things-considered *permitted* to do so. Gloomylanders would certainly owe Brightlanders apologies, and possibly also compensation, if with the passing of time they succeeded in rebuilding their society and generating some surplus.

In sum, the normative framework I have developed implies that, in a world of fully independent political communities, only justice-based duties of non-interference, and duties of humanitarian assistance, apply. Readers will have realized that this account of international justice resembles statists', and specifically Rawls's. In Rawls's society of peoples, political communities are to a large extent self-sufficient, internally well ordered, respectful of one another's self-determination, and ready to help one another when the need arises. If we assume a 'separate islands' model of the international arena, my normative framework delivers broadly statist conclusions.

8.3.2 Global Polity

Consider a world in which all persons relate to one another like fellow citizens. Here, there are no independent political communities, but a truly global political structure shaping persons' relations across the globe. In this imaginary scenario, there is interactional coercion on the part of the global state against its citizens as well as worldwide forms of systemic coercion that cannot be straightforwardly attributed to the agency of the state itself – unless the state has absolute control over its citizens, which is hardly ever the case even within existing, smaller-scale societies.

Under these circumstances, individual political communities are no longer the primary *locus* of justice and freedom: the global state is. If we were to ask about the implications of equal respect for this particular configuration of the global political order, we would reach the straightforward conclusion that familiar principles of domestic justice should apply to it. The world state should be so designed as to implement a mutually justifiable distribution of freedom among its citizens, which, as we know from Chapter 7, involves equal civil and political rights, as well as adequate socio-economic rights.

This conclusion is typically reached by cosmopolitan accounts of justice: whatever principles of justice apply domestically should, *mutatis mutandis*, apply globally. Under these circumstances, justice beyond borders would make no reference to the sovereignty and independence of individual political communities, but would look directly at how each individual is faring under a world-large institutional apparatus. In other words, our thinking about justice would have no international dimension, but would instead be fully global, as most cosmopolitans recommend.

So far, I have looked at two opposite configurations of the international arena, the 'separate-islands' and 'global-polity' models, and considered the implications of my normative framework when it is applied to each of them. It has emerged that, when applied to the first scenario, my framework delivers broadly statist conclusions: international morality requires justice-based non-interference and humanitarian assistance. By contrast, when applied to the second scenario, my framework leads to cosmopolitan conclusions: international justice corresponds to domestic justice writ large. As is probably apparent, both positions are implausible as accounts of what justice requires in the world today, because they both rest on oversimplified pictures of the international arena. Given that this is neither made up of independent islands, nor under the rule of a global state, what structure does it have?

8.4 THE WORLD TODAY: A NESTED-ISLANDS MODEL

Today we, human beings, are neither denizens of independent islands nor citizens of a global polity – instead, we are somewhere between these two extremes. If, on the one hand, we are members of our political communities, on the other, we (and our communities) are becoming increasingly vulnerable to decisions that are taken outside our borders. While national membership remains the first *locus* of realization of persons' right to freedom, the state's power to act on principles of justice is increasingly affected by exogenous factors. International institutions and informal rules heavily constrain states' and their members' opportunities to act. It looks as though politics today is neither fully international nor fully global. In the words of Andrew Hurrell,

> [w]e are not dealing with a 'now vanished Westphalian world' (to paraphrase Allan Buchanan) but rather with a world in which...cosmopolitan models of governance coexist, usually rather unhappily, with many aspects of the old Westphalian order.[10]

If we were to give a schematic representation of contemporary international practice in relation to the hypothetical scenarios described earlier, we would probably obtain a 'nested-islands' model. Individual societies are trapped in a dense and intricate network of bridges. What happens within them partly depends on what happens outside them and *vice versa*. Moreover, some of these islands are more closely interlinked than others; some are more powerful

---

[10] Andrew Hurrell, 'Global Inequality and International Institutions', *Metaphilosophy*, 32 (1/2) (2001), 34–57, p. 43.

than others, and hence in a much better position to control the movement of people and goods across the bridges. The freedom of those who live in weaker islands is thereby strongly affected by the choices of the inhabitants of powerful ones. On the one hand, the weak depend on the strong for their own subsistence – autarchy and self-sufficiency are just a mirage, and the prospect of cutting all bridges is therefore unacceptable. On the other hand, thanks to their better bargaining position and greater resources, wealthier, more prosperous, islands can use bridges on terms that are most advantageous to them.

This picture suggests that the coercive system we find within domestic societies has started to expand beyond them, resulting in a highly inhomogeneous and asymmetrical set of limits on freedom.[11] This feature of the international arena is what Hurrell calls 'deformity'. In the contemporary international scenario, some areas are clearly more integrated than others both geographically and functionally – consider, for instance, the case of the European Union or that of global trade. Moreover, when it comes to the design of rules and institutions with global reach, '[t]he vast majority of weaker actors are increasingly "rule takers" over a whole range of issues that affect all aspects of social, economic and political life'.[12]

If this is the situation with which we are confronted today, a plausible theory of justice for the world at large should be able to justify the constraints states and individuals place on one another's freedom not only directly but also indirectly, through the intricate nest of bridges forming the background against which they exist and interact. Can my coercion-based normative framework help us construct a theory of global justice appropriate for the current 'circumstances of international politics'?[13] Thanks to its dual focus on interactional and systemic coercion, it can.

As I have been emphasizing all along, the state remains a central *locus* of coercion and a crucial actor in the international arena. This suggests that a first set of principles of international justice should concentrate on the justification of states' internal and external conduct – setting limits to *domestic coercion*, and to *international interactional coercion*. In addition, such principles need to be supplemented by further principles, justifying *global systemic coercion*. This is the sort of coercion states, corporations, individuals, and international institutions exercise over one another by engaging in stable patterns of international interaction, and sustaining a global (or near-global) system of rules.

---

[11] I borrow this image from Julius, 'Nagel's Atlas', pp. 189ff.
[12] Hurrell, 'Global Inequality and International Institutions', p. 43.
[13] Joshua Cohen and Charles Sabel, 'Extra Rempublicam Nulla Justitia?', *Philosophy and Public Affairs*, 34 (2) (2006), 147–75.

8.5 INTERNATIONAL JUSTICE: INTERSTATE INTERACTIONAL COERCION

Statist principles of international justice are typically devoted to the justification of interstate interactional coercion. From the perspective of my coercion-based approach, there are clearly good reasons for engaging in this justificatory exercise, but the way statists have done so has proven defective. As I showed in Chapter 4, Rawlsian statists' advocacy of 'familiar principles of international law and practice' rests on shaky grounds. Their appeal to the notion of a people is misleading, as it injects a moralized dimension in what ought to be a descriptive account of the subjects of international justice. Moreover, their acceptance of illiberal societies as legitimate members of the international community, and their refusal to apply principles of socio-economic justice beyond the state, are dubious and poorly defended.

In light of these deficiencies, I put forward a set of principles of international justice, aimed at the justification of interstate interactional coercion, which is only partly inspired by statists', and specifically Rawls's, outlook on justice. Even though their *content* is very much in line with Rawls's theory – indeed, I deliberately use almost identical formulations – their *interpretation* differs in significant respects.

The principles in question cover three dimensions of international moral concern: internal legitimacy; sovereign equality; and just war. In my discussion, I only focus on the first two areas – given that the topic of just war theory is addressed in a rich separate literature that I cannot discuss here. One point, however, is worth emphasizing. If my conceptual framework is correct, then it shows that discussions about global justice and just war theory address the same normative concern: the justification of coercion. This makes my conceptual framework particularly attractive, allowing us to give unified meaning to the different ways in which the notion of justice is used at the international level.[14]

1. *Internal legitimacy*: states ought to be reasonably just, that is, they ought to distribute freedom among their citizens in a way that is in principle acceptable to all of them.
2. *Sovereign equality*: states ought to be free and independent, and their freedom and independence ought to be respected by other states (this entails further principles such as: 'States ought to observe treaties and undertakings'; 'States ought to be equal and parties to the agreements that bind them'; 'States are to observe a duty of non-intervention').

---

[14] See the arguments in Terry Nardin, 'International Political Theory and the Question of Justice', *International Affairs*, 82 (3) (2006), 449–65.

3. *Just War*: 'States have the right of self-defense but no right to instigate war for reasons other than self-defense', and 'States are to observe certain restrictions in the conduct of war'.[15]

8.5.1 Internal Legitimacy

As I have argued in Chapters 4, 6, and 7, from the perspective of my framework, states matter only insofar as they protect and enable individual freedom. My view attaches no independent moral importance to political communities that do not meet fundamental requirements of justice. A tyrannical or oppressive state, for example, is not entitled to the privileges of sovereignty. Similarly, a state that fails to respect the sovereignty of other legitimate states loses its status as an equal member of the international community.

If states matter only so long as they protect their citizens' right to freedom, stringent requirements of internal legitimacy must be placed on them. The distribution of freedom existing within a particular society must be justifiable in the eyes of all citizens. When this criterion is met – specifically, when equal civil and political rights, and socio-economic rights, are fulfilled – it is wrong to interfere with states' internal affairs as this would show disrespect towards their populations, who have a right to lead their lives in accordance with their conceptions of the good, and to determine the socio-economic implications of the right to freedom, beyond a fixed minimum – as argued in Chapter 7.

If, however, a state falls considerably short of this threshold of legitimacy, it is no longer owed equal respect on the part of other legitimate political communities. A state that does not meet such a threshold is one where a smaller or larger part of the population is unjustifiably coercing the rest. When this happens, a state loses its status as a sovereign equal. But what does sovereign equality amount to?[16]

8.5.2 Sovereign Equality

Sovereignty indicates the cluster of powers and rights that ought to be equally enjoyed by legitimate states. These include the authority to govern those living within their territories, the power to use and dispose of the resources present on their territories, the right not to be interfered with by other states, and so forth.[17] When a state is sovereign, it is free and independent; it has, and can

---

[15] Cf. Rawls's list in *The Law of Peoples* (Cambridge, MA: Harvard University Press, 1999), p. 37.
[16] I here draw on Antonio Cassese, *International Law* (Oxford: Oxford University Press, 2001), pp. 88ff.
[17] See A. John Simmons, 'On the Territorial Rights of States', *Philosophical Issues*, 11 (1) (2001), 300–26, esp. p. 305. In his account, Simmons refers to David Copp's 'The Idea of a Legitimate State', *Philosophy and Public Affairs*, 28 (1) (1999), 3–45, p. 19.

exercise, the capacity to be the 'maker of its own fate'. Sovereignty can be seen as having both normative and positive conditions. *Normative conditions* are those that determine whether a particular state is *entitled* to being sovereign. *Positive conditions* are those that any state must enjoy in order to be able to take advantage of the privileges of sovereignty.

From a normative point of view, a state ought to be treated as sovereign only so long as it is internally legitimate and respects the sovereignty of other legitimate states. In other words, a state's sovereign status ought to be conditional on its compliance with domestic and international norms of justice. Failure to respect these norms ought to result in a state's loss of the privileges of sovereignty, from the right to cooperate with other legitimate states on equal terms, to the rights to self-determination and territorial integrity.

Legitimate states, for instance, have a duty of justice not to enter into agreements and do business with illegitimate ones – unless this is done on condition that they modify their domestic practices. When legitimate states trade on equal terms with rogue regimes, they immediately become complicit in injustice, by pursuing their interests with no regard for these states' poor and oppressed populations.[18]

The so-called 'resource curse' offers an example of this type of injustice. It is well known that populations of resource-rich countries (especially in Africa) tend to experience surprisingly high levels of poverty and destitution, and to be governed by authoritarian regimes. This unfortunate phenomenon is fuelled by the international habit of trading with these regimes as if they were legitimate. In contemporary international practice, so long as a regime has effective control of a country's territory, it can freely borrow and use resources in the country's name. This has the effect of incentivizing corrupt officials to seize power in already underprivileged societies, rendering the goal of development ever more remote.[19] By recognizing illegitimate states as sovereign, other 'would-be legitimate' ones confer the power on them to perpetrate grievous injustices and are thus at least partly responsible for them.[20]

In addition to losing the privileges to trade and make alliances on equal terms, a failure to respect norms of justice renders a particular state in principle open to external intervention: ranging from criticism, to full-blown military action. A state that actively massacres part of its population is in

---

[18] Allen Buchanan, 'Recognitional Legitimacy and the State System', *Philosophy and Public Affairs*, 28 (1) (1999), 46–78, p. 58. Notice, however, that there might be exceptions to this general rule, for instance if the populations of an illegitimate state were to be excessively burdened by a trade embargo.

[19] This example has been discussed by Pogge in *World Poverty and Human Rights: Cosmopolitan Responsibilities and Reforms* (Cambridge: Polity Press, 2002), esp. Introduction and ch. 4.

[20] For further discussion, see Joseph E. Stiglitz, *Making Globalization Work* (London: Penguin, 2006), ch. 5; and Leif Wenar, 'International Property Rights and the Resource Curse', *Philosophy and Public Affairs*, 36 (1) (2008), 2–32.

principle vulnerable to intervention on the part of other states. Of course, whether intervention is warranted 'all-things-considered' will depend on a host of other considerations, going beyond the target's own lack of legitimacy (e.g. likelihood of success, legitimacy of the intervention itself, and so forth). But it still remains true that failing to meet the normative requirements of sovereignty is a necessary, though not a sufficient, condition for the moral appropriateness of external interference.[21]

Having briefly discussed the normative conditions of sovereignty, and what failure to respect them entails, let me now turn to the positive ones. Under what conditions can a state be in a position to act freely and have effective control over its territory, resources, and population? Plainly, when it is internally well functioning (i.e. not a failed state), and *de facto* free from interference. If a state's functioning is continuously disrupted by exogenous factors outside its control, it becomes unclear how it could be regarded as the maker of its own fate, or as having the *capacity* (hence the duty) to secure its citizens' right to freedom. If a state is routinely assaulted, or pressured into adopting particular policies, it cannot be counted as substantively, as opposed to merely formally, sovereign: what it does is to a large extent dependent on the will of others.[22]

Examples of this lack of the positive conditions of sovereignty are sadly familiar in human history. It suffices to think of European colonial expansion in Africa towards the end of the nineteenth century. As is well known, France, Belgium, Great Britain, Italy, Germany, Spain, and Portugal all 'raced' to conquer as much African land as possible. The conquered territories were then (variously) subjected to laws and policies dictated by the Mother Country in *its own* interest. Colonizers and colonized did not come together to constitute a single people. Instead, the former subjugated and exploited the latter. After the Second World War, direct colonial expansion of this kind was increasingly perceived as illegitimate and is now no longer regarded as an acceptable means of promoting national interests. But rule through colonial domination is just the most blatant form of interference.

For more recent examples of wrongful interference, think about the Soviet Union's control of Eastern Europe after the Second World War. Or even more strikingly, consider US foreign policy during those years, especially with regard to Latin American countries such as Panama, Honduras, Chile, Nicaragua, and Guatemala. Particularly notorious amongst such interventions are the Bay of Pigs Invasion (1961), a failed attempt to remove Fidel Castro's communist regime from power in Cuba, or the CIA's secret campaign against the election

---

[21] Cf. Laura Valentini, 'Human Rights: A Freedom-Centered View' (manuscript).

[22] Cf. the notion of effective sovereignty independently developed by Miriam Ronzoni, 'The Global Order: A Case of Background Injustice? A Practice-dependent Account', *Philosophy and Public Affairs*, 37 (3) (2009), 229–56, p. 248, and the distinction between positive and negative sovereignty in Robert H. Jackson, *Quasi-States: Sovereignty, International Relations and the Third World* (Cambridge: Cambridge University Press, 1990).

of Salvador Allende to the presidency of Chile (1964) and its subsequent support of Augusto Pinochet's dictatorial regime (1970s).[23]

The disruptive effects of such interventions on countries' sovereignty become all the more evident when it is recalled that, at the domestic level, persons' autonomy (what one might call their sovereignty over themselves) is threatened *not only* by *actual control* of one person over another, but also by the mere *possibility of interference*. If property laws are not generally complied with, or if I know that I am susceptible to others' intervention in my affairs, my capacity to set and pursue my own ends is severely undermined. A similar dynamic may also occur at the international level. Actual intervention does indeed undermine sovereignty. But the very lack of assurance against intervention does so too. It is not hard to imagine that a country that – for good reason – constantly feels threatened by another, more powerful, nation will try to design its policies in such a way as to reduce the likelihood of intervention. Such policies, however, might not correspond to those that would best realize citizens' right to freedom. Being subject to the power of another agent – even if the relation of subjugation is not formally acknowledged – undermines a country's sovereignty all the same.[24]

These examples of violations of the positive conditions of sovereignty can be fully accounted for from an interactional perspective. They are overt forms of intervention, actual or counterfactual, perpetrated by one or more countries against others. They are obvious examples of interactional coercion, and specifically of *unjust* interactional coercion. But in an increasingly globalized world, interference and intervention also take a more subtle form, which cannot be fully captured simply by looking at interstate relations. What I am referring to are the constraints imposed on states and their citizens by global rules, incentives, and patterns of interaction that limit their ability to 'determine' their own fate, and protect their citizens' right to freedom.[25]

Among such rules, those underlying the global economy are the most consequential for states and their prosperity. If there is a system of rules that, against any plausible baseline, would come out as coercive, it is the global economy.[26] As I will argue in greater detail in the next section, the constraints this system imposes on states and their citizens clearly stand in need of

---

[23] See Eric Cavallero, 'Coercion, Inequality, and the International Property Regime', *Journal of Political Philosophy*, 18 (1) (2010), 16–31 for discussion of these examples.

[24] For further discussion of this point in relation to the republican notion of freedom, see Cécile Laborde, 'Republicanism and Global Justice: A Sketch', *European Journal of Political Theory*, 9 (1) (2010), 48–69.

[25] For an analysis of the challenges confronting sovereignty in a era of globalization, specifically with reference to Southeast Asia, see Mark Beeson, 'Sovereignty under Siege: Globalisation and the State in Southeast Asia', *Third World Quarterly*, 24 (2) (2003), 357–74.

[26] On the power dynamics characterizing globalization, see David Singh Grewal, *Network Power: The Social Dynamics of Globalization* (New Haven and London: Yale University Press, 2008).

justification: they are appropriate objects of assessment for principles of justice. This means that, in our globalized world, sovereign equality takes on a complex, systemic dimension that Rawlsian statists have largely neglected. This deficit in statist theory must be remedied through principles of 'global' justice.

At this point, one caveat is needed. Even though I will restrict my discussion to the global economic system, this does not mean that it represents the only instance of global systemic coercion. There may very well be other, more subtle, global coercive practices, which also merit our attention. For the limited purposes of my discussion, however, I focus on the global economic system because it is most readily associated with globalization, and clearly constrains the freedom of (at least) states and their citizens against any plausible baseline. Even though there may be other global coercive systems, it is reasonable to think that, if the global economy were governed in accordance with principles of justice, many of the existing global injustices would disappear.

8.6 GLOBAL SOCIO-ECONOMIC JUSTICE: THE PROBLEM OF SYSTEMIC COERCION

But what do I mean by the global economic system? And in what ways might it be said to place constraints on the sovereignty of states and the freedom of their citizens? What I have in mind, here, are the rules and conventions governing global trade and finance, whose existence rests on the support of very many agents: from states to corporations, and from international organizations to individual buyers and sellers. Those rules clearly place severe constraints on (some) countries' ability to secure justice at home.

8.6.1 Global Trade

Consider, for example, the bulk of the rules crystallized in the WTO multilateral trade agreements. The main goal of these agreements is to foster trade liberalization through the abolition of trade barriers. Whether trade liberalization is a blessing or a curse though, depends on the background conditions against which it is implemented. As observed by Joseph Stiglitz, trade liberalization brings benefits 'when there are good risk markets, when there is full employment, when an economy is mature. But none of these conditions are satisfied in developing countries'.[27]

---

[27] Joseph Stiglitz, 'Social Justice and Global Trade', *Far Eastern Economic Review*, 169 (2) (2006), 18–22, p. 19.

Developing countries, whose industrial sector is still at the early stages, cannot compete with advanced market economies. Moreover, even those economic sectors in which developing countries are stronger, such as agriculture and textile, have suffered under the rules governing global trade. Because of the availability of cheaper alternatives imported from abroad, small farmers have great difficulties in finding markets for their products. This has generated poverty, unemployment, and dependence on foreign goods. Similar considerations apply to developing countries' textile sector. In Kenya, for instance, 'the liberalisation of textiles and footwear has led to imports flooding the domestic market and to a more limited market for domestically produced textiles and footwear'.[28] The result has been a massive shrinking in cotton production leading to lower incomes, unemployment, and even greater hunger.

These examples show how the rules underpinning liberalized trade have had obviously detrimental effects on the economy of (many) developing countries and, consequently, on their ability to secure their citizens' right to freedom. How can these countries be seen as fully sovereign? How can we hold them responsible for failing to secure justice at home if what happens within their borders is to a large extent determined by exogenous factors outside their control? These countries may be formally sovereign, but not substantively so.

This becomes all the more evident when we acknowledge that the erosion of trade barriers has been accomplished asymmetrically: with developing countries being forced to open their markets, while developed nations continued to protect those sectors in which developing countries would otherwise have been most competitive, namely agriculture and textile industries. As Stiglitz again points out, trade negotiations at the WTO 'provide a field day for special interests'.[29] Even though their task is to write the rules of a global game,

> they reflect the interests of advanced industrial countries – or, more particularly, special interests (like agriculture and oil) within those countries. This imbalance is in some cases the result of distorted voting rights; at other times, it comes from the sheer economic power of the countries and interests involved.[30]

As studies have shown, the formally consensus-based decision procedures characterizing WTO meetings are an expedient kept in place by its most powerful participants both to maintain an appearance of legitimacy in the eyes of their domestic populations, and to obtain relevant information on the preferences of other negotiators, so as to strike bargains that unfairly favour

---

[28] John Madeley, 'Trade and Hunger: An Overview of the Impact of Trade Liberalization on Food Security', *Globala Studier*, 4 (2000), 1–77, pp. 11–12, http://www.ppl.nl/bibliographies/wto/files/645.pdf (last accessed 31 October 2011).
[29] Stiglitz, 'Social Justice and Global Trade', p. 20.
[30] Stiglitz, *Making Globalization Work*, pp. 276–80, esp. p. 276.

their national interests.[31] Thanks to their superior bargaining power, rich countries unfairly foster their national economic interests 'through tariffs, quotas, anti-dumping duties, and subsidies'.[32] The trade rules negotiated in WTO settings therefore end up bestowing considerable advantages on developed countries, and on specific industrial sectors within them, at the expense of the poor in developing ones.[33] In the current global economy, then, states are not 'equally' sovereign, some are clearly more sovereign than others, that is, considerably more capable of shaping their future, at the expense of the future of others.

8.6.2 Global Finance

In addition to free trade, the current global economic system is characterized by considerable financial and capital mobility. Here too, already advanced industrial societies, with strong financial and economic institutions, find themselves in a position where they can benefit from trade and monetary liberalization, and can often (though not always) successfully manage the risks associated with it. This is not the case for developing countries. Instead of strengthening their economy, capital liberalization might easily increase their vulnerability. As Barry Eichengreen argues, 'high capital mobility is a problem for countries where risk management is underdeveloped, where supervision and regulation are weak, and where the banking system is an instrument for development policy'.[34]

Notice, however, that extreme global capital mobility has had detrimental effects not only on developing countries but also on developed ones. A particularly problematic consequence of capital mobility is tax competition. In order to attract capital and investment, countries are incentivized to adopt less progressive tax policies, thereby diminishing the funds with which to promote social justice at home.[35] There is an unofficial rule within

---

[31] Richard H. Steinberg, 'In the Shadow of Law or Power? Consensus-based Bargaining and Outcomes in the GATT/WTO', *International Organization*, 56 (2) (2002), 339–47.

[32] Thomas W. Pogge, '"Assisting" the Global Poor', in Deen K. Chatterjee (ed.), *The Ethics of Assistance: Morality and the Distant Needy* (Cambridge: Cambridge University Press, 2004), p. 277. See also Stiglitz, *Making Globalization Work*, esp. ch. 3.

[33] As Robert H. Wade puts it, '[d]eveloped states seek to shape the internal regimes of emerging markets in ways that favour the expansion of the property and profits of their own producers, through both bilateral relations and multilateral organizations'. Robert H. Wade, 'Should We Worry about Income Inequality?', in David Held and Ayse Kaya (eds.), *Global Inequality* (Cambridge: Polity Press, 2007), 104–31, p. 123.

[34] Barry Eichengreen, 'The Global Gamble of Financial Liberalization: Reflections on Capital Mobility, National Autonomy, and Social Justice', *Ethics and International Affairs*, 13 (1) (1999), 205–26, p. 221.

[35] Reuven S. Avi-Yonah, 'Globalization, Tax Competition, and the Fiscal Crisis of the Welfare State', *Harvard Law Review*, 113 (7) (1999–2000), 1573–676, pp. 1575–6. See also Joseph Stiglitz,

the global economy that says 'if you want to attract or retain investment, you need to apply significant discounts on taxes on foreign capital'.

Even though, as I have mentioned, this phenomenon concerns both developed and developing countries, the latter have been more adversely affected than the former. While developed countries have often been able partly to compensate for lower tax rates by broadening their tax base, developing countries have not, thus experiencing a significant decline in their tax revenues.[36] This appears all the more morally troublesome if one thinks that, in developing countries, revenue is needed to support even the most basic social services.[37] In sum, both developing and developed countries are vulnerable to the effects of tax competition. The only entities that stand to benefit from it are tax havens, and international investors.[38]

Another blatant example of how the current structure of international finance may place significant constraints on state sovereignty and erode the basic conditions for domestic justice is offered by the multiple financial crises witnessed over the past three decades. Consider, first, the so-called 'Década Perdida' (the lost decade), namely the period of extreme financial instability that characterized Latin America in the 1980s. Next, recall the Asian Financial Crisis in the 1990s. The crisis began in Thailand in 1997, when turmoil in its financial institutions led investors to withdraw capital from the country. The insecurity quickly spread to Indonesia, Malaysia, and the Philippines, whose currencies also ended up being dramatically depreciated as a result.[39] In response to the crisis, many of these countries adopted policies of liberalization, deregulation, and privatization, further eroding the presence of the state in public life.

Finally, think of the financial crisis that erupted in late 2007, where the burst of a housing 'bubble' in the United States led to an abrupt reduction in property prices, which eventually gave rise to a global recession. Many businesses (if not entire countries) went bankrupt, thereby increasing poverty and unemployment rates. To help their economies pick up, and reduce their deficits, European countries have resorted to drastic public funding cuts, predictably leading to a deterioration of domestic social justice.

'Globalization and the Economic Role of the State in the New Millennium', *Industrial and Corporate Change*, 12 (1) (2003), 3–26, p. 3.

[36] See Thomas Rixen, 'Tax Competition and Inequality' (manuscript), and Michael Keen and Alejandro Simone, 'Is Tax Competition Harming Developing Countries more than Developed?', *Tax Notes International*, 34 (2004), 1317–25.

[37] See Reuven S. Avi-Yonah, 'Globalization and Tax Competition: Implications for Developing Countries', *Cepal Review*, 74 (2001), 59–66, p. 62.

[38] See Peter Dietsch, 'Rethinking Sovereignty in International Fiscal Policy', *Review of International Studies* 37 (5) (2011); and also Peter Dietsch and Thomas Rixen, 'Justice and International Tax Competition' (manuscript).

[39] Ngaire Woods, 'International Political Economy in an Age of Globalization', in John Baylis and Steve Smith (eds.), *The Globalization of World Politics* (Oxford: Oxford University Press, 2005), 325–48, p. 341.

As lamented by the 2010 Human Development Report, the crisis 'caused 34 million people to lose their jobs and 64 million more people to fall below the $1.25 a day income poverty threshold'.[40]

Such recurrent crises are a predictable consequence of unconstrained international financial speculation.[41] That is, the current international financial system is foreseeably and avoidably conducive to frequent crises, eroding states' capacity to secure justice at home.[42]

This admittedly brief overview of some of the effects of the existing global economic system illustrates the claim that this system is coercive (i.e. it places foreseeable and avoidable constraints on some agents' freedom, compared to alternative systems) and, plainly, unjustly so. The particular distribution of freedom it engenders is not in principle universally justifiable to all persons in the world. Its detrimental effects on state sovereignty render individual political communities less capable of securing their citizens' right to freedom. But what alternative system could meet the demands of justice?

Before asking what measures could be taken to bring about a just (or at any rate more just) world, I need to respond to an objection global justice sceptics are likely to raise. This is that at least many of the international rules I have identified as coercive are, in fact, far from being so. Critics might, for example, point at international organizations such as the IMF and the WTO and suggest that what they do is inappropriately described as coercive.[43]

For instance, when the WTO 'invites' a developing country D, to join the organization, it arguably increases, rather than curtails, its freedom.[44] In all likelihood, by not participating in the WTO, a developing country would be severely disadvantaged, lacking vital opportunities to trade with other states. This being the case, it looks like the WTO widens, rather than restricts, D's freedom and thus cannot be appropriately described as (interactionally) coercive. On this view, the WTO is beyond justice-based scrutiny. In some sense, one might even say that 'it helps' the poor.[45]

Similarly, even though it is true that the IMF places *some* constraints on (developing) countries when it makes its loans conditional on financial liberalization, and domestic privatization, the fact that developing countries

---

[40] UN, 'Overview', *Human Development Report* (2010), p. 9, http://hdr.undp.org/en/media/HDR_2010_EN_Overview_reprint.pdf (last accessed 31 October 2011).

[41] James Tobin, 'Prologue', in Mahbib ul Haq, Inge Kaul, and Isabelle Grunberg (eds.), *The Tobin Tax: Coping with Financial Volatility* (New York and Oxford: Oxford University Press, 1996), ix–xviii.

[42] Aaron James, 'Distributive Justice without Sovereign Rule: The Case of Trade', *Social Theory and Practice*, 31 (4) (2005), 533–59, p. 554.

[43] The next few paragraphs draw on Valentini, 'Coercion and (Global) Justice'.

[44] For a description of the process of accession to the WTO, see http://www.wto.org/english/thewto_e/acc_e/acces_e.htm (last accessed 31 October 2011).

[45] Mathias Risse, 'Do We Owe the Global Poor Assistance or Rectification?', *Ethics and International Affairs*, 19 (1) (2005), 9–18, p. 13.

accept such loans suggests that these loans make them better off, more free, overall. How, then, can these institutions be accused of 'coercing' developing nations, let alone unjustly so?

These are correct observations, but they fail to disprove my argument. If anything, they further support my more general theoretical claim that, when thinking about justice, we should keep in mind *both* interactional and systemic perspectives. The objector is here looking at the WTO and the IMF as specific group agents, making offers and issuing threats. This interactional perspective is important and worth retaining. We can certainly consider both the WTO and the IMF interactionally, and judge the coerciveness (or lack thereof) and justice of specific policies or decisions taken by them. But this interactional perspective is ill-suited to evaluate the effects of the global economic system as a whole.

While the WTO and the IMF *qua* organizations certainly participate in, and contribute to supporting this system, the system as such is not reducible to them. Its existence and operating mechanisms depend on the cooperation of very many agents, ranging from international institutions to states, and from big transnational corporations to individual consumers. In short, the fact that, at least in certain instances, the WTO (or the IMF) is not interactionally coercive of particular agents, does not mean that: (*a*) the WTO (or the IMF) does not contribute to supporting the existing international economic system; and (*b*) this economic system is not appropriately seen as both coercive and unjust.

But what would make global systemic coercion ultimately justified? A template for answering this question is already given by the logic of my coercion-based view, as articulated in relation to the domestic context in Chapters 5 and 6. Recall that, on this view, to become compatible with the freedom of all, systemic coercion in pre-societal conditions requires regulatory institutions: specifically, a just governing authority such as the state. If this is the case domestically, why not think that something similar will also be the case internationally? What we need at the global level are international or global institutions capable of effectively regulating the international economy in such a way as to make it compatible with everyone's right to freedom.[46]

8.7 GLOBAL SOCIO-ECONOMIC JUSTICE: JUSTIFYING SYSTEMIC COERCION

What principles should govern the international economy? What institutions should implement the relevant principles? In this section, I sketch an answer

---

[46] For similar views, see Iris Marion Young, 'Responsibility and Global Justice: A Social Connection Model', *Social Philosophy and Policy*, 23 (1) (2006), 102–30; and Miriam Ronzoni, 'The Global Order: A Case of Background Injustice?'.

to these questions. I say 'sketch' because I am not in a position to establish what specific regulatory mechanisms should be adopted to render the international economy compatible with everyone's right to freedom. It would be both naive and hubristic for a political philosopher alone to try and prescribe a set of rules for the fair regulation of the global economy. The issue is too complex, and clearly requires interdisciplinary research including economists, sociologists, lawyers, IR scholars, and experts from other fields. Although I cannot propose *specific* institutional solutions for governing the global economy, I can still flash out some of the ideals that those institutions should promote, and the broad form such institutions should take.

8.7.1 Ideals and Principles

In terms of ideals and principles, our governing rule should be the equal (substantive) sovereignty of states understood, in turn, as a precondition for realizing their citizens' right to freedom. Only states that are substantively sovereign have the capacity, and hence the duty, to secure domestic justice. Even though the global and domestic arenas should both be so organized as to be compatible with every person's right to freedom, this does not entail that the principles of justice any particular society defends at the domestic level should apply to the world at large.

First, what qualify as mutually acceptable socio-economic arrangements in one context need not immediately transpose onto a different one. Whether certain economic inequalities, for example, lead to domination and oppression depends on the particular social background we are confronted with. Even though we may analogize states and individuals, the analogy is not a perfect one. The conditions for individual and societal self-determination are likely to differ, at least to some extent. Plainly, it would be absurd to give states a right to education, health care, or freedom of movement. The interests of states, and the background against which they interact, are not *identical to* the interests and background conditions of individuals' actions. To that extent, what socio-economic justice requires is likely to vary from the domestic to the global arena.[47]

Second, as we saw in Chapter 7, there may be *reasonable disagreements* between citizens about what counts as a mutually acceptable distribution of freedom within society, specifically in relation to matters of economic justice. Such reasonable disagreements are all the more likely to arise when we move from the domestic to the international arena, given the latter's greater social

---

[47] See also the discussion in Laura Valentini, 'Global Justice and Practice-Dependence: Conventionalism, Institutionalism, Functionalism', *Journal of Political Philosophy*, 19 (4) (2011), 399–418.

complexity and pluralism. The normative perspectives we need to reconcile are many, and the facts on the basis of which judgements about justice and injustice have to be made are complex and often not easily ascertainable.

Given the cultural diversity and social complexity characterizing the global economy, instead of aiming for a specific and complete account of what global socio-economic justice requires, we are once again on firmer ground simply establishing what it must exclude. Instead of offering an account of perfect justice, we focus on identifying existing injustices and suggesting how to remedy them. From this perspective, we can certainly agree with David Miller, who argues that:

> a fair [just] international order cannot simply mean a free market in which nations and corporations pursue their interests without regard to the consequences for vulnerable poor people. The responsibility of citizens of rich countries is to ensure fairness [justice] in this sense – an international order whose rules [*robustly*] allow poor societies adequate opportunities to develop.[48]

But what might this require, from a more concrete point of view?

8.7.2 Sample Policy Proposals and Institutional Reforms

At the very least, global socio-economic justice would seem to require symmetry in the rules applying to different countries and accountability in the processes establishing them, with no profitable exceptions for the most powerful. This is unlikely to be enough, though: when agents' strengths and starting positions are widely different, symmetry in the establishment of rules need not guarantee fairness. Perfectly symmetrical rules may still be unfair.

Consider, for instance, the effects of symmetrical rules in societies characterized by racial or gender inequality. Colour- or sex-blind laws are likely to perpetuate, rather than put an end to, the injustices plaguing the societies in question.[49] Similar considerations can also be advanced, *mutatis mutandis*, in relation to the global order. This suggests that trade liberalization should be conducted asymmetrically, but this time with asymmetries positively discriminating in favour of developing countries, allowing them to protect their emergent economies.

Alternatively, liberalization could be symmetrical, but accompanied by *redistributive measures* aimed at allowing developing countries to sustain

---

[48] David Miller, *National Responsibility and Global Justice* (Oxford: Oxford University Press, 2007), p. 253.
[49] See Darrel Moellendorf, 'The World Trade Organization and Egalitarian Justice', *Metaphilosophy*, 36 (1/2) (2005), 145–62, p. 153. Unfairness is also generated by the choice of regulated sectors; for instance, intellectual property regulation tends to favour developed countries. See also Thomas W. Pogge, 'Human Rights and Global Health: A Research Program', *Metaphilosophy*, 36 (1/2) (2005), 182–209.

their emergent industries, and make their prices competitive on the global plane without having to lower labour standards.[50] In turn, compensating developing countries for the otherwise adverse effects of liberalization will probably require establishing new international authorities, with the capacity and moral entitlement to extract revenue for international redistributive purposes. One way of raising the said revenue could be, for instance, Thomas Pogge's Global Resources Dividend: a global tax on the use of natural resources, which is estimated to raise considerable funds each year. The revenue raised from this tax could then be employed to support developing countries' emergent economies.[51]

In addition to introducing forms of 'positive discrimination' and/or redistributive measures in favour of developing countries, a just global order, in which each society has the power to secure social justice at home, would have to be one where capital mobility does not end up eroding states' ability to raise revenue through capital taxation. As we have seen, in today's international economy, states compete for investment by lowering taxes on foreign capital. It again seems that the key to solving this particular problem lies in greater coordination, and tax regulation, between different societies. Unless international institutions are established with the authority to oversee and harmonize, or at least balance, different tax regimes across the globe, tax competition will jeopardize state sovereignty and domestic justice.[52]

Greater regulation will also be necessary in order to avoid repeat performances of the financial crises that have shaken the world during the second half of the twentieth century until the present time. A proposal that has generated considerable attention in this respect is the so-called Tobin tax, consisting of a tax (proposed rates vary between 0.1 and 1 per cent) on all foreign exchange transactions. The tax, it is argued, would both help reduce financial volatility, which is one of the main causes of financial crises, and generate revenue that could be used for development purposes.[53]

These are just a few examples of the sorts of reforms that might be necessary in order to move the world towards greater justice. As I said, identifying exactly what policy measures would achieve this goal goes beyond what I set out to do in this book. Even so, one might still want to ask how change towards

---

[50] Moellendorf, 'The World Trade Organization and Egalitarian Justice', p. 152.
[51] Pogge, *World Poverty and Human Rights*, ch. 8.
[52] See Peter Dietsch, 'Tax Competition and Its Effects on Domestic and Global Justice', in Ayelet Banai, Miriam Ronzoni, and Christian Schemmel (eds.), *Social Justice, Global Dynamics: Theoretical and Empirical Perspectives* (London: Routledge, 2011), and 'Rethinking Sovereignty in International Fiscal Policy'. See also Gillian Brock, *Global Justice: A Cosmopolitan Account* (Oxford: Oxford University Press, 2009), ch. 5.
[53] See James Tobin, 'Prologue'; and Simon Caney, 'Global Justice: From Theory to Practice', *Globalizations*, 3 (2) (2006), 121–37, pp. 126ff.

global justice should be pursued, and what a just global order would roughly look like, on the view I advocate.

From a practical point of view, the wisest approach to global institutional reform, especially given its complexity and the inevitable uncertainty concerning its effects, is gradualism.[54] We need to start with the institutions that we have and slowly but steadily create new ones, as well as improve the performance of those that already exist: ranging from voting rules to agenda setting, from areas of competence to policy instruments.

In the long run, piecemeal reform should lead to the establishment of institutions with relatively independent and accountable decision-making power.[55] Without independent authorities, the robustness of persons' freedom could not be guaranteed: the most powerful would still be in a position to 'dominate' or unduly constrain the freedom of the powerless, as is often the case in our existing political reality. So long as institutions at the international or global level are governed by bargaining among actors with different power positions, their structure and policies will continue to promote the interests of a small subset of the world's population.

The line of reasoning underpinning this conclusion reflects the rationale behind the justification of the state at the domestic level. If solving the problem of justice in the state of nature requires building a sovereign arbiter that regulates individual transactions so as to protect persons' right to freedom, a similar solution will also be necessary at the international level. We need to replace lawless coercion with law-governed coercion: coercion that is compatible with everyone's right to freedom.

This, however, does not imply that we ought to strive to create a global state. Functionally differentiated institutions could also realize the objective of guaranteeing the right to freedom for all. As Thomas Pogge points out, the experience of federal states shows that sovereignty need not be absolute, but can be successfully dispersed across functionally differentiated institutional units.[56] In turn, such institutions would have to be designed so as to be accountable to those whose freedom they shape and constrain, in the same way in which we think domestic institutions should be accountable to their populations.

On the picture of the world I am envisaging, even though we would witness a partial transfer of sovereignty from the state to the supranational level, such a transfer would not be conducted in order to diminish the power of the state. As we have seen, unless appropriate regulation is in place, states themselves

---

[54] See the discussion about our epistemic limits in relation to global institutional reform in Chapter 2.

[55] This point is made, specifically in relation to the WTO, by Elisa Orrù and Miriam Ronzoni, 'Which Supranational Sovereignty? Criminal and Socio-Economic Justice Compared', *Review of International Studies*, 37 (5) (2011).

[56] Pogge, *World Poverty and Human Rights*, ch. 7.

find their agency severely restricted, and their sovereignty undermined, by the effects of the global economic system. Our ultimate aim is not to annihilate the state as an institution, but to enable all states to perform the functions that justify their existence, by building new institutions at the global level.[57] Depending on the shape, capacities, and mandate of the institutions in question, different regulative principles will apply to them, which will have the same general aim as domestic principles of justice – namely preserving everyone's right freedom to – but will presumably pursue it on the basis of different *rules* of conduct.

This conclusion should not be so surprising after all. As I argued earlier in this chapter, when it comes to the international arena, our relations are neither entirely reducible to interactions between states, nor identical to those we share with our fellow citizens. In light of this, the suggestion that a just global order would have to include authorities with limited competences, thus being neither as loosely regulated as a Westphalian system of states, nor as tightly organized as a world state, is a natural one to advance.

8.8 CONCLUSION

In this chapter, I have explored the implications of my coercion-based conceptual framework for the question of global justice. I have argued that, because the international arena is characterized by interactional coercion between states as well as global systemic coercion, especially of an economic nature, a good theory of global justice should contain principles for the justification of both. A plausible liberal approach to justice for our world should be neither fully statist, nor fully cosmopolitan. Justice cannot be secured simply by careful domestic policies, and non-intervention between internally just states, as statists typically recommend. However, neither does justice require replicating domestic arrangements and principles at the global level. Justice for the world is located somewhere between these two extremes.

A just world is one in which states both have the capacity to secure their citizens' right to freedom and act so as to secure it. For this to be the case, states must not only meet criteria of internal legitimacy but also be in a position to act freely. I have argued that, in increasingly globalized settings, the latter condition is hardly ever met. What happens within societies, and to their ability to realize justice domestically, is heavily influenced by processes that lie outside their control. Under these circumstances, justice requires the establishment of additional institutional forms with the capacity

---

[57] For proposals in this direction, see Orrù and Ronzoni, 'Which Supranational Sovereignty?'

to effectively regulate international transactions so as to avoid the continued erosion of state sovereignty. While both domestic and international institutions should be geared towards the realization of persons' right to freedom, the rules governing them will likely differ in content, given the different contexts in which they operate.

What specific rules should govern these institutions, and what precise shape they should take, is a question I have only gestured at, and one I am not in a position to address in the present book. But I do nevertheless hope to have developed a normative framework generating an appealing and coherent liberal approach to global justice.

9

Conclusion

9.1 INTRODUCTION

I started this book by setting out what I called 'the question of extension', asking whether we can plausibly extend principles of liberal-egalitarian justice from the domestic to the international arena. I identified two main answers to this question, cosmopolitanism and statism, and argued that each of them presents to both theoretical and practical difficulties. Theoretically, while statists' defence of the moral primacy of peoples seemed contrary to liberal normative individualism, cosmopolitans' commitment to global egalitarianism appeared intolerant and imperialistic. Practically, while statists' 'familiar principles of international law and practice'[1] seemed biased towards the *status quo*, cosmopolitans' globalization of domestic standards of justice struck many as hopelessly idealistic. In the light of these difficulties, I further qualified my question, asking *whether there can be a coherent liberal answer to the question of extension capable of overcoming the theoretical and practical difficulties with cosmopolitanism and statism*. Does the normative framework developed in this book meet these challenges? I argue that it does: its answer to the question of extension is neither illiberal nor intolerant, and neither *status-quo* biased nor implausibly idealistic.

In this short concluding chapter, I show how my normative framework helps us reconceptualize and advance the debate on global justice beyond the cosmopolitan and statist paradigms. In Section 9.2, I consider how my framework overcomes the justificatory difficulties with cosmopolitanism and statism, and proves to be fully consistent with the liberal commitment to equal respect for persons. In Section 9.3, I turn to what I called the 'practical' difficulties with cosmopolitanism and statism and explain why they do not arise in the context of my framework. In Section 9.4, I illustrate how my view helps us reframe the debate on global justice, and why it enables us to make

---

[1] John Rawls, *The Law of Peoples* (Cambridge, MA: Harvard University Press, 1999), p. 37.

progress within it. Finally, in Section 9.5, I briefly consider the grounds and nature of our responsibilities for global justice.

9.2 OVERCOMING THEORETICAL DIFFICULTIES

Is my coercion-based normative framework consistent with the fundamental commitments of liberalism? It is. The framework is grounded in the principle of equal respect for persons *qua* rational and autonomous agents, which in turn gives rise to two types of duties: duties of justice and duties of humanity. Duties of justice determine under what conditions we may permissibly constrain one another's freedom. Duties of humanity establish what we ought to do for others when they find themselves in need. Together, these two types of duties capture the most important ways we may express respect for persons *qua* rational and autonomous agents: by refraining from interfering with their entitlements, and by helping them when their agency is compromised or at risk. Like cosmopolitanism, then, my approach is firmly committed to the moral primacy, and equality, of persons. Unlike cosmopolitanism, however, it cannot be charged with being imperialistic or inattentive to the value of self-determination.

This is thanks to its nuanced account of freedom: of the necessary social conditions to lead autonomous lives. First, my view explicitly acknowledges the historical situatedness of autonomy, and therefore the impossibility of offering a fully determinate and universally valid account of what distribution of freedom can be justified in the eyes of all. As we have seen, this gives rise to a modest outlook on justice, setting minimal standards that any political community must meet, without advocating the universal validity of domestic economic egalitarianism (see Chapters 7 and 8). Of course, even though my view does not support a unique standard of justice, it is not neutral across *all* possible ways of organizing society either. Illiberal communities, which fail to recognize the fundamental moral equality of persons, are illegitimate on the view I have defended. As I argued in Chapters 4 and 7, this is a conclusion any liberal view must endorse. Failure to respect the moral equality of persons is incompatible with a truly liberal morality.

Second, my normative framework is sensitive to the moral importance of political communities insofar as they constitute the primary *locus* of respect for individuals' right to freedom. The value of each society rests on it representing the result of a collective endeavour aimed at defining and protecting the right to freedom.[2] My coercion-based framework therefore shows how a commitment

---

[2] For an excellent Kant-Rousseau inspired defence of this view, see Anna Stilz, *Liberal Loyalty: Freedom, Obligation, and the State* (Princeton, NJ: Princeton University Press, 2009).

to normative individualism is fully consistent with statists' emphasis on national self-determination and the importance of communal ties. But once again, in order for such an emphasis to be fully liberal, it must be compatible with the ideal of the fundamental moral equality of persons. If communal ties and self-determination do not serve this ideal, they carry very little moral weight. If, however, they do, we have reason to respect, promote, and defend them. It is in this spirit that, in Chapter 8, I have advocated principles of socio-economic justice extending to the global realm. Perhaps paradoxically, in an increasingly globalized world, a concern with sovereignty and self-determination prompts us to take seriously the question of global socio-economic justice statists tend to downplay.

Now that the domestic and international realms are deeply intertwined, especially through global trade and finance, non-interference between political communities is almost unattainable. We are so intensely interconnected that we interfere with one another all the time: even when we do not do so overtly. Under these circumstances, what is needed, in order to make sure that each community is genuinely sovereign and self-determining, is a set of institutions capable of regulating international transactions so as to prevent the erosion of state sovereignty.

On the view defended here, global socio-economic justice does not amount to an extension of the parochial intuition that 'nobody should be worse off through no fault of her own'. Rather, it requires so arranging the world that individual societies can be genuinely self-determining, and hence capable of protecting their citizens' right to freedom.

9.3 OVERCOMING PRACTICAL DIFFICULTIES

Is my normative framework hopelessly idealistic or problematically *status-quo* biased? It is not. Regarding hopeless idealism, there are two crucial ways in which my framework is not guilty of it. First, as I have been emphasizing all along, the framework is designed by taking seriously the psychological limits of human nature. It represents what, in Chapter 2, I called an 'embedded' approach to justice, one that focuses on human beings as they are, and on the circumstances of moderate scarcity that characterize human existence. From this methodological perspective, we cannot expect individuals to be concerned with making everyone else as well off as they are, to act as impartiality operators. Rather, as argued in Chapter 4, we should interpret the principle of equal respect as having an impartial component, as well as a 'partial' one.

Each person's life counts equally from an impartial point of view, yet each has a special responsibility for her or his life going well. This being the case, we should limit stringent demands of justice to those situations in which some are undermining others' right to freedom. Helping others who enjoy the necessary social conditions to lead autonomous lives and yet are not as well off as we are through no fault of our own might be generous and praiseworthy, but is not a requirement of justice. To think otherwise would be to fail to take seriously what we can and should reasonably expect from beings like ourselves.

Even though the view I have defended is not implausibly demanding, it is also not implausibly complacent. From the perspective of my framework, ignoring others' disadvantage, when one has contributed to causing it, is morally unacceptable, as is unacceptable to ignore others' suffering and destitution, even if one has not contributed to bringing them about. Justice and humanity do place important demands on us, without presupposing that human beings are selfless, fully altruistic creatures.

Moreover, the normative framework I have proposed does not lead to the defence of a utopian picture of what a just world would be like. Rather, it remains relatively open-ended with respect to the particular types of institutional arrangements that justice demands. Instead of asking what a morally perfect world ought to be like, if we were to start from scratch, my framework is meant to enable us to assess existing institutions and patterns of interaction from the viewpoint of justice, and identify under what conditions they could be justified in the eyes of all.[3] Starting from the world as it is, the view does not defend an implausibly detached and idealistic account of justice, but directs our attention towards piecemeal reform of existing institutions and practices. It is certainly true that, on my account, global justice in all likelihood requires building stronger international and supranational institutions. However, this feature of the view hardly makes it utopian. If anything, it simply accentuates a tendency we are already witnessing in real-world international politics, embodied in institutions such as the UN, EU, ICC, WTO, and IMF.

So far, I have argued that my framework does not lead to implausibly idealized conclusions, but what about the charge of *status-quo* bias? Once again, in relation to my framework, this charge is misplaced. This is because the framework explicitly rejects the view that only the state, understood as a powerful and authoritative group *agent*, can bear duties of justice (especially of a socio-economic kind). Since no global state exists, this claim has deeply conservative implications, confining concerns of justice to the domestic arena. As I argued in Chapters 5 and 6, however, this view of the state mistakes its role with respect to principles of justice. The state is not the sole trigger of demands of justice; rather, under appropriate conditions, it is primarily a response to them. All that is needed for questions of justice to arise is coercion.

---

[3] For the distinction between these two types of theorizing, see Michael Blake 'Distributive Justice, State Coercion, and Autonomy', *Philosophy and Public Affairs*, 30 (3) (2001), 257–96, pp. 261ff.

In particular, the framework's dual focus on interactional and systemic coercion allows us to detect and (if necessary) condemn the ways in which political communities affect one another's fate not only directly – for example, through military intervention – but also indirectly, through systemically coercive global practices. My coercion-based view therefore does not declare our duties to help the world's poor a mere matter of assistance. Rather, it sees them as being, to a large extent, a question of structural justice, concerning the rules currently shaping the international economic system. To the extent that statism's bias towards the *status quo* is generated by its inability to capture the systemic dimension of international politics and its normative significance, the coercion view is immune from it.

In addition, my framework is also uncompromising when it comes to the fundamental liberal commitment to equal respect. While statists often consider societies whose political cultures fail to honour the moral equality of persons as legitimate, such compromises with existing political reality are unwarranted from the perspective advocated here. As I argued in Chapter 4, unless it can be shown (and it is unclear how it could) that a world in which the moral equality of persons is universally upheld is impossible, liberals have no reason to consider as legitimate societies whose structure and values are contrary to human freedom and equality. The *fact* of pluralism is not a reason for a liberal to accept illiberal views.

9.4 REFRAMING THE DEBATE

Not only does my coercion-based normative framework avoid the difficulties detected in cosmopolitanism and statism, but it also allows us to see these two views as answers to the *same* question. From within my coercion-based approach, both cosmopolitanism and statism may be interpreted as answers to the question of what principles should justify coercion beyond state borders. While statists focus on interactional coercion between states, cosmopolitans concentrate on its systemic counterpart. Once these two outlooks are looked at from this perspective, the connection between justice and socio-economic equality becomes clearer.

Justice is fundamentally about mutually acceptable distributions of freedom, of the social conditions for persons to lead autonomous lives. Whether persons' right to freedom requires simple (yet robust) non-interference or socio-economic distributive principles is a contingent matter that depends on the particular social practice at hand. In a world of independent states, for example, justice would generate no distributive requirements. As argued in Sections 3.3 and 8.3, the only such requirements would be demands of humanity, aimed at relieving absolute deprivation. By contrast, against a background of sufficiently intense interaction and interdependence, justice does have a socio-economic dimension, perhaps even egalitarian in kind.[4] Since cosmopolitanism and statism presuppose different accounts of our global political practices – cosmopolitans emphasize global interdependence, statists (especially Rawls) relative independence – the former concludes that respecting persons' right to freedom worldwide requires socio-economic redistribution, the latter denies it.

The view I have developed allows us so to reframe the debate on global justice, thanks to its distinctive flexibility. Such flexibility contrasts with the relative rigidity of the Rawls-inspired basic-structural outlook that has so far been dominant in the literature. Although the coercion approach is closely related, and owes much, to this outlook, it is also more nuanced and adaptable. As I have shown, very often cosmopolitan theorists find themselves in the difficult position of having to argue for the claim that there exists a global basic structure. Since the notion of a basic structure has been coined in the context of debates on domestic justice, it is natural to equate it with the set of institutions governing individual societies.

Once we turn our attention from the domestic context to the international arena, taking 'the basic structure as subject' forces us to address a rather artificial all-or-nothing dilemma: either there is a global basic structure, in which case principles of domestic justice apply globally, or there is not, in which case no 'systemic' principles of justice apply worldwide. Such a focus on the basic structure is what renders the relational cosmopolitan conclusion that principles of domestic justice should be extended to the world at large suspicious. As we clearly do not live in a global society *just like* domestic ones, the claim that there is a global basic structure stands on shaky ground.

By contrast, my coercion-based framework provides a more flexible account of the subject of justice. Coercion is a broad phenomenon of which there can be multiple manifestations, both interactional and systemic. What matters is the presence of non-trivial constraints on freedom avoidably and foreseeably generated by responsible agents, or systems of social rules. This allows the coercion view to think about the 'subject' of justice in distinctly functional terms. What makes a certain agent or entity an appropriate subject of justice, on this view, is not primarily its constitution (e.g. it being a state, it being a basic structure, etc.); rather, it is the way it affects persons' freedom. Even though different standards of justice apply to different forms of coercion, what brings them together is their aim: that of making coercion compatible with everyone's right to freedom.

In sum, the coercion view provides a distinctly liberal normative framework in terms of which we can make sense of both the disagreement between

---

[4] Depending on the context and on the presence of *reasonable* disagreement about what justice requires. See Section 7.5.

cosmopolitans and statists, and the grounds of our domestic, and international, moral duties.

9.5 WHAT TO DO?

Those who find the view I have advocated plausible, may still wonder what our global justice-related responsibilities are. It is all well and good to say, in broad terms, what the function of justice is and what it broadly requires; it is another thing to identify how, and how much, each should contribute to its realization. This question becomes all the more difficult when it is asked against a background as complex as that of the current global order. What should we do then?

Surely, we all have humanitarian duties to help the poor in need so long as this is not unreasonably costly to ourselves. But what about our duties of justice? From the perspective of the normative framework I have developed, these duties will be of at least two types: (*a*) duties we bear *qua* citizens of our states, seen as group agents; and (*b*) duties we bear *qua* individual participants in systemically coercive processes. For instance, *qua* citizens we may be liable to paying reparations for injustices committed by our states in wars of conquest (so long as the conditions outlined in Chapter 6 for responsibility of group members hold). Calculating what exactly we owe in terms of reparations is an extremely complex task, and one that must be carried out on a case-by-case basis.[5] Equally complex is the task of understanding what we ought to do *qua* participants in systemically coercive mechanisms.

With respect to the latter, as I have mentioned in Chapter 6, our overall degree of responsibility will depend on the degree of involvement of our agency in these systemically coercive dynamics. Those who benefit the most from them, or are most involved, bear greater duties to rectify their harmful (unjust) effects.[6] What exactly each of us owes remains an open question. As I have emphasized in Chapter 6, the justice-based duties we bear in relation to collective outcomes are almost always imperfect in kind. Many actions are possible, including raising public awareness about the nature and extent of current global injustice, supporting charities or NGOs, joining public protests, developing and backing possible reform proposals of international institutions, and so forth. What matters, when we consider the justice-based nature of these duties, is that we bear in mind that the actions we perform to fulfil

---

[5] Daniel J. Butt, *Rectifying International Injustice: Principles of Compensation and Restitution between Nations* (Oxford: Oxford University Press, 2009).

[6] See the discussion in Iris Marion Young, 'Responsibility and Global Justice: A Social Connection Model', *Social Philosophy and Policy*, 23 (1) (2006), 102–30.

them are in some sense owed to the victims of global injustice. They have a right, however ill-defined, that we do something about it. And the more our actions are implicated in their plight, the more demanding and stringent are our duties to address it.

In these circumstances, each individual agent is best placed, on the basis of considerations such as those advanced in this book, to establish how much of a contribution she/he ought to give, and what is the best way for her/him to discharge it. Even though there is certainly room for further developing, and applying, the conceptual framework I have defended here, theorists – whether normative or positive – can only do so much. Morality, including political morality, is not just a matter of principle, but also one of personal judgement. There is bound to be a point where theory ends and, from then on, the rest is up to you.

Bibliography

Abizadeh, Arash, 'Cooperation, Pervasive Impact, and Coercion: On the Scope (not Site) of Distributive Justice', *Philosophy and Public Affairs*, 35 (4) (2007), 318–58.
—— 'Democratic Theory and Border Coercion: No Right to Unilaterally Control Your Own Borders', *Political Theory*, 36 (1) (2008), 37–65.
—— 'Democratic Legitimacy and State Coercion: A Reply to David Miller', *Political Theory*, 38 (1) (2010), 121–30.
Altman, Andrew and Wellman, Christopher Heath, *A Liberal Theory of International Justice* (Oxford: Oxford University Press, 2009).
Anderson, Elizabeth, 'What is the Point of Equality?', *Ethics*, 109 (2) (1999), 287–337.
Anderson, Scott, 'Coercion', in Edward N. Zalta (ed.), *The Stanford Encyclopedia of Philosophy* (Spring 2006 edition), http://plato.stanford.edu/archives/spr2006/entries/coercion
Armstrong, Chris, 'Defending the Duty of Assistance', *Social Theory and Practice*, 35 (3) (2009), 461–82.
Arneson, Richard J., 'Luck Egalitarianism and Prioritarianism', *Ethics*, 110 (2) (2000), 339–49.
—— 'Two Cheers for Capabilities', in Harry Brighouse and Ingrid Robeyns (eds.), *Measuring Justice. Primary Goods and Capabilities* (Cambridge: Cambridge University Press, 2010), 101–28.
Avi-Yonah, Reuven S., 'Globalization, Tax Competition, and the Fiscal Crisis of the Welfare State', *Harvard Law Review*, 113 (7) (1999–2000), 1573–676.
—— 'Globalization and Tax Competition: Implications for Developing Countries', *Cepal Review*, 74 (2001), 59–66.
Barry, Brian, 'Humanity and Justice in Global Perspective', in Brian Barry, *Liberty and Justice: Essays in Political Theory 2* (Oxford: Clarendon Press, 1991), 182–210.
Barry, Christian and Valentini, Laura, 'Egalitarian Challenges to Global Egalitarianism: A Critique', *Review of International Studies*, 35 (3) (2009), 485–512.
Beeson, Mark, 'Sovereignty under Siege: Globalisation and the State in Southeast Asia', *Third World Quarterly*, 24 (2) (2003), 357–74.
Beitz, Charles R., 'Justice and International Relations', *Philosophy and Public Affairs*, 4 (4) (1975), 360–89.
—— 'Cosmopolitan Ideals and National Sentiment', *The Journal of Philosophy*, 80 (10) (1983), 591–600.
—— 'Social and Cosmopolitan Liberalism', *International Affairs*, 75 (3) (1999), 515–29.
—— *Political Theory and International Relations* with a new afterword (Princeton, NJ: Princeton University Press, 1999).
—— 'Rawls's Law of Peoples', *Ethics*, 110 (4) (2000), 669–96.
Benn, S. I. and Weinstein, W. L., 'Being Free to Act, Being a Free Man', *Mind*, 80 (318) (1971), 194–211.
Berlin, Isaiah, *Four Essays on Liberty* (London: Oxford University Press, 1969).
Blake, Michael, 'Distributive Justice, State Coercion, and Autonomy', *Philosophy and Public Affairs*, 30 (3) (2001), 257–96.

Blake, Michael and Risse, Mathias, 'Two Models of Equality and Responsibility', *Canadian Journal of Philosophy*, 38 (2) (2008), 165–99.
Brennan, Timothy, 'Cosmopolitanism and Internationalism', *New Left Review*, 7 (2001), 75–84.
Brighouse, Harry, *Justice* (Cambridge: Polity Press, 2004).
—— Robeyns, Ingrid (eds.), *Measuring Justice. Primary Goods and Capabilities* (Cambridge: Cambridge University Press, 2010).
Brock, Gillian, *Global Justice: A Cosmopolitan Account* (Oxford: Oxford University Press, 2009).
Brown, Chris, 'The Construction of a "Realistic Utopia": John Rawls and International Political Theory', *Review of International Studies*, 28 (1) (2002), 5–21.
Buchanan, Allen, 'Justice and Charity', *Ethics*, 97 (3) (1987), 558–75.
—— 'Recognitional Legitimacy and the State System', *Philosophy and Public Affairs*, 28 (1) (1999), 46–78.
—— 'Rawls's Law of Peoples: Rules for a Vanished Westphalian World', *Ethics*, 110 (4) (2000), 697–721.
—— *Justice, Legitimacy, and Self-Determination* (Oxford: Oxford University Press, 2004).
Butt, Daniel J., *Rectifying International Injustice: Principles of Compensation and Restitution between Nations* (Oxford: Oxford University Press, 2009).
Caney, Simon, 'Cosmopolitan Justice and Equalizing Opportunities', *Metaphilosophy*, 32 (1/2) (2001), 113–34.
—— 'International Distributive Justice', *Political Studies*, 49 (5) (2001), 974–97.
—— 'Cosmopolitanism and the Law of Peoples', *Journal of Political Philosophy*, 10 (1) (2002), 95–123.
—— *Justice beyond Borders: A Global Political Theory* (Oxford: Oxford University Press, 2005).
—— 'Global Justice: From Theory to Practice', *Globalizations*, 3 (2) (2006), 121–37.
—— 'Global Poverty and Human Rights: The Case for Positive Duties', in Thomas Pogge (ed.), *Freedom from Poverty as a Human Right: Who Owes What to the Very Poor?* (Oxford: Oxford University Press, 2007), 275–302.
Carens, Joseph H., 'Realistic and Idealistic Approaches to the Ethics of Migration', *International Migration Review*, 30 (1) (1996), 156–70.
Carrington, Damian, 'BP oil spill report lists series of failures – mostly by others – that led to disaster', *The Guardian*, 8 September 2010, http://www.guardian.co.uk/environment/2010/sep/08/bp-oil-spill-failures
Carter, Ian, *A Measure of Freedom* (Oxford: Oxford University Press, 1999).
—— 'A Critique of Freedom as Non-domination', *The Good Society*, 9 (3) (2000), 43–6.
—— Kramer, Matthew H., and Steiner, Hillel (eds.), *Freedom: A Philosophical Anthology* (Oxford: Blackwell, 2007).
—— 'Positive and Negative Liberty', in Edward N. Zalta (ed.), *The Stanford Encyclopedia of Philosophy* (Fall 2008 edition), http://plato.stanford.edu/archives/fall2008/entries/liberty-positive-negative/
Cassese, Antonio, *International Law* (Oxford: Oxford University Press, 2001).
Cavallero, Eric, 'Coercion, Inequality, and the International Property Regime', *Journal of Political Philosophy*, 18 (1) (2010), 16–31.
Cohen, G. A., 'The Structure of Proletarian Unfreedom', *Philosophy and Public Affairs*, 12 (1) (1983), 3–33.

Cohen, G. A., 'On the Currency of Egalitarian Justice', *Ethics*, 99 (4) (1989), 906–44.
—— 'Where the Action Is: On the Site of Distributive Justice', *Philosophy and Public Affairs*, 26 (1) (1997), 3–30.
—— 'Facts and Principles', *Philosophy and Public Affairs*, 31 (3) (2003), 211–45.
—— 'Expensive Taste Rides Again', in Justine Burley (ed.), *Dworkin and His Critics* (Oxford: Blackwell, 2004), 3–29.
—— *Rescuing Justice and Equality* (Cambridge, MA: Harvard University Press, 2008).
Cohen, Joshua and Sabel, Charles, 'Extra Rempublicam Nulla Justitia?', *Philosophy and Public Affairs*, 34 (2) (2006), 147–75.
Copp, David, 'The Idea of a Legitimate State', *Philosophy and Public Affairs*, 28 (1) (1999), 3–45.
Curtis, Polly, 'Budget 2010: Public-sector cuts a "declaration of war", says union', *The Guardian*, 22 June 2010, http://www.guardian.co.uk/uk/2010/jun/22/budget-public-sector-cuts-unions
D'Agostino, Fred, 'The Legacies of John Rawls', in Thom Brooks and Fabian Freyenhagen (eds.), *The Legacy of John Rawls* (London: Continuum, 2005), 195–212.
Daniels, Norman, 'Equal Liberty and Unequal Worth of Liberty', in Norman Daniels (ed.), *Reading Rawls: Critical Studies on Rawls' 'A Theory of Justice'* (Stanford, CA: Stanford University Press, 1975), 253–81.
—— *Just Health: Meeting Health Needs Fairly* (New York and Cambridge: Cambridge University Press, 2008).
Dietsch, Peter, 'Rethinking Sovereignty in International Fiscal Policy', *Review of International Studies* 31 (5) (2011).
—— 'Tax Competition and Its Effects on Domestic and Global Justice', in Ayelet Banai, Miriam Ronzoni, and Christian Schemmel (eds.), *Social Justice, Global Dynamics: Theoretical and Empirical Perspectives* (London: Routledge, 2011), 95–144.
—— Rixen, Thomas, 'Justice and International Tax Competition' (manuscript).
Dworkin, Ronald, *Law's Empire* (Cambridge, MA: Harvard University Press, 1986).
—— *Sovereign Virtue: The Theory and Practice of Equality* (Cambridge, MA: Harvard University Press, 2000).
Eichengreen, Barry, 'The Global Gamble of Financial Liberalization: Reflections on Capital Mobility, National Autonomy, and Social Justice', *Ethics and International Affairs*, 13 (1) (1999), 205–26.
Erskine, Toni, 'Assigning Responsibilities to Institutional Moral Agents: The Case of States and Quasi-States', *Ethics and International Affairs*, 15 (2) (2001), 67–85.
Fabre, Cécile, 'Guns, Food and Liability to Attack in War', *Ethics*, 120 (1) (2009), 36–63.
Feinberg, Joel, *Harm to Self* (New York: Oxford University Press, 1986).
Flikschuh, Katrin, 'Reason, Right, and Revolution: Kant and Locke', *Philosophy and Public Affairs*, 36 (4) (2008), 375–404.
Forst, Rainer, 'Towards a Critical Theory of Transnational Justice', *Metaphilosophy*, 32 (1/2) 2001, 160–79.
Freeman, Samuel, 'The Law of Peoples, Social Cooperation, Human Rights, and Distributive Justice', *Social Philosophy and Policy*, 23 (1) (2006), 29–68.
French, Peter, *Collective and Corporate Responsibility* (New York: Columbia University Press, 1984).
Gallie, W. B., 'Essentially Contested Concepts', *Proceedings of The Aristotelian Society*, 56 (1956), 176–98.

Gaus, Gerald F., 'The Demands on Impartiality and the Evolution of Morality', in Brian Feltham and John Cottingham (eds.), *Partiality and Impartiality* (Oxford: Oxford University Press, 2010).

Gilabert, Pablo, 'The Feasibility of Basic Socio-economic Human Rights: A Conceptual Exploration', *Philosophical Quarterly*, 59 (237) (2009), 659-81.

—— 'Kant and the Claims of the Poor', *Philosophy and Phenomenological Research*, 81 (2) (2010), 382-418.

Goodin, Robert E., 'Apportioning Responsibilities', *Law and Philosophy*, 6 (2) (1987), 167-85.

Grewal, David Singh, *Network Power: The Social Dynamics of Globalization* (New Haven and London: Yale University Press, 2008).

Hart, H. L. A., *The Concept of Law* (Oxford: Clarendon Press, 1961).

Herman, Barbara, 'Mutual Aid and Respect for Persons', *Ethics*, 94 (4) (1984), 577-602.

Hurrell, Andrew, 'Global Inequality and International Institutions', *Metaphilosophy*, 32 (1/2) (2001), 34-57.

Jackson, Robert H., *Quasi States: Sovereignty, International Relations and the Third World* (Cambridge: Cambridge University Press, 1990).

James, Aaron, 'Constructing Justice for Existing Practice: Rawls and the Status Quo', *Philosophy and Public Affairs*, 33 (3) (2005), 281-316.

—— 'Power in Social Organization as the Subject of Justice', *Pacific Philosophical Quarterly*, 86 (1) (2005), 25-49.

—— 'Distributive Justice without Sovereign Rule: The Case of Trade', *Social Theory and Practice*, 31 (4) (2005), 533-59.

Julius, A. J., 'Basic Structure and the Value of Equality', *Philosophy and Public Affairs*, 31 (4) (2003), 321-55.

—— 'Nagel's Atlas', *Philosophy and Public Affairs*, 34 (2) (2006), 176-92.

Kamminga, Menno R., 'Why Global Distributive Justice Cannot Work', *Acta Politica*, 41 (1) (2006), 21-40.

Kant, Immanuel, 'On the Common Saying: This May be True in Theory, but It Does Not Apply in Practice' (1793), in Hans Reiss (ed.), *Kant's Political Writings* (Cambridge: Cambridge University Press, 1970), 61-92.

—— 'Perpetual Peace: A Philosophical Sketch' (1795), in Hans Reiss (ed.), *Kant's Political Writings* (Cambridge: Cambridge University Press, 1970), 93-130.

—— *The Metaphysics of Morals* (1797), translated by Mary Gregor (Cambridge: Cambridge University Press, 1991).

—— *The Metaphysical Elements of Justice: Part I of the Metaphysics of Morals* (1797), translated by John Ladd (Indianapolis/Cambridge: Hackett, 1999, 2nd ed.).

Keen, Michael and Simone, Alejandro, 'Is Tax Competition Harming Developing Countries more than Developed?', *Tax Notes International*, 34 (2004), 1317-25.

Kramer, Matthew H., *The Quality of Freedom* (Oxford: Oxford University Press, 2003).

Kukathas, Chandran, 'The Mirage of Global Justice', *Social Philosophy and Policy*, 23 (1) (2006), 1-28.

Kuper, Andrew, 'Rawlsian Global Justice: Beyond the Law of Peoples to a Cosmopolitan Law of Persons', *Political Theory*, 28 (5) (2000), 640-74.

Kutz, Christopher, *Complicity: Ethics and Law for a Collective Age* (New York: Cambridge University Press, 2000).
Kymlicka, Will, *Contemporary Political Philosophy: An Introduction* (Oxford: Oxford University Press, 2002, 2nd ed.).
Laborde, Cécile, 'Republicanism and Global Justice: A Sketch', *European Journal of Political Theory*, 9 (1) (2010), 48–69.
Lamont, W. D., 'Justice: Distributive and Corrective', *Philosophy*, 16 (61) (1941), 3–18.
List, Christian, 'Republican Freedom and the Rule of Law', *Politics, Philosophy & Economics*, 5 (2) (2006), 201–20.
—— Pettit, Philip, *Group Agency: The Possibility, Design, and Status of Corporate Agents* (Oxford: Oxford University Press, 2011).
Locke, John, *Second Treatise of Government* 1689 (Oxford: Basil Blackwell, 1966, 3rd ed.).
Loriaux, Sylvie, 'Beneficence and Distributive Justice in a Globalising World', *Global Society*, 20 (3) (2006), 251–65.
Madeley, John, 'Trade and Hunger: An Overview of the Impact of Trade Liberalization on Food Security', *Globala Studier*, 4 (2000), 1–77, http://www.ppl.nl/bibliographies/wto/files/645.pdf
Martin, Rex, 'Rawls on International Distributive Economic Justice: Taking a Closer Look', in Rex Martin and David Reidy (eds.), *Rawls's Law of Peoples: A Realistic Utopia?* (Oxford: Blackwell, 2006), 226–42.
Mason, Andrew, 'Just Constraints', *British Journal of Political Science*, 34 (2) (2004), 251–68.
May, Larry, *Sharing Responsibility* (Chicago: University of Chicago Press, 1992).
McGregor, Joan, 'Bargaining Advantages and Coercion in the Market', *Philosophy Research Archives*, 14 (1988–1989), 23–50.
McMahan, Jeff, 'Self-Defense and the Problem of the Innocent Attacker', *Ethics*, 104 (2) (1994), 252–90.
McMahon, Christopher, 'The Indeterminacy of Republican Policy', *Philosophy and Public Affairs*, 33 (1) (2005), 67–93.
Meckled-Garcia, Saladin, 'International Justice, Human Rights and Neutrality', *Res Publica*, 10 (2) (2004), 153–74.
—— 'On the Very Idea of Cosmopolitan Justice: Constructivism and International Agency', *Journal of Political Philosophy*, 16 (3) (2008), 245–71.
—— 'International Law and the Limits of Global Justice', *Review of International Studies*, 37 (5) (2011).
Miller, David, 'Constraints on Freedom', *Ethics*, 94 (1) (1983), 66–86.
—— *Liberty* (Oxford: Oxford University Press, 1991).
—— *On Nationality* (Oxford: Clarendon Press, 1995).
—— 'Justice and Global Inequality', in Andrew Hurrell and Ngaire Woods (eds.), *Inequality, Globalization, and World Politics* (Oxford: Oxford University Press, 1999), 187–210.
—— *Principles of Social Justice* (Cambridge, MA: Harvard University Press, 1999).
—— 'Distributing Responsibilities', *Journal of Political Philosophy*, 9 (4) (2001), 453–71.
—— 'Caney's "International Distributive Justice": A Response', *Political Studies*, 50 (5) (2002), 974–7.

Miller, David, '"Are They My Poor?": The Problem of Altruism in a World of Strangers', *Critical Review of Social and Political Philosophy*, 5 (4) (2002), 106–27. Reprinted in Jonathan Seglow (ed.), *The Ethics of Altruism* (London: Frank Cass, 2004), 106–27.
—— 'Against Global Egalitarianism', *The Journal of Ethics*, 9 (1/2) (2005), 55–79.
—— *National Responsibility and Global Justice* (Oxford: Oxford University Press, 2007).
—— 'Political Philosophy for Earthlings', in David Leopold and Marc Stears (eds.), *Political Theory: Methods and Approaches* (Oxford: Oxford University Press, 2008), 29–48.
—— 'Democracy's Domain', *Philosophy and Public Affairs*, 37 (3) (2009), 201–28.
—— 'Why Immigration Controls Are not Coercive: A Reply to Arash Abizadeh', *Political Theory*, 38 (1) (2010), 111–20.
Miller, Richard W., 'Cosmopolitan Respect and Patriotic Concern', *Philosophy and Public Affairs*, 27 (3) (1998), 202–24.
—— *Globalizing Justice: The Ethics of Poverty and Power* (Oxford: Oxford University Press, 2010).
Mills, Charles W., '"Ideal Theory" as Ideology', *Hypatia: A Journal of Feminist Philosophy*, 20 (3) (2005), 165–84.
Moellendorf, Darrel, *Cosmopolitan Justice* (Boulder, CO: Westview Press, 2002).
—— 'The World Trade Organization and Egalitarian Justice', *Metaphilosophy*, 36 (1/2) (2005), 145–62.
Moltchanova, Anna, 'Collective Agents and Group Moral Rights', *Journal of Political Philosophy*, 17 (1) (2009), 23–46.
Nagel, Thomas, *Equality and Partiality* (Oxford: Oxford University Press, 1991).
—— 'The Problem of Global Justice', *Philosophy and Public Affairs*, 33 (2) (2005), 113–47.
Nardin, Terry, 'International Political Theory and the Question of Justice', *International Affairs*, 82 (3) (2006), 449–65.
Naticchia, Chris, 'The Law of Peoples: The Old and the New', *Journal of Moral Philosophy*, 2 (3) (2005), 353–69.
Newsweek, 'How to feed the world' (19 May 2008), http://www.newsweek.com/id/136360/page/8
Nozick, Robert, 'Coercion', in Sidney Morgenbesser, Patrick Suppes, and Morton White (eds.), *Philosophy, Science, and Method: Essays in Honor of Ernest Nagel* (New York: St Martin's, 1969), 440–72.
—— *Anarchy, State, and Utopia* (Oxford: Blackwell, 1974).
Nussbaum, Martha, 'Women and the Law of Peoples', *Politics, Philosophy & Economics*, 1 (3) (2002), 283–306.
O'Neill, Martin, 'What Should Egalitarians Believe?', *Philosophy and Public Affairs*, 36 (2) (2008), 119–56.
O'Neill, Onora, 'The Most Extensive Liberty', *Proceedings of The Aristotelian Society*, 80 (1980), 45–59.
—— 'Abstraction, Idealization and Ideology in Ethics', in J. D. G. Evans (ed.), *Moral Philosophy and Contemporary Problems* (Cambridge: Cambridge University Press, 1988, copyright 1987), 55–69.
—— *Towards Justice and Virtue: A Constructive Account of Practical Reasoning* (Cambridge: Cambridge University Press, 1996).

—— *Bounds of Justice* (Cambridge: Cambridge University Press, 2000).
Orrù, Elisa and Ronzoni, Miriam, 'Which Supranational Sovereignty: Global Criminal and Socio-Economic Justice Compared', *Review of International Studies*, 37 (5) (2011).
Parent, W. A., 'Freedom as the Non-Restriction of Options', *Mind*, 83 (331) (1974), 432–4.
Pattison, James, 'Humanitarian Intervention and a Cosmopolitan UN Force', *Journal of International Political Theory*, 4 (1) (2008), 126–45.
Pettit, Philip, 'Freedom as Antipower', *Ethics*, 106 (3) (1996), 576–604.
—— *Republicanism: A Theory of Freedom and Government* (Oxford: Clarendon Press, 1997).
—— *A Theory of Freedom: From the Psychology to the Politics of Agency* (Cambridge: Polity Press, 2001).
—— 'The Determinacy of Republican Policy: A Reply to McMahon', *Philosophy and Public Affairs*, 34 (3) (2006), 275–83.
Pevnick, Ryan, 'Political Coercion and the Scope of Distributive Justice', *Political Studies*, 56 (2) (2008), 339–413.
Pogge, Thomas W., *Realizing Rawls* (Ithaca, NY: Cornell University Press, 1989).
—— 'Cosmopolitanism and Sovereignty', *Ethics*, 103 (1) (1992), 48–75.
—— 'An Egalitarian Law of Peoples', *Philosophy and Public Affairs*, 23 (3) (1994), 195–224.
—— 'On the Site of Distributive Justice: Reflections on Cohen and Murphy', *Philosophy and Public Affairs*, 29 (2) (2000), 137–69.
—— 'Critical Study: Rawls on International Justice', *The Philosophical Quarterly*, 51 (203) (2001), 246–53.
—— 'Moral Universalism and Global Economic Justice', *Politics, Philosophy & Economics*, 1 (1) (2002), 29–58.
—— *World Poverty and Human Rights: Cosmopolitan Responsibilities and Reforms* (Cambridge: Polity Press, 2002).
—— 'The Incoherence between Rawls's Theories of Justice', *Fordham Law Review*, 72 (5) (2004), 1739–59.
—— '"Assisting" the Global Poor', in Deen K. Chatterjee (ed.), *The Ethics of Assistance: Morality and the Distant Needy* (Cambridge: Cambridge University Press, 2004), 260–88.
—— 'Severe Poverty as a Violation of Negative Duties', *Ethics and International Affairs*, 19 (1) (2005), 55–83.
—— 'Human Rights and Global Health: A Research Program', *Metaphilosophy*, 36 (1/2) (2005), 182–209.
—— 'Cohen to the Rescue!', *Ratio*, 21 (4) (2008), 454–75.
—— 'A Critique of the Capability Approach', in Harry Brighouse and Ingrid Robeyns (eds.), *Measuring Justice. Primary Goods and Capabilities* (Cambridge: Cambridge University Press, 2010), 17–60.
Räikkä, Juha, 'The Feasibility Condition in Political Theory', *Journal of Political Philosophy*, 6 (1) (1998), 27–40.
Rawls, John, 'Justice as Fairness', *Philosophical Review*, 67 (2) (1958), 164–94.
—— 'The Independence of Moral Theory', *Proceedings and Addresses of The American Philosophical Association*, 48 (1974–75), 5–22.
—— *Political Liberalism* (New York: Columbia University Press, 1996).

Rawls, John, 'The Law of Peoples' (1993), in Samuel Freeman (ed.), *John Rawls: Collected Papers* (Cambridge, MA: Harvard University Press, 1999), 529–64.
—— *A Theory of Justice* (Oxford: Oxford University Press, 1999 rev. ed.).
—— *The Law of Peoples* (Cambridge, MA: Harvard University Press, 1999).
—— *Justice as Fairness: A Restatement* (Cambridge, MA: Harvard University Press, 2001).
Raz, Joseph, *The Morality of Freedom* (Oxford: Oxford University Press, 1986).
Reddy, Sanjay, 'The Role of Apparent Constraints in Normative Reasoning: A Methodological Statement and Application to Global Justice', *The Journal of Ethics*, 9 (1/2) (2005), 119–25.
Reidy, David A., 'Rawls on International Justice: A Defense', *Political Theory*, 32 (3) (2004), 291–319.
—— 'A Just Global Economy: In Defense of Rawls', *The Journal of Ethics*, 11 (2) (2007), 193–236.
Ripstein, Arthur, 'Authority and Coercion', *Philosophy and Public Affairs*, 32 (1) (2004), 2–35.
—— 'Private Order and Public Justice: Kant and Rawls', *Virginia Law Review*, 92 (7) (2006), 1391–438.
Risse, Mathias, 'Do We Owe the Global Poor Assistance or Rectification?', *Ethics and International Affairs*, 19 (1) (2005), 9–18.
—— 'What to Say About the State?', *Social Theory and Practice*, 32 (4) (2006), 671–98.
Rixen, Thomas, 'Tax Competition and Inequality' (manuscript).
Rodrik, Dani, 'Feasible Globalizations', in Michael M. Weinstein (ed.), *Globalization: What's New?* (New York: Columbia University Press, 2005), 196–213.
Ronzoni, Miriam, 'Two Concepts of the Basic Structure and their Relevance to Global Justice', *Global Justice: Theory Practice Rhetoric*, 1 (2008), 68–85, http://www.theglobaljusticenetwork.org/wp-content/uploads/6_ronzoni.pdf
—— Valentini, Laura, 'On the Meta-Ethical Status of Constructivism: Reflections on G. A. Cohen's "Facts and Principles"', *Politics, Philosophy & Economics*, 7 (4) (2008), 403–22.
—— 'What Makes a Basic Structure Just?', *Res Publica*, 14 (3) (2008), 203–18.
—— 'The Global Order: A Case of Background Injustice? A Practice-dependent Account', *Philosophy and Public Affairs*, 37 (3) (2009), 229–56.
Rousseau, Jean-Jacques, *Rousseau's Political Writings*, translated by Julia Conaway Bondanella (New York and London: Norton, 1987).
Sangiovanni, Andrea, 'Global Justice, Reciprocity, and the State', *Philosophy and Public Affairs*, 35 (1) (2007), 3–39.
—— 'Justice and the Priority of Politics to Morality', *Journal of Political Philosophy*, 16 (2) (2008), 137–64.
Scanlon, Thomas M., 'The Diversity of Objections to Inequality', *Lindley Lecture*, University of Kansas (Lawrence, Kansas: 1996).
—— *What We Owe to Each Other* (Cambridge, MA: Harvard University Press, 1998).
Scheffler, Samuel, 'What Is Egalitarianism?', *Philosophy and Public Affairs*, 31 (1) (2003), 5–39.
Schemmel, Christian, 'On the Usefulness of Luck Egalitarian Arguments to Global Justice', *Global Justice: Theory Practice Rhetoric*, 1 (2007), 54–67, http://www.theglobaljusticenetwork.org/wp-content/uploads/5_schemmel.pdf
Sen, Amartya K., 'Well Being, Agency and Freedom', *Journal of Philosophy*, 82 (4) (1985), 169–221.

—— 'Welfare, Preference, and Freedom', *Journal of Econometrics*, 50 (1/2) (1991), 15–29.
—— 'What Do We Want from a Theory of Justice?', *Journal of Philosophy*, 103 (5) (2006), 215–38.
—— *The Idea of Justice* (Cambridge, MA: Harvard University Press, 2009).
Shue, Henry, 'Mediating Duties', *Ethics*, 98 (4) (1988), 687–704.
—— *Basic Rights: Subsistence, Affluence and U.S. Foreign Policy* (Princeton, NJ: Princeton University Press, 1980, 2nd ed. 1996).
—— 'Rawls and the Outlaws', *Politics, Philosophy & Economics*, 1 (3) (2002), 307–23.
Simmons, A. John, 'On the Territorial Rights of States', *Philosophical Issues*, 11 (1) (2001), 300–26.
—— 'Ideal and Nonideal Theory', *Philosophy and Public Affairs*, 38 (1) (2010), 5–36.
Singer, Peter, 'Famine, Affluence, and Morality', *Philosophy and Public Affairs*, 1 (3) (1972), 229–43.
Skinner, Quentin, *Liberty before Liberalism* (Cambridge: Cambridge University Press, 1998).
Steinberg, Richard H., 'In the Shadow of Law or Power? Consensus-based Bargaining and Outcomes in the GATT/WTO', *International Organization*, 56 (2) (2002), 339–47.
Stiglitz, Joseph E., 'Globalization and the Economic Role of the State in the New Millennium', *Industrial and Corporate Change*, 12 (1) (2003), 3–26.
—— 'Social Justice and Global Trade', *Far Eastern Economic Review*, 169 (2) (2006), 18–22.
—— *Making Globalization Work* (London: Penguin, 2006).
Stilz, Anna, *Liberal Loyalty: Freedom, Obligation, and the State* (Princeton, NJ: Princeton University Press, 2009).
—— 'Collective Responsibility and the State', *Journal of Political Philosophy*, 19 (2) (2011), 190–208.
Swanton, Christine, *Freedom: A Coherence Theory* (Indianapolis: Hackett, 1992).
Tan, Kok-Chor, 'Liberal Toleration in Rawls's Law of Peoples', *Ethics*, 108 (2) (1998), 276–95.
—— *Justice without Borders: Cosmopolitanism, Nationalism and Patriotism* (Cambridge: Cambridge University Press, 2004).
Taylor, Charles, 'What's Wrong with Negative Liberty?', in Charles Taylor, *Philosophy and the Human Sciences* (Cambridge: Cambridge University Press, 1985), 211–29.
Tobin, James, 'Prologue', in Mahbib ul Haq, Inge Kaul, and Isabelle Grunberg (eds.) *The Tobin Tax: Coping with Financial Volatility* (New York and Oxford: Oxford University Press, 1996), ix–xviii.
Tomlin, Patrick, 'Survey Article: Internal Doubts about Cohen's Rescue of Justice', *Journal of Political Philosophy*, 18 (2) (2010), 228–47.
United Nations, 'Overview', *Human Development Report* (2010), http://hdr.undp.org/en/media/HDR_2010_EN_Overview_reprint.pdf
Valentini, Laura, 'On the Apparent Paradox of Ideal Theory', *Journal of Political Philosophy*, 17 (3) (2009), 332–55.
—— 'Cosmopolitan or Social Liberal? Review of David Miller's *National Responsibility and Global Justice*', *Global Justice: Theory Practice Rhetoric*, 1 (2) (2009), 50–3.
Valentini, Laura, 'Coercion and (Global) Justice', *American Political Science Review*, 105 (1) (2011), 205–20.

Valentini, Laura, 'Global Justice and Practice-Dependence: Conventionalism, Institutionalism, Functionalism', *Journal of Political Philosophy*, 19 (4) (2011), 399–418.
—— 'A Paradigm Shift in Theorizing about Justice? A Critique of Sen', *Economics and Philosophy*, 27 (3) (2011), 297–315.
—— 'Justice and Democracy' (manuscript).
—— 'Human Rights: A Freedom-Centered View' (manuscript).
—— 'Justice, Charity, and Misery: What, if Anything, Is Owed to Haiti' (manuscript).
Wade, Robert H., 'Should We Worry about Income Inequality?', in David Held and Ayse Kaya (eds.), *Global Inequality* (Cambridge: Polity Press, 2007), 104–31.
Waldron, Jeremy, 'Theoretical Foundations of Liberalism', *The Philosophical Quarterly*, 37 (147) (1987), 127–50.
—— 'Special Ties and Natural Duties', *Philosophy and Public Affairs*, 22 (1) (1993), 3–30.
—— 'Minority Cultures and the Cosmopolitan Alternative', in Will Kymlicka (ed.), *The Rights of Minority Cultures* (Oxford: Oxford University Press, 1995), 93–119.
Walzer, Michael, *Spheres of Justice: A Defense of Pluralism and Equality* (New York: Basic Books, 1983).
Wearden, Graeme, 'BP to admit partial blame for Deepwater oil spill', *The Guardian*, 8 September 2010, http://www.guardian.co.uk/business/2010/sep/08/bp-deepwater-report
Wenar, Leif, 'International Property Rights and the Resource Curse', *Philosophy and Public Affairs*, 36 (1) (2008), 2–32.
Wertheimer, Alan, *Coercion* (Princeton, NJ: Princeton University Press, 1987).
Woods, Ngaire, 'International Political Economy in an Age of Globalization', in John Baylis and Steve Smith (eds.), *The Globalization of World Politics* (Oxford: Oxford University Press, 2005), 325–48.
Young, Iris Marion, 'Responsibility and Global Labor Justice', *Journal of Political Philosophy*, 12 (4) (2004), 365–88.
—— 'Responsibility and Global Justice: A Social Connection Model', *Social Philosophy and Policy*, 23 (1) (2006), 102–30.
Ypi, Lea L., 'Statist Cosmopolitanism', *Journal of Political Philosophy*, 16 (1) (2008), 48–71.
—— 'Justice and Morality beyond Naïve Cosmopolitanism', *Ethics & Global Politics*, 3 (3) (2010), 171–92.
Zimmerman, David, 'Coercive Wage Offers', *Philosophy and Public Affairs*, 10 (2) (1981), 121–45.

Index

Abizadeh, Arash, 59n36, 60n41, 103n18, 111n31, 112n32, 115n43, 118n49, 128n18
action guidance (*see* guidance critique)
agency-based approach
   cosmopolitanism and, 63–4
   statism and, 100–7
Allende, Salvador, 192
Altman, Andrew, 66n61
altruism, 25–6, 34, 181, 183, 208
Anderson, Elizabeth, 29n21, 56n32
Anderson, Scott, 126n11, 135n38
Armstrong, Chris, 74n9
Arneson, Richard, 29n24, 167n32
Asian Financial Crisis, 196
assistance (*see* duties of justice versus humanitarian assistance; principles of humanity)
autonomy
   coercion and, 123–5, 128, 134, 140n45, 142–3
   freedom and, 156–64, 166
   social conditions for, 116, 112–23, 123n4, 156–7
   societal cooperation and, 109–10
Avi-Yonah, Reuven S., 195n35, 196n37

Barry, Brian, 8n18&n20, 59–60, 59n37, 60n38, 108n24
Barry, Christian, 35n43, 42n67, 60n41, 102n16, 110n27, 181n4
basic structure of society, 6, 210
   cooperation for mutual advantage and, 59–60, 111
   cosmopolitanism and, 58–62, 68
   international interdependence and, 17, 59, 72, 109
   rule-governed social system and, 60–2
   statism and, 107, 112n32
Bay of Pigs Invasion, 191–2
Beeson, Mark, 192n25
Beitz, Charles, 6, 10n23, 37n49, 41, 45n3, 46, 48n14, 50n19, 58n35, 59n37, 60, 61n43, 62n47, 63n53, 65, 82n33, 88n50, 90, 121n2
Benn, S.I., 157n3
Blake, Michael, 7, 46, 72, 73n4, 75, 80n22, 112–14, 115n44, 124n5, 141n50, 208n3
Berlin, Isaiah, 134n32, 157n3, 165n27

Brennan, Timothy, 12n28
Brighouse, Harry, 25n4
British Petroleum (BP), 132, 148
Brock, Gillian, 3n5, 74n9, 201n52
Brown, Chris, 82n30
Buchanan, Allen, 9n22, 36, 73n7, 82n33, 186 (Allan), 190n18
Butt, Daniel, 211n5

Caney, Simon, 6, 23n2, 42n69, 45, 45n3&n4, 46n8, 47n11, 57, 82n33, 85n40, 201n53
capitalism, 136, 144–5, 151–2
Carens, Joseph, 33–4
Carrington, Damian, 148n64
Carter, Ian, 113n36, 134n32, 157n3&n4, 158n6&n7, 159n8, 160n12, 163n22, 164n24&n25, 165n26, 167n30, 174n41
Cassese, Antonio, 189n16
Castro, Fidel, 191–2
Cavallero, Eric, 115n42, 192n23
Central Intelligence Agency (CIA), 191–2
Chile, 191–2
coercion
   autonomy and, 123–5, 128, 134, 140n45, 142–3
   basic-structural approach and, 143–4
   broad definition of, 15
   capitalism and, 136, 144–5, 151–2
   contested concept of, 126–30
   domestic, 115–16, 141–6, 187
   egalitarianism and, 121–6, 130, 132n6, 142–3, 154
   freedom and, 15, 18, 122–5, 128–47, 151–6, 163–4, 168–73, 178
   generalized, 130–41
   interactional, 15, 19–20, 130–6
     (*see also* interactional coercion)
   lawless, 125, 142, 202
   legitimacy of, 124, 128, 149
   liberalism and, 123–5
   narrow, 121–2, 129–30, 135, 141, 154
   non-trivial constraints on freedom and, 134–5, 139
   principles of justice and, 4, 121–4, 128, 154
   relational approach and, 112–18
   respect for persons and, 123–4
   responsibility for, 122, 131–3, 146–53, 211
   scope of justice and, 179–88, 192–203

coercion (*cont.*)
  statism and, 112–18, 121–5, 132, 141, 154, 157
  suitable baseline for, 135–7, 139–41
  systemic, 19–20, 137–41
  (*see also* systemic coercion)
Cohen, G.A., 24–31, 48, 144
Cohen, Joshua, 3n4, 66n61, 187n13
constructivism, 61, 93–4, 98
contractualism, 103, 114
cooperation
  autonomy and, 109–10
  cosmopolitanism and, 27, 41, 59–60
  interaction and, 110–12
  mutually advantageous, 59–60, 111
  scope of justice and, 198
  statism and, 81, 87, 92–9, 108–12, 114
Copp, David, 189n17
cosmopolitanism
  assessing ideal of, 23–43
  cooperation for mutual advantage and, 59–60
  defined, 23
  embedded approach and, 24–8, 30–2, 34, 42–4, 48
  fictional scenarios and, 50–8
  guidance critique and, 16, 24, 28, 32–42
  impasse with statism and, 9–20, 205–11
  international interdependence and, 59
  justification of, 44–68
  liberalism and, 2–3, 6, 10, 40
  luck-egalitarianism and, 29, 31, 47–57
  methodological critique of, 44–68
  non-relational, 6n14, 13, 16, 44–58, 68
  pluralism and, 40–1, 62, 66–7
  poverty and, 13, 49–50, 54–7
  practical implications of, 7, 16, 23, 37–9
  relational, 6, 12–13, 16, 44, 46n5, 58–61, 64, 66–8, 121, 210
  transcendent approach and, 24–5, 28–32, 42–4, 48, 54
  utopianism and, 13, 40
  weak, 17, 65, 110, 121n2
Cuba, 191–2
Curties, Polly, 133n31

D'Agostino, Fred, 28n17
Daniels, Norman, 3n4, 175n43
Década Perdida, 196
Deepwater Horizon, 148
democracy, 19
  cosmopolitanism and, 36–7, 47
  equality and, 177–8
  freedom and, 177–8
  statism and, 81, 83, 85, 88
despotism, 14, 16, 40–1, 64n54, 77, 82–3, 124

Dietsch, Peter, 196n38, 201n52
duties
  of justice versus humanitarian assistance, 8–10, 49–58, 74n9, 180–2, 206
  perfect versus imperfect, 153n77
  permissibly enforced, 52–3
  stringency of, 181
Dworkin, Ronald, 2n2, 4n7, 78n18, 93–4, 98

egalitarianism, 16
  coercion and, 121–6, 130, 132n6, 142–3, 154
  cooperation view and, 108–12
  cosmopolitanism and, 6, 23, 29, 35, 38, 42n67, 45–50, 54–8, 61–8, 210
  deep value pluralism and, 62, 66–7
  domestic level and, 2–3, 17, 206
  fair returns and, 108
  freedom and, 155, 171, 175
  liberalism and, 6–7, 9, 12–13
  luck and, 183–4
  rule-governed social system and, 61–7
  statist rejection at the global level, 77–81
  weak, 29
Eichengreen, Barry, 195
embedded approach, 26–8, 43n70
equality
  cosmopolitanism and, 4, 7–8, 16, 20, 23, 29–32, 46–7, 55–8, 66, 206
  democracy and, 177–8
  distributive, 29, 46, 56
  economic, 7–8, 19, 155–6, 177–8, 209
  fair returns and, 108
  freedom and, 155–6, 173–4, 177–8
  gender, 48, 124, 138, 144, 200
  global, 4, 16, 23, 47, 179, 188–93, 200
  humanity and, 180–3
  importance of, 55–8
  luck and, 29, 31, 169, 171, 176
  moral (with regard to persons), 6, 12–13, 98n9, 206–9
  natural resource redistribution principle and, 50n19, 75n11
  racial, 48, 55–6, 142–4, 200
  respect and, 3–8, 10, 12, 14, 19, 46–7, 55–8, 61, 66–7, 78–81, 84, 91, 112–17, 123–4, 173, 175, 179–85, 189, 205–9
  scope of justice and, 179–95, 199–200
  socio-economic, 12, 19, 46, 71, 155–6, 178, 209
  sovereign, 188–93
Erskine, Toni, 133n30
Europe, 12, 97, 108, 117, 187, 191, 196

Fabre, Cécile, 53n24
fair returns, 108
Feinberg, Joel, 127n16

financial crises, 137, 196–7, 201
Flikschuh, Katrin, 102n17
foreign policy, 73, 87, 98–9, 191
Forst, Rainer, 3n4, 177n48
freedom, 19
  autonomy and, 156–62, 166
  civil rights and, 174–7
  coercion and, 15, 18, 122–5, 128–47, 151–6, 163–4, 168–73, 178
  as contested concept, 157
  defining, 155–64
  democracy and, 177–8
  distribution of, 155–6, 164, 168, 172–7
  egalitarianism and, 155, 171, 175
  equality and, 155–6, 173–4, 177–8
  as independence, 155–64, 168–78
  measuring, 164–8
  mutually justifiable degree of, 124
  negative, 157n3, 160n12
  as non-domination, 134, 159, 162, 163n22
  as non-interference, 134, 156–63, 166, 169
  non-trivial constraints on, 134–5, 139
  as option-availability, 157–62, 169, 171, 178
  poverty and, 157, 171–2
  primary goods approach and, 173–4, 176
  Rawls and, 162, 167n30, 173–6
  slavery and, 134, 160–1, 166, 168
  sovereign equality and, 189–93
  substance of, 173–4
Freeman, Samuel, 60n41, 83n34, 108n24
French, Peter, 133n30

Gallie, W.B., 128
Gaus, Gerald, 175n44
gender equality, 48, 124, 138, 144, 200
Gilabert, Pablo, 52n23, 105n20
Global Resource Dividend, 201
Goodin, Robert, 147n61
Grewal, David, 192n26
Guatemala, 191
guidance critique
  action-guiding theory of justice and, 32
  agent motivation and, 32–3
  cosmopolitanism and, 16, 24, 28, 32–42
  ideal theory and, 37–8
  immediate applicability and, 34–5
  interpretation I and, 32–4
  interpretation II and, 34–9
  interpretation III and, 39–42
  non-ideal circumstances and, 37–8
  Rawls and, 32, 37, 40–1
  statism and, 17–18, 85–90

Hart, H.L.A., 20n33
Hayek, F.A., 161–2
Herman, Barbara, 78n20

Honduras, 191
humanity (*see* duties of justice versus humanitarian assistance; principles of humanity)
human rights, 1, 7
  cosmopolitanism and, 37
  Rawls and, 81–4
  statism and, 74–5, 81–4
  underfulfilments of, 105n20
Hurrell, Andrew, 186–7

imperialism, 12, 36, 47, 66, 205–6
independence
  freedom as, 73, 155–64, 168–78
  global, 182, 185
Indonesia, 196
interactional coercion
  agential status and, 131–3
  defined, 122, 168
  freedom and, 139, 168
  function of justice and, 122, 130–7, 148–51
  group, 131–3, 148–51
  individual, 131–3
  interstate, 19, 188–93
  scope of justice and, 183, 185, 187–93, 203
  suitable baseline for, 135–7
internal legitimacy, 188–9
international interdependence, 17, 59, 72, 109, 210
International Monetary Fund (IMF), 97, 116, 132, 197–8, 208
interpretive approach
  defined, 93
  Dworkin and, 93–4, 98
  Rawls and, 93, 95, 97–9
  statism and, 92–101, 118
  virtues/vices of, 95–100
Iraq, 97

Jackson, Robert 191n22
James, Aaron, 3n4, 93–5, 141n47, 145n60, 197n42
Julius, A.J., 3n4, 26n10, 62n45, 64n55, 182n7, 187n11
justice (*see also* scope of justice)
  basic structure of society and, 6, 16, 27, 45, 107, 112n32, 121, 143–4
  coercion and, 121–54 (*see also* coercion)
  cooperation for mutual advantage and, 59–60, 111
  domestic, 2, 5, 7, 9, 18–19, 23, 45–6, 59, 65–8, 75, 77, 91, 123, 141–6, 178, 182, 185–6, 196, 199–201, 210
  embedded approach to, 24–8, 30–2, 34, 42–4, 48, 207
  global, 179–204

justice (cont.)
  humanity and (see duties of justice versus humanitarian assistance)
  natural resource redistribution principle and, 50n19, 75n11
  original position and, 5, 27–8, 46, 114, 174–5
  question of extension and, 2, 5, 7, 14–15, 20, 59, 205
  Rawls and, 185, 188, 193
  (see also Rawls, John)
  rule-governed social system and, 60–7
  third wave of debate, 3
  transcendent approach to, 24–5, 28–32, 42–4, 48, 54

Kamminga, Menno, 39n58
Kant, Immanuel, 1, 35, 102, 125, 153n77, 159n9
Keen, Michael, 196n36
Kramer, Matthew, 158n5&n6&n7, 160n12, 164n24
Kukathas, Chandran, 36
Kuper, Andrew, 41n65, 82n33
Kutz, Christopher, 138n40
Kymlicka, Will, 4n7

Laborde, Cécile, 56n33, 163n23, 192n24
Lamont, W.D., 8n19
Law of Peoples, The (Rawls), 14n31, 38n56, 40, 72–3, 85–91, 93, 95, 98–9
liberalism, 206
  coercion and, 123–5
  contemporary, 4–6, 10, 123–5
  contractualism and, 103, 114
  cosmopolitanism and, 2–3, 6, 10, 40
  domestic, 81–4
  egalitarianism and, 2–7, 9, 12–13
  (see also egalitarianism; equality)
  freedom and, 166
  fundamental commitments of, 4–5
  statism and, 6, 10, 81–4, 95, 98–9, 115–16
libertarians, 132n26, 171
liberty (see freedom)
List, Christian, 110n29, 129n21, 132, 149n66, 160
Locke, John, 103
Loriaux, Sylvie, 8n18

Madeley, John, 194n28
Malaysia, 196
Martin, Rex, 8n16
Mason, Andrew, 29n24
May, Larry, 153n74
McGregor, Joan, 127n17
McMahan, Jeff, 53n24

McMahon, Christopher, 163n22
Meckled-Garcia, Saladin, 63, 82n33, 95n6, 100–1, 103, 106n23, 117n46, 136n39
Middle East, 97
Miller, David, 3n5, 7, 12n29, 181n3, 200
  coercion and, 115n43, 128, 131n22&n25, 134n34&n36, 139n42
  cosmopolitanism and, 23n1&n2, 32–3, 39n57, 47n12, 48n13, 50n19, 54n26, 55n28, 62n49
  embedded approach and, 26n7
  freedom and, 158n7
  responsibility distribution and, 144n55, 146n61, 149n65, 150n68&n69, 152n73
  statism and, 71–5, 80, 90n58, 91, 101
Miller, Richard, 3n4, 80, 97n7, 112
Mills, Charles, 85n42
Moellendorf, Darrel, 6, 12n26, 23n3, 58n35, 61n43, 200n49, 201n50
Moltchanova, Anna, 132n28
Mugabe, Robert, 96

Nagel, Thomas, 4n7, 7, 8n16, 36, 72–3, 75–8, 101, 112, 141
Nardin, Terry, 188n14
Naticchia, Chris, 84n38
nationalism, 2, 3n5, 71n1, 89
nested-islands model, 186–7
Nicaragua, 191
nongovernmental organizations (NGOs), 1, 9n21, 132, 211
non-interference, 207, 209
  coercion and, 134
  freedom and, 134, 156–63, 166, 169
  scope of justice and, 179, 182–6, 191–2
  statism and, 74–5, 91, 95, 99, 103
normative framework
  coercion and, 15, 121–54, 206–7
  freedom and, 155–78
  reconceptualization of justice debate and, 205, 209–11
  scope of justice and, 18–20, 179–204
Nozick, Robert, 107, 126n12, 127n15, 171n36
Nussbaum, Martha, 84n37, 173n38

oil supply, 97
O'Neill, Martin, 56n31, 175n42, 183n9
O'Neill, Onora, 35, 127n13, 166, 170n35, 181n2
original position, 5, 27–28, 46, 114, 174–5
Orrù, Elisa, 65n59, 106n21, 202n55, 203n57

Panama, 191
Parent, W.A., 157n3
Pattison, James, 65n58
Perpetual Peace (Kant), 1

Pettit, Philip, 110n29, 129n21, 132, 133n30, 134n33, 149n66, 159n9&n10, 160n12, 162–3
Pevnick, Ryan, 117n46
Philippines, 196
Pinochet, Augusto, 192
pluralism, 209
   cosmopolitanism and, 40–1, 62, 66–7
   statism and, 82–4
Pogge, Thomas, 6, 8n16, 11n24, 12n26&n27, 13n30
   critique of transcendent approach and, 26n7, 29, 31
   coercion and, 122n3, 131n24, 138n40, 139n43
   cosmopolitanism and, 41n65, 42n66, 50n19, 52n21&n22, 54, 56n30, 58n35, 61n43
   freedom and, 157n2
   scope of justice and, 181n6, 190n19, 195n32, 200n49, 201–2
   statism and, 82n33, 83–6, 87n43, 88n49&n50, 89, 105n20
Political Liberalism (Rawls), 25n6, 61n44, 95, 98–9, 102n17
political morality, 2, 10, 66–7, 82, 86, 172, 212
Pollan, Michael, 11
poverty, 1, 10
   causes of, 11, 86–90
   cosmopolitanism and, 13, 49–50, 54–7
   freedom and, 157, 171–2
   statism and, 86–90
primary goods, 47, 94, 111, 173–4, 176
principles of humanity, 8–10, 14, 49–55
   (*see also* duties of justice versus humanitarian assistance)
principles of justice, 3, 8–10, 208–9
   (*see also* justice; duties of justice versus humanitarian assistance)

question of extension, 5, 7, 15, 20
   cosmopolitanism and, 2–3, 23, 33–4, 39, 41–2, 59, 66, 205
   statism and, 2–3, 13–14, 17–18, 205

racial equality, 48, 55–6, 142–4, 200
Räikkä, Juha, 36n48
Rawls, John, 210
   basic structure of society and, 6, 16, 27, 45, 107, 112n32, 121, 143–4, 210
   cosmopolitanism and, 24–8, 30, 32, 37, 40–1, 46–7, 59–68
   duty of assistance and, 8, 74n9, 90
   embedded approach and, 24–8, 30
   freedom and, 162, 167n30, 173–6

   guidance critique and, 32, 37, 40–1
   human rights and, 81–4
   ideal/non-ideal theory and, 37–8
   interpretive approach and, 93, 95, 97–9
   The Law of Peoples and, 14n31, 38n56, 40, 72–3, 85–91, 93, 95, 98–9
   original position and, 5, 27–8, 46, 114, 174–5
   Political Liberalism and, 25n6, 61n44, 95, 98–9, 102n17
   primary goods and, 47, 94, 111, 173–4, 176
   realistic utopia and, 76, 82–3, 88
   reflective equilibrium and, 167n30
   statism and, 7, 10–11, 72–7, 81–91, 93, 95, 97–9, 102, 106n23, 107, 114
reciprocity, 74, 95–6, 109
reflective equilibrium, 167n30
Raz, Joseph, 156n1
Reddy, Sanjay, 90n57
Reidy, David, 7, 8n16, 41, 63n50, 67n62
relational approach
   coercion and, 92–3, 112–18
   cooperation and, 92–3, 108–12
   cosmopolitanism and, 44, 46n5, 58–61, 64, 66–8, 121, 210
   statism and, 92, 107–18
respect
   coercion and, 123–4
   cosmopolitanism and, 46–7, 55–8, 61, 66–7
   equality and, 3–8, 10, 12, 14, 19, 46–7, 55–8, 61, 66–7, 78–81, 84, 91, 112–17, 123–4, 173, 175, 179–85, 189, 205–9
   freedom and, 173–5
   statism and, 78–81, 84, 91, 112–17
   violations of, 55–6
responsibility, 207
   causal, 11
   CEOs and, 151–2
   coercion and, 122, 131–3, 146–53, 211
   group, 131–3, 148–51, 211
   individual, 131–3, 146–8
   moral, 11
   national, 47–8
   outcome, 131, 146n61, 147, 181n3
   shared, 151–3
Ripstein, Arthur, 129n20, 160, 162n17
Risse, Mathias, 46, 90n57, 116–17, 197n45
Rixen, Thomas, 196n36, 196n38
Rodrik, Dani, 110n27
Ronzoni, Miriam, 3n4, 28n20, 65n56&n59, 66n61, 89n51, 106n21, 112n33, 125n9, 142n52, 144n54, 191n22, 198n46, 202n55, 203n57
Rousseau, Jean-Jacques, 102

228

Index

Sabel, Charles, 3n4, 66n61, 187n13
Sangiovanni, Andrea, 3n4, 6n14, 7, 44n1, 49n16, 55n29, 73, 75, 98n9, 108n24, 109, 139n44
Scanlon, T.M., 114, 131n22&n23, 175n42
Scheffler, Samuel, 56n32
Schemmel, Christian, 48n15, 49n16, 55n29
scope of justice, 179–204
    equality and, 179–95, 199–200
    global finance and, 195–8
    global trade and, 193–5
    interactional coercion and, 187–93
    nested-islands model and, 186–7
    non-interference and, 179, 182–6, 191–2
    normative framework and, 18–20, 179–204
    separate-islands model and, 182–5
    sovereign equality and, 189–93
    systemic coercion and, 193–203
self-determination, 7
    cosmopolitanism and, 48
    liberalism and, 12
    statism and, 71, 74–5, 78, 89, 91, 94, 97–9, 115, 180, 190, 199, 207
Sen, Amartya, 25n5, 42n68, 158n6, 166n29, 167n31, 175n44
sense of community, 62–3
Shue, Henry, 9n22, 76, 154n77, 176n47
Simmons, A. John, 37n51, 189n17
Simone, Alejandro, 196n36
Singer, Peter, 49, 51, 80n23
Skinner, Quentin, 159n9
slavery, 33, 81, 98, 134, 160–1, 166, 168
sovereign equality, 188–93
statism
    agency-based approach and, 100–7, 109, 112, 118
    assessing ideal of, 71–91
    coercion and, 92–3, 108, 112–18, 121–5, 132, 141, 154, 157
    contractualism and, 103, 114
    cooperation and, 81, 87, 92–9, 108–12, 114, 118
    democracy and, 81, 83, 85, 88
    egalitarianism and, 7, 17, 71–81, 90, 92–3, 99–118
    equality and, 4, 71, 96, 102–5, 110
    human rights and, 74–5, 81–4, 97, 99, 105n20
    impasse with cosmopolitanism and, 9–20, 205–11
    international interdependence and, 72, 109
    interpretive approach and, 92–101, 118
    justification of, 92–118
    liberalism and, 6, 10, 81–4, 95, 98–9, 115–16
    methodological critique of, 92–118
    nationalism and, 2, 3n5, 71n1, 89, 207

    overview of, 72–5
    pluralism and, 82–4
    relational approach and, 92, 107–18
    self-determination and, 71, 74–5, 78, 89, 91, 94, 97–9, 115, 190, 199, 207
    status-quo bias of, 71–2, 75–80, 84–94, 98n9, 99–100, 105–9, 118, 121, 205, 207–9
status quo bias, 13, 17–18, 33, 66, 71–2, 75–81, 84–92, 98n9, 99–100, 107, 109, 118, 121, 205, 207–9
    global egalitarianism and, 77–81
    guidance critique and, 33–4, 39, 41–2
    statism and, 71–2, 75–80, 84–94, 98n9, 99–100, 105–9, 118, 121, 205, 207–9
Steinberg, Richard, 195n31
Stiglitz, Joseph, 190n20, 193–4, 195n32&n35
Swanton, Christine, 128n13
systemic coercion, 19–20, 209
    defined, 122, 137
    domestic justice and, 141–6
    freedom and, 139, 170, 172
    global finance and, 195–8
    global trade and, 193–5
    individual responsibility for, 146–8
    justification of, 198–203
    problem of (at the global level), 193–8
    responsibility for, 146–8, 151–3
    scope of justice and, 179–80, 185, 187, 193–203
    suitable baseline for, 139–41

Tan, Kok-Chor, 6, 8n16, 10n23, 38n55, 45n3, 82n33
tax evasion, 95
Taylor, Charles, 158
Tobin, James, 197n41, 201
Tomlin, Patrick, 29n23
trade liberalization, 1, 111, 193, 200
transcendent approach, 24–5, 28–32, 42–4, 48, 54
Transocean, 148

unemployment, 132, 136, 138, 194, 196
United Nations, 97, 208
United States, 11–12
    Bay of Pigs Invasion and, 191–2
    housing bubble of, 196
utopianism, 208
    cosmopolitanism and, 13, 40
    Rawls and, 76, 82–3, 88
    realistic, 82
    statism and, 76, 82–3, 88

Wade, Robert, 175n43, 195n33
Waldron, Jeremy, 5–6, 26n9, 62n46, 79n21

Walzer, Michael, 98n10
war, 188–91
Wearden, Graeme, 148n63
Weinstein, W.L., 157n3
Wellman, Christopher, 66n61
Wenar, Leif, 190n20
Wertheimer, Alan, 126n12
Westphalian model, 36, 186, 203
Woods, Ngaire, 196n39

World Trade Organization (WTO), 97, 111, 193–8, 202n55, 208
World War II, 191

Young, Iris, 104n19, 105n22, 125n9, 151–2, 138n40, 142n51, 146n61, 198n46, 211n6
Ypi, Lea, 3n4

Zimbabwe, 96
Zimmerman, David, 52n20, 144n57

Lightning Source UK Ltd.
Milton Keynes UK
UKOW06n1531101116

287229UK00017B/420/P